MW00952220

Publisher: Golden Rule Press
Cover Design: Sarah Andrews
Production and Composition: Golden Rule Productions

This publication is designed to provide accurate and authoritative information in regard to the subject matter covered. It is sold with the understanding that the publisher is not engaged in rendering legal or accounting services. If legal advice or other expert assistance is required, the services of a competent professional should be sought.

Physical Therapy Marketing For The New Economy by Nitin Chhoda

ISBN-l0: 1463751176

ISBN-13: 978-1463751173

Printed in the United States of America

Nitin Chhoda, PT, DPT

For Ritika

Forever in your debt

In this life and the next

CONTENTS

SECTION I

SECTION II

SECTION I

NO NONSENSE CLINIC

Grow Your Practice

CHAPTER 1

Developing The Mindset of a Successful Private Practice Owner

Welcome to the chapter on *"Developing the mindset of a successful private practice owner."*

Using some elements of my own life story, I will teach you how to build a successful practice and how you can train your staff to do all the work for you.

Over the years, I have coached thousands of private practice owners and helped them grow their practice using media like live events, workshops, and members-only websites. I want to thank you for trusting me with your time and reading this book. I welcome you to a world of abundance in your practice and your life. For an immigrant from India who first arrived in the United States in 2002, your support and encouragement has been more than I ever expected.

I promise that you will learn the *'four steps needed to quickly flood your practice with new patients and how to motivate your staff to do the work for you'* as a part of reading this book.

Let's dive in.

You have begun reading this book today for a reason...for some of you, it's to find ways to get more patients by increasing the number of your referral sources; or perhaps you are not getting enough referrals from physicians. For others, it may be that your clinic is doing okay, but your gut tells you it could be doing a lot better and you just don't know what's missing.

I have talked with thousands of private practice owners just like you and the recurring theme is that most private practice owners are **overwhelmed** with too many things to take care of. What they've told me, time-after-time, is how exhausting and overwhelming it can be trying to work in the clinic, build a solid financial future, and **still have the time and energy to spend with family and friends**.

Like you, they've been struggling to put together all the *"business stuff"* that goes into running a successful clinic. The fact is that no one teaches us these things in school. Like you, they've spent thousands of dollars on one random thing after another that yielded failure after failure.

The harsh reality is that a lot of private practice owners have been unsuccessful in marketing their clinic by themselves. You might feel the same way. Sometimes, you feel so intimidated by all of the moving parts that you haven't even tried to learn how to take control of your practice. Instead, your practice is controlling you. **All that is about to change today.**

I am about to explain to you that **referral generation is a process, not an event**. It is the end result of **sequences and**

scripts to communicate with **4 types of individuals** using **4 different modes of communication**.

4 TYPES OF INDIVIDUALS
4 MODES OF COMMUNICATION

In a nutshell, we sequence the whole process using the 4 modes to communicate with 4 types of individuals in order to help you grow your practice.

It's that simple.

If for some reason you are not following a system like this, it's likely that your practice is stagnant and you're frustrated or even fearful for its long-term survival.

You've been looking for someone, anyone, to tell you in simple terms exactly what you need to do. You want to move forward from where you're at now to where you want to be, in order to finally reach all the things you want to achieve.

You are looking for answers, like we all are. Up until now, your search has not given you answers. You've only found more frustration and expenses, with half-baked solutions that just haven't given you the returns you've always wanted.

If this describes your situation, there are two things I would like to do: First, I'd like to congratulate you for making the right decision to read this book.

Second, and this is very important so please read carefully... THE FUTURE OF YOUR PRIVATE PRACTICE IS IN YOUR HANDS, BUT YOU MUST TAKE ACTION STARTING TODAY IF YOU WANT TO BE SUCCESSFUL. If you want to serve patients better while growing your clinic and increasing your income at the same time, then you have to be willing to accept change by learning from the experts. You have to be willing to take action in the process.

As the Indian philosopher and legend Mahatma Gandhi once said,

"Be the change you want to see in the world."

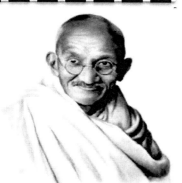

What this means is that you need to take bold, decisive action in order to change your life and the lives of people around you.

Speaking of "taking action", it is also noteworthy to mention something else that Gandhi once said:

"You may never know what results come of your action, but if you do nothing there will be no result."

Chapter 1   5

That's why it is important for you to take action to grow your clinic. By reading this book, you have already set into motion a chain of events that will bring you one step closer to financial freedom. Since you entrusted me with your time and energy, I'd like to tell you a little bit about me. As you probably already know, I've been helping private practice owners, just like you, for several years. I have created technologies like *Therapy Newsletter* and *Clinical Contact* to help clinics market themselves affordably and effectively by taking full advantage of the technology that is available to us today. I have written several books and have been featured on amazon.com. I speak, write, and train clients on practice management internationally. I have also been called the world's leading consultant for private practices according to Wikipedia. I've come a long way from living with my brother and parents in a tiny one-bedroom apartment in Mumbai, India and a lonely, broke immigrant in the United States.

Now, in addition to the "done-for-you" technologies like Therapy Newsletter and Clinical Contact, I have also conducted sold-out live events like the Private Practice Summit and the Private Practice Formula in New Jersey and other parts of the country. My private practice mastermind-coaching program is currently closed for registration and has a waiting list of private practice owners ready to participate as soon as slots open up.

However, this book is not about me. This is about you and what I can do for you.

My story is the classic 'rags to riches' story, with a few unusual twists and turns. If I had to sum it up in one sentence, I'd say it is the story is that of a desperate, broke immigrant physical therapist in New Jersey who discovered the amazing secret to making more than $350,000 a year working only 20 hours a week.

I'm home most evenings and weekends to spend time with my family, just like a normal person. Whoever made this silly law that says you have to have lots of staff and overhead in order to succeed as a private practice owner? I was able to earn the respect and income I deserved and live life to the fullest with a simple, accidental discovery that I am about to share with you. What I am about to share will allow you to succeed as a private practice owner regardless of competition, referral sources, and reimbursements.

If you are really serious about learning the truth about how to generate multiple six figures in your practice without undermining yourself and being pushy, then this will be the most important information you will ever read.

I have been a private practice owner, just like you, out there every day trying to do top quality work and earn a respectable living in the process.

I'm willing to bet that there is one big difference between you and me. I get an average of at least 30-40 new calls from new patients seeking appointments every week, automatically. What may come as a shock to you is that I have not solicited a single physician to ask for referrals in almost three years.

Let me explain to you how this all happened.

My early years as a private practice owner were a constant struggle for survival. Day after day I came into the office to face the bone numbing humiliation of calling hundreds of physicians and reaching their gatekeepers who did not want to talk to me. I was just hoping to find the ones who would let me introduce myself (before they hung up on me). After enduring hundreds of rejections, I found myself at the brink of despair and burnt out. I consulted my brother for advice and he said, "*Keep your chin up, hang in there... It's still possible, shake it off and keep going. Things will be just fine.*"

Yeah, right. As if somehow I could forget being hung up on, cursed at, and being treated like I had the plague.

I got into private practice because I wanted to help patients, not to pester physicians for referrals. I hated selling, being looked at like I was a car salesman. I had simple systems to stay in touch with patients and physicians and they kept me afloat. What tore me apart was the fact that some of my colleagues were using manipulative tactics to get patients from the same physicians who rejected me.

So I did what most people do when they are looking for answers... I went to the library and read a bunch of books. I went online and did a lot of research, trying to learn how to grow my clinic.

I even ended up buying dozens of CDs and books from marketing experts, but none of them taught me how to connect with physicians and bond better with patients. They were all teaser courses, designed to identify the 'big fish' and get them to fork over tens of thousands of dollars for actionable content. This was money that I simply did not have. I tried to learn as much as I could on my limited budget. No matter how much I role-played physician meetings, I'd always choke up and freeze each time I got in front of a physician. I just couldn't do it. I saw the funds in my checking account dwindle. Before long, I was on the verge of bankruptcy.

I was barely hanging on; the stress to get new patients was rising as I was drowning under a sea of bills. To top it all off, I was recently married at the time and my wife Ritika, the driving force behind everything in my life, had no idea how deeply I was in debt when we got married. We lived in a tiny one-bedroom apartment in Hackensack, New Jersey and as much as I wanted to, I could not have my mom (who lives in India) come to visit us since there was no room for her in our apartment. Things were not looking good.

The pressure was rising. I was ashamed and embarrassed. I did not have the heart to tell my wife (also a physical therapist) that I was struggling financially. I was being pushed into a corner and my confidence was shattered.

On one hand, I thought of shutting down the practice; but on the other hand, I was desperate to prove to Rita and to myself that I could weather the storm. I had to do something, anything to create cash flow and reluctantly took a part time job working for another private practice owner down the street. I was almost out of options as I reached my breaking point.

I was almost ready to give in and then...

Chapter 1   7

EVERYTHING CHANGED

It happened when I discovered the ***Referral Ignition System.*** I am about to teach you the fundamentals of this system in the upcoming chapters. From my 'simple systems' emerged a discovery so exhilarating that it shook me to my core. I could not sleep all night after I saw the results of a system that helped me get a flood of patients. When I looked closely at some of the patterns that were generating referrals, I realized I had stumbled upon a pattern that was so ingenious that it turned out to be the answer to all my prayers.

The discovery was this… physicians and patients rewarded me with referrals in a fairly predictable manner if I took the right steps and approached them the right way. I observed that some patients preferred email, others phone calls, while some responded well to letters. Whatever their preference, they started sending me friends and family referrals. I also found that many potential patients (I call these individuals prospects) became patients as long as I maintained contact with them with specific scripts using specific modes of communication.

Physicians responded with a flood of referrals when I positioned them as experts in front of my patients and every single member in my community started recognizing me as a 'trusted provider.'

My life changed.

It was almost as if the blindfold had been removed from my eyes after months of groping in the darkness.

Was this the solution I was desperately looking for or was it a fluke?

There was only one way to find out. I had to try these systems in my own private practice.

The results exceeded my wildest dreams. I got 77 new patients, 21 new physicians became referral sources and I had to hire TWO clinicians just to keep up with the patient volume... and that's not even the best part. What happened next was unbelievable. All this happened in SIX weeks. The best part is yet to come. The ***Referral Ignition System*** delivered all these patients automatically, no cold calling, and no rejections; all thanks to its simplicity and effectiveness.

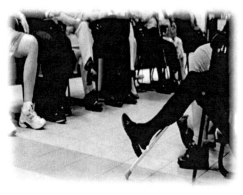

It was astounding. At first I thought it was a fluke, but I continued to duplicate my success by implementing this system and refining it.

For years I silently implemented this system and improved it.

Now for the first time ever, I am going to reveal this groundbreaking system to you so it can help you to grow your practice.

Despite my efforts to keep the system under wraps, word about my success eventually started leaking out and I was besieged with requests to consult and speak across the country. My articles started appearing in national and trade level magazines and my books, audio, and video courses appeared on Amazon.

My life changed within a matter of months. We bought a new house, my mother visited us from India and **for the first time in her life, my mother had a room of her own when she visited my home in Denville, New Jersey.**

Being able to take care of my wife and now my mother was the proudest moment in my life.

All of this was possible thanks to my system, which ignited a wave of referrals each time it was implemented, which is why Ritika coined the name "*Referral Ignition*".

It was not my original idea, but Ritika pointed out that it was time for me to share my system with other private practice owners, since I owe it to the profession and to other private practice owners to end the misery of trying to find new patients. I was astonished when she showed me the hundreds of emails and letters from private practice owners requesting information. In fact, they begged me to teach them the system. I was not sure if I could handle the responsibility, but I reluctantly agreed.

HOW MY STORY CAN HELP YOU

I am about to show you how my little story can help your practice, but before I get to that I want you to know something. In the last several years, I've worked with tens of thousands of private practice owners and I always start by asking them one simple question.

My question is, "*What do you really want from your practice?*"

Here's what they tell me.

"I want autonomy so that I feel certain and in control of my future."

"I want a business where I can treat patients the way I want, give them high quality care without having to cut corners. I want to treat them the right way"

"I want a business that makes me proud and shows the world what I'm capable of doing."

However, if I ask these same private practice owners a follow-up question, if I ask them to tell me **how it's really going**, a very different picture emerges.

They're not generating the type of revenue they dream of. In fact, the reality is way short of their goals. They've spent so much money on false promises and push-button solutions that they're embarrassed and concerned. They're now worried because if things continue as they are; they'll never have what they really want. They're uncertain because they don't know how to fix their situation.

I'm going to tell you exactly what the difference is between having your ideal practice and what you have right now.

You see, there are hidden strategies; in fact, there is a 'success blueprint' behind every private practice success story. This is the blueprint that helps you ignite referrals, hire staff, manage staff, and grow your practice.

There is a process behind the success of all the private practice owners that live the dream lifestyle you want.

I know, because I've worked with almost all of them.

In fact, the things I am about to teach you are very different than what you've been both sold on and told to do in the past. Yet, the things I am about to share with you represent the missing components that have created all of the big success stories you see in private practice clinics. Before we're through, they'll be yours to use both to grow and market your practice. I've had several testimonials from individuals who have had **life altering moments** after my workshops and live events.

Hundreds of emails and phone calls are testimony to the fact that the strategies I am about to share with you and has the potential to change your practice forever.

This blueprint will help you grow your practice no matter what stage you are in. It doesn't matter if you're on the verge of retirement or you're much, much younger. It also doesn't matter where you're starting from; meaning, how much or how little technical, marketing, or business knowledge you currently have. The approach I'm going to walk you through is **systematic** and **proven** to help you to grow your clinic.

Now, whenever I speak at a conference or one of my own live events, private practice owners always come up and thank me. They always say, "*I wish I had known all of this earlier.*"

I think you're going to be thinking the same way by the end of this book, **especially when you learn about the resources I have in store for you. So I respectfully ask that you please commit your undivided attention as you read this book and take advantage of the resources that you come across in different chapters**.

I want you to know that because you're here and you made the decision to pay attention and absorb my message, it puts you miles ahead of the overwhelming majority who are attempting to grow their clinic with outdated strategies and a self-entitlement attitude.

This means you now have an advantage over everyone else who is still stuck in the old ways of growing a practice, even though they know at some level that what they're doing doesn't work and never will.

This is the exact same method that has worked for my private coaching clients and will work for you also. It requires just a few small changes in your way of thinking, while fully leveraging who you are. It's not a new tactic you need to learn. This is going to be a radical new approach in the way you approach marketing and referral generation.

The fact is, when you open your mind up to new possibilities and new strategies, you will see a change in your financial future; just like the private practice owners who have previously attended my workshops and courses.

You'll find as you go through this training that one idea can be worth tens of thousands of dollars for your practice. It's often that single bullet that can trigger that "a-ha moment" and ignite the future for your practice, like it has for my students all over the world. It's that game changing moment after which your practice expands effortlessly.

Section I   10

Now before I get into the nitty-gritty, let me explain something. Clarity in all things is the key to success. In your business, clarity causes you to succeed and as you read this book and make notes, it will greatly increase your payoff. I have a short exercise that's certain to give you greater clarity and success right now.

Take out a pen and piece of paper. I'm going to ask you to answer three simple questions that will give you the clarity you need. Your answers can be a sentence, a phrase, or even a word; it doesn't matter as long as it's true for you.

Now, this is extremely important and it's easy, so go ahead and do it.

Please do not skip this, because it will help you take full advantage of what you are about to discover in this book.

WHY ARE YOU READING THIS BOOK?

First, write down your reason for reading this book right now.

Okay, now let's take this a step further. Look at the answer you just wrote down and now write your answer to this next question.

WHAT'S IMPORTANT ABOUT THAT?

Remember your answer can be a phrase, a word, or a sentence; but write down what is important about your first answer? In other words, why is that important to you?

For example, if you wrote "I am reading this book because I want to increase the number of visits in my clinic each week."

The reason that is important to you is probably because "It will help me increase my revenue" or "It will help me hire another clinician so I can step away from my clinic and focus more on management and marketing" or something along those lines.

Great, now you have two answers written down. I want you to look at both of them and write down your answer to this final question.

WHAT WILL HAVING THIS DO FOR YOU?

What will having those things – meaning your answers to one and two – do for you?

Let me say it again, what will having those things, when you look at the answers to questions one and two, do for you?

In the example I gave you, your answer will be something along the lines of "This will help me spend more time with my spouse and children, or take a week off and go to Europe like I've always dreamed of."

I hope you have been writing these things down so far. Once again, DO NOT trivialize this – the readers who spend a couple of minutes writing these things down **gain tremendous insight** into their business lives and will get the best results from this book. Period.

If you have been writing things down, then I have to tell you that...

SO FAR YOU ARE DOING <u>GREAT</u>

You should be clearer now on why you're reading this and you know what it'll do for you to understand it. Here's the really great thing…

As we go through this training, I want you to run everything I share with you through those answers that you just wrote down. Use your answers as filters so that you can see and hear how my systems and teachings will help you reach your goals. I want you to see how my systems and teachings will help you grow your clinic so you can achieve everything you have just written down on that piece of paper.

Look, I want you to know I value both your time and I value my own time. Just trust the process for now.

You might not understand during this training why I'm asking you to do certain things like writing things down, but if you suspend your judgment until you're through with this book, you will have a breakthrough. In fact, you will have several breakthroughs. You'll be on your way to being a successful private practice owner and this is how I can help you achieve it. Make this time, our time together, as powerful as it can be.

Since we have so much to cover, it's important you get the big picture right up front. You see, my sole focus since I started my company, **Referral Ignition**, has been and still is to turn struggling private clinicians into successful private practice owners. That's what we do, that's all we do, and we do it all day after day.

And here's how we do it.

The way we help our clients achieve results is with the use of systematic sequences and scripts to ignite referrals from multiple sources. In fact, you should write that down.

Let me repeat that. **The way we help our clients achieve results is with the use of systematic sequences and scripts to ignite referrals from multiple sources**.

As mentioned earlier, referral generation is a process and not an event.

Once you can wrap your head around this, you'll understand why we get unmatched results for our clients. You'll understand why we get success stories from all over the world. The fact is that everything is based on one simple premise and it's this: *always have multiple referral sources to grow your clinic.*

I'm not saying there is no work involved. This is not a magic pill. This is real business and when you try to ignite referrals from multiple sources you're never going to be distracted or overwhelmed by all the other things that can go wrong. Instead, you are going to have a clear plan of action, just like you will have at the end of this book. In other words, if you get this, if you really get this, and put the strategies into action, you <u>will</u> succeed.

Before you take action, it's important for you to have the right coach or system and the right set of guiding principles for growth. With all the clients I have worked with, the approach made all the difference. I can say from personal experience that my growth in my own practice was a result of a small shift in my approach that caused a massive shift in my financial future.

It will be the same for you too. It's not all about you; it's about your systems which are taught to you by your coach. When you change your systems, your results will improve dramatically.

The single approach responsible for the biggest impact in your practice is going to be the **diversity of your referral sources**. The more referral sources you have, the faster your practice will be able to grow. This is the first and most important success trait for private practice owners.

The second success trait is the importance of **focusing on high lifetime value activities**. In your practice, high lifetime value activities include strategy development, consulting with experts on the phone and in person, marketing decisions that establish your authority and expertise with patients and referral sources, staff management, and financial planning.

Other activities can be classified into high dollar value (treatment, teaching) and low dollar value (answering phones, responding to emails, faxes, and getting involved in billing and paperwork).

Most private practice owners focus a disproportionately large amount of time on the low dollar value and the high dollar value activities and almost ZERO time is spent on the high lifetime value activities.

All of that is about to change **right now!**

If you're frustrated with your progress, if you're overwhelmed with your workload, or if you're just plain exhausted do we still have to wonder why?!

Even if you were going to delegate it all, ask yourself this… How would you manage all the staff that would be required to get everything done?

You see, the main problem here isn't a staffing problem, it's a strategy problem. Remember that. It's not a manpower problem, it's a strategy problem.

Think for a second about all the time and all the money you'd save if you stopped going to outdated marketing seminars and utilizing overpriced consultants that dump more and more tactics (that you're not going to get done) onto your plate.

Think about it. How much easier would it be to succeed if you had a lot less to focus on and a lot less to think about while you increased your revenue, spent less time in your clinic, and you enjoyed your practice and your life more?

As a private practice owner, your goal is to have the best possible strategy for your current situation. Know how to get the greatest outcome as quickly as possible from the smallest amount of effort and the smallest amount of resources.

At any time, during any day, there is one obvious and distinctly right next thing that needs to be done in order to grow your practice. Not five, not ten, not twenty: but just one obvious action which is going to make all the difference in your practice in the next day, in the next week, in the next month, and in the next year.

Let me ask you a question and be brutally honest with yourself right now. At this very moment do you know the exact steps that you need to take, in the right sequence, which will take you from where you are right now to where you want to end up?

Do you know the steps you need to take in order to ignite an avalanche of referrals into your practice?

Do you know your precise plan of action to get to where you want to end up?

If it takes you more than a second or two to come up with an answer, then you're not there yet.

Now if *that describes you* then don't worry, you are not alone.

Chapter 1   13

In fact, it's not your fault. They don't teach us these things in school. If you don't have a plan yet, it's ok because **that's where I come in to help you**. That's what we are going to fix with this book.

Let me tell you exactly what your plan should be. The goal with the *Referral Ignition* principle is to get the greatest result from the least amount of effort, with the least amount of resources, in the shortest amount of time.

You want the greatest result (most number of patients, referrals, and referral sources).

You want to do this with the least amount of effort (find that single letter, script, or ad that opens the floodgates and brings in lots of new patients)

You want to use a minimal amount of resources (use low cost or zero cost measures that are proven to work).

Finally, you want to do so as quickly as possible, because time is money. In fact, each day that you are not using these principles is **another day you are potentially losing money in your clinic.**

That's exactly how Jason felt when he first started consulting with me. He was (and still is) an excellent clinician, but when it came to the business side of his new private practice he didn't know where to begin.

JASON'S STORY

He was seeing 19 new patients each week and had two physicians as referral sources in December 2009. I helped him overcome both of those challenges in a few weeks. Jason now has THREE full time physical therapists working in his clinic and works six hours a week treating patients. Last year alone, his gross income was $1 million.

How long would it take you to achieve comparable results? I'd like you to estimate the time frame.

The great news is that you don't have to struggle through this alone, because I'll help you get there much faster than you ever thought possible.

Based on my years of experience, here's my promise to you – together I'll help you get to that dream practice and income level in at least half the time of your original estimate. For many of you, it'll be a quarter of the time of your original estimate. For a few of you, I'll get you there in one-tenth the time of your original estimate.

WHAT'S STANDING IN YOUR WAY?

As I explained to Jason, it all starts with the FOUR main challenges faced by MOST private practice owners.

1. Trying to get new patients to come in.
2. Get more referrals from existing patients or reactivate former patients.
3. Get physicians and referral sources to send more patients.
4. Become the expert in your community, so that people recognize you and look up to you.

Honestly, the formula for success in your private practice is really simple
Everything comes down to 4 things that **REALLY MATTER**

❖ You want to get new patients.
❖ You want to do an outstanding job of reactivating former patients or increasing referrals from existing patients.
❖ You want to increase referrals from physicians and other referral sources including local, non-competing businesses.
❖ Finally, you want every single member of your community to recognize you as the leading provider of your professional services.

YOU CAN ACHIEVE ALL THIS WITH TEMPLATES AND SCRIPTS THAT HAVE BEEN PROVEN TO WORK EVERY SINGLE TIME

Most importantly, you want to achieve this with templates and scripts that SAVE YOU TIME, MONEY AND RESOURCES and that work every single time.
This is the Referral Ignition system.
As soon as I explained this to Jason, he became anxious to apply all these things as quickly as possible. I appreciated his willingness to take action right away, which is an important trait of all successful private practice owners. However, I had to warn him; there is no magic pill. Scripts and templates can only take you so far.

I explained to him, just as I am explaining to you now, that the survival of your practice depends on systems. If you don't have a system, things can change very quickly.

Truth be told, things tend to get out of control and I will show you what I mean in just a second.

You have probably heard of the research firm Dun and Bradstreet, which keeps records on over 140 million businesses and has been tracking business for over a century. Their records show that of the small businesses that fail, 90% do so because of a lack of skills and knowledge on the part of their owner. You see, success in business is not common sense; it's actually uncommon sense and it's also uncommon skills.

Dun & Bradstreet

By the time you're through reading this book, you'll not only know what these skills are, you'll also know the fastest and easiest ways for you to leverage them to grow your clinic.

If that wasn't enough to get you thinking, here's some important research information from SCORE and US Bank. For 70% of small business failures, a key factor was that the owner did not recognize or simply ignored a weakness and did not seek help.

Now, let me share an astonishing statistic that hits even closer to home… According to research firm Bizminer, 43.42% of physical therapy private practices failed in 2009.

Again, an average of 43.32% of physical therapy private practices failed in 2009 alone.

That equates to 8,280 clinics.

Fortunately, Jason was not one of them and I want a similar, if not bigger success story for you at the end of this training manual.

If you analyze these alarming statistics a little bit, **you will realize that it's probably going to get worse because…**

The way the economy is going, reimbursements will continue to decline – patients are going to feel the crunch and "skip therapy" to avoid co-pays, or "bear the pain" instead.

Add to all of this the increasing competition from physicians opening their own clinics, large hospitals with deep pockets ruthlessly expanding in your territory, and insurance companies determined to find faults with every claim. That's why thousands of clinics failed in 2010.

Those corporate giants are not going away anytime soon.

Not to mention the unreported cases of clinics that sink without a trace.

So it's possible the number of clinics that fail will get even higher.

Clearly, this is not a good sign. In fact, it is a BIG warning sign of things to come. What this means is, and this is the unvarnished truth, the harsh reality if you will…

THERE WILL BE A THINNING OF THE HERD

Only the strongest and the most intelligent practices will survive. The question is are you going to survive and thrive like Jason did, or are you going to be slaughtered like over 43% of private practices?

As a side note, I want to point out to you some of my observations from this research.

I believe private practice owners fail not because they're not marketing, but because they are doing the wrong kind of marketing and spending time on the wrong kind of tasks.

They spend very little time on the high lifetime value activities and are instead focusing on the low dollar value activities and they don't even realize it. This is why they don't seek out help or guidance until it's too late; they become a part of the 43% of failing practices every year.

The overwhelming majority of private practice owners get the exact opposite of what they were hoping and dreaming for when they first started their business. Think about that for a second. Think about how tragic this is; all the time that you put into your practice, all the sacrifices that you make for your practice, and all the money that you invest in your practice and instead of achieving the lifestyle and freedom that you desire, the overwhelming majority of private practice owners end up worse off financially and mentally.

The exceptions are individuals like Jason, who sought help and took action immediately and focused on the systems that really mattered.

The big reason behind the 43% failure rate is the lack of diversity from the referral sources and the inability to spend time on the high lifetime value tasks.

While I know it can be disturbing to see recent trends, the good news is that you're getting greater clarity on what you need to do by reading this book.

Now, I said at the beginning of this book that you can generate more revenue, a lot more, while at the same time working a lot less. It's now time for me to show you how it's done. You'll see why no matter where you are right now, this is the path for getting everything you listed on that piece of paper at the start of this book.

So what are those critical things that ignite growth in your practice – what are those few things that matter most? What are those things that'll have you working less, increasing revenue, and building your dream practice while enjoying the freedom that comes along with it?

This brings us to the reason why you are reading this RIGHT NOW.

Are you facing one of these <u>FOUR</u> problems?

- ✓ Are you struggling to get new patients?
- ✓ Would you like to reactivate former patients and increase referrals from existing patients?
- ✓ Would you like to increase referrals from other medical and non-medical professionals?
- ✓ Last but not the least, would you like to gain expert status in your community so everyone recognizes you as the trusted expert?

Let me ask you again – Are you facing any one of these problems? If you don't have each and every one of these areas completely dialed in with templates, scripts, and processes using multiple modes of communication, then you are not able to exploit the full growth potential of your practice. Whether you realize it or not, the

truth is that most practices face one or more of these problems. In fact, Jason was facing all of these problems and we transformed all of his obstacles into opportunities.

If you are facing one, many, or all of these problems; let me share something with you…

It's not your fault that you are struggling with marketing…

YOU WERE NOT TRAINED IN
THE BUSINESS OF PRIVATE PRACTICE!

Like I mentioned earlier, most private practice owners are not trained in the business of private practice. What I am about to reveal to you today are FOUR of the most common problems faced by most private practice owners and I can virtually guarantee that the same issues lie at the root of your struggles too. In fact, these are problems you may not even know about…

Every single issue related to the growth of your practice falls under one of these FOUR major categories.

For example, let's say you are unable to get new patients.

(THE "THIS WON'T WORK PHILOSOPHY")

Here is why this happens. Most practices don't have a '*hook*' to attract new patients. There is way too much of the 'me too' approach in private practice. There is absolutely no follow up after initial contact. Even if there is follow up, it is a fragmented approach that involves one or two attempts at contact and one or two modes of contact. There is also that self-defeating thought that '*this will not work for my clinic*" when it comes to marketing.

In a nutshell, there is no direction, there is no system. There is a naïve sense of optimism and a false expectation that the same old approaches will somehow bring patients towards your clinic.

I have news for you. It does not work that way. You must be able to magnetically attract patients instead of trying to 'push' them to come to you.

Here are the solutions. For starters, you must specialize in something.

It's a lot better to be the 'shoulder injury expert' than the 'physical therapy clinic'. You must have hooks in place like books, audio CDs, DVDs, and free reports to attract new patients to your clinic.

You must have segmented lists of prospects and patients like past patients, present patients, and discharged patients. You **must communicate with them regularly using 4 different modes of contact – email, phone, text messaging, and regular mail.** There are several opportunities to contact patients throughout the year. Their birthday and national holidays is one small piece of the equation. You want to automate the **entire process using scripts that work and technology that helps automate the entire process**. This is exactly what will drive growth in your practice.

I call this *prospect ignition*. It is the process of getting as many people as possible interested in coming to your clinic. It is the process of identifying possible patients for your practice, even before they recognize the need for your services.

Do you want to reactivate former patients or increase word of mouth referrals from existing patients?

Here's why most clinics fail at this:

Once a patient walks in, there are several opportunities to get them to know, like, and trust you; all of which are completely missed.

Every single contact during the treatment process is a valuable opportunity to bond with that patient.

Also, there are very few attempts to collect testimonials from patients.

What every clinic needs is a process to transform patients into referral sources and this process is usually lacking.

Here's the most important part – staff must be conditioned to get involved in the *'referral conditioning process,'* which most practice owners struggle with.

In a nutshell, every single patient is a powerful referral source and there are several stages during the 'lifecycle' of this patient where there is a potential to ignite referrals and construct a meaningful relationship with that individual.

The fact is you can expect zero patient referrals unless you have a conditioning system and scripts in place to transform a patient into a raving fan and then into a human billboard. This includes the use of email, print, video newsletters, and text message appointment reminders to increase compliance and minimize cancellation rates. It also includes voice broadcasts to remind patients how much you care about them. You also want to use automated greeting cards to thank new patients for coming in, greeting them on meaningful occasions like their birthday and during national holidays.

You also want to organize patient appreciation days to recognize and thank patients for their part in the success of your clinic and tie in the medical community in the process, which I will get to in a moment. You need to firmly and politely make patients aware of cancellation policies and here's the BIG missing component for most clinics – your staff should say the right things at the right times to obtain testimonials.

The thing about testimonials is that they need to be in multiple formats – video, audio, typeset, and handwritten. You need to be able to nurture at least THREE patients a month who can become 'human billboards' for your clinic, since these patients will help your practice grow beyond your imagination. Essentially, you move patients up the ascension ladder from prospects to patients, patients to raving fans, and raving fans into human billboards.

You just have to implement systems to be able to condition present patients to refer and reactivate discharged patients so they come back to your clinic, bringing a herd of friends and family with them

Chances are that you don't have a system like this in place.

It's ok… Because you will **still get referrals…**

But it's likely that they will come from mom, dad and Aunt Martha… You know what I mean ☺

Of course, I was just kidding, but the point I was trying to get across to you is that there MUST BE A SYSTEM; a system to condition patients to refer.

I call this *patient ignition.* It is the process of getting the maximum number of referrals from existing patients and reactivating former patients using systematic communication sequences and leveraging technology and different forms of media in the process. That's how you get patients to give you lots of referrals.

Speaking of referrals, area number THREE that most clinics struggle with is getting physicians and other non-medical referral sources (case managers, attorneys, and other local businesses) to send patients to your clinic.

The problem is that everyone uses the same old boring approach towards physicians without facing the reality that most physicians are immune to the same old solicitations. Here are some of the common mistakes… Offering free consultations to their patients, taking the physician and his staff to lunch (which positions you as an 'attention seeker' like a pharmacy rep instead of a trusted expert), dropping off brochures and trying to get past gatekeepers with the same old slogan *"I am a good PT and a nice person – please send me patients"* **will no longer work.** As they say, the definition of insanity is doing the same thing over and over again and expecting different results.

If you are trying the same approach and it's not working, **please stop.** You know this is true, because you have tried everything in the past and it **has not worked for you.**

It probably caused you more heartache, more frustration, and you had nothing to show for it except a 'devaluation' of your status as an expert. This leads me to my next point; let me say this… out of respect for your time and mine, let me be upfront with you. If you don't agree with me, it's ok. Please close this book and take that deli menu out to order some more sandwiches for physicians. You can also call your printer for more brochures that will never, ever be read.

As a strategic private practice owner, I think you get the point. You need to do different things to get noticed by physicians and other referral sources in order to get on their radar. I call it the 'third dimension' approach, which physicians and referral sources are not accustomed to.

What does this do you for you? It results in instant expert status positioning for you and your clinic. Do you know why this works? Because **no one else is doing it!**

YOU MUST BE DIFFERENT FROM EVERYONE ELSE.
YOU MUST BE THE KNIGHT IN SHINING ARMOR.

If you want physicians and other referral sources to notice you, you must never ask for a referral outright. The referral should be your 'endgame'. You want to introduce yourself with a giving hand; offer to feature physicians in your newsletter, ask them to speak at your patient appreciation days, approach education directors at local hospitals to position yourself as an expert and offer books, CDs, DVDs and Consumer Reports for their patients. You want to approach them with a giving hand, with the intention of helping their patients and in a sense, feeding their ego in the process. The goal is to build a relationship, not to get a patient (which emerges as a natural end result).

I call this process *physician ignition*. It is the process of strategically approaching physicians and other professionals in the medical community, positioning yourself as an expert so they want to send their patients to you. It is the creation of a magnetic identity based upon the principle of 'relationship building' which leads to referral generation.

All that being said, it's important to recognize the fourth component in the success of your private practice; becoming a well-known individual in your community, an expert.

STRATEGIC VISIBILITY IN THE COMMUNITY POSITIONS YOU AS THE UNDISPUTED LOCAL EXPERT

Now, unfortunately very few private practice owners understand the importance of this. That's the reason why clients of mine go through an entire module early on in my program to identify and then learn how to become an expert in their local community. You need to use press releases to get featured in local newspapers and negotiate regular columns with them, which instantly positions you as an expert. We also give our clients 'done for you' PowerPoint presentations on over 20 different subjects from low back pain to shoulder pain and fall prevention.

Here's another big tip to help you become the 'local celebrity' in your community: get local businesses to promote you as an expert to their clients. Every business has a list of local clients, imagine what would happen if you positioned yourself as an expert in front of those clients. The best way to do this is to create a 'syndicate' in your community. This is essentially your own version of the local chamber of commerce, with affiliates and potential partners. When you choose members in your 'syndicate', try to pick the non-competitive individuals who will offer the best service to your patients and help promote each other's businesses. For your practice, an endorsement by a local business owner to their clients (using postcards, letters) is the best low cost or zero cost marketing decision you can ever make. Individuals with the biggest local syndicates are going to gain a 'celebrity' status faster than businesses that rely on expensive advertising.

Community ignition is the construction of the celebrity status or the 'trusted expert' status in your community through leveraged visibility in the local media. It also involves the creation of your own 'syndicate' of referral sources that feed the growth of your practice.

Now, for most private practice owners like you, who want to enjoy explosive and immediate income growth in your clinic, you will find that the sweet spot lies somewhere in between these four elements.

In fact, that's exactly what I teach clients in my training programs; to find that

critical intersection between prospect, patient, physician, and community ignition that results in explosive growth.

I call this sweet spot "*Referral Ignition.*"

In fact, the difference between clients like Jason who thrive and everyone else who survives is precisely this; finding the trigger, the sweet spot that ignites growth in your clinic.

The ones who are barely surviving are always frazzled, uncertain, and wishful. Individuals who follow my system feel certain, confident, and experience peace of mind because they (and soon you will) see the rewards of their efforts quickly and therefore have the certainty that they're doing the right things.

The big breakthrough for *Referral Ignition* clients, one that I mentioned at the beginning of this book, is that successful private practice owners have the ability to focus on **high lifetime value tasks.**

Here's how you can tell: if you are working on the high lifetime value tasks, you will be surprised by how quickly your practice is growing. If you find yourself with more and more free time while your practice is gaining momentum and growing faster and faster, you are focusing on the high lifetime value tasks. So three cheers to you!

HIGH LIFETIME VALUE TASKS INCLUDE:

- ✓ **STRATEGY DEVELOPMENT**
- ✓ **CONSULTING WITH EXPERTS ON THE PHONE OR IN PERSON**
- ✓ **MARKETING DECISIONS**
- ✓ **STAFF MANAGEMENT**
- ✓ **FINANCIAL PLANNING**

Now, as you can see… this book right here, right now, is a system reset for your financial future. You see, before this book, you were just like me during my years of struggle. What I mean is, we both made the same mistakes as we were trying to grow a clinic. If you want to break free from your old habits and chart your own future trajectory you have to make a decision from this point forward, just like Jason did.

Imagine what this can do for your life. In fact, your private practice is the biggest financial bet of your life: because how your practice does right now will be the biggest indicator of whether you're going to be rich or poor; whether you're going to be financially free or continuously struggling. It is very important that you realize how high the stakes are.

The decision you are about to make will also determine whether you'll ultimately be free to enjoy your life or you'll be shackled with constantly having to work the sidelines. It will determine the amount of time you get to spend with your family in addition to all the things you can provide for them.

Look back at the piece of paper from the start of this book. Think about how proud you would be to give your family all the finer things in life and be able to spend the time with them to watch them enjoy it. So for all those reasons, your destiny hinges on the success or failure of your practice.

Think about this vision for your business and your life, your income depends on it. Your self-esteem is influenced by it. Your lifestyle is determined by it. Your family is relying on it. Your free time is controlled by it and your happiness is derived from what you're doing in it. With the stakes that high, with your wealth, your happiness, your freedom, and your family all impacted by your business's performance doesn't it only make sense to approach your practice the right way, the way in which you can ignite referrals systematically?

Now, I want you to take a minute and really think about your answer to this question – how big of an impact do you believe getting personally mentored by me is going to have on you and your practice? How quickly do you think it's going to take us to get you to the level of success that you desire?

Now, ask yourself, are you ready to work with me to take your practice from where it is today to where you imagine it could be?

Look, if you've gotten this far I know you want to grow a successful practice for yourself, for your family, and for your life. You want the freedom that comes along with having a successful business of your own. You want the freedom that comes along with having enough income coming in that you don't have to worry about whether you'll be able to pay your bills next month or whether you'll be able to afford that vacation you might have dreamed about.

So if you're willing, then it's time to start transforming yourself into a successful private practice owner today. This means meaning that right now you are willing to end negative habits like procrastination, indecisiveness, and self-doubt; that you are willing to work together with me and the unique processes that I've designed for you so together we can design and build your dream practice using the principles in this book.

You know, there's a quote from Albert Einstein, I'm sure you've heard it 100 times

> *"The definition of insanity is doing the same thing and expecting a different result."*

So you have to ask yourself and you need to be really honest with yourself; if you just keep doing what you've been doing, 30 days from now are you going to be anywhere different than where you are right now, today? Are you really going to have your practice growing, on track? Are you going to have increasingly more and more money coming in? Are you going to be on track with that practice that you've been dreaming about for years now?

If not, I have a resource for you. Remember, I've been where you are. I understand what you've been through. I understand the frustration, the fear, and even the skepticism you might feel right now.

What I want you to know is that I care deeply about your success, having gone through a lot of struggle in the early years of my practice that I'm going to do absolutely everything I possibly can to make sure you get exactly what it is you want. I am going to train you to think like a private practice owner in the next section on "The 7 habits of highly successful private practice owners". Before I do that, I'd like to present you with a resource that will help you grow your practice.

RESOURCE

I know it's challenging to work in your practice treating patients all day and marketing your clinic to increase revenue at the same time. Like you, I am on a mission to provide my patients with the best quality of care and earn a respectable living at the same time. If you've had a journey similar to mine, you've often struggled with the same burning question…

Why Is My Practice Not Growing Fast Enough?

Are you frustrated with the painfully slow growth of referrals, high cancellation rates (despite the increasing number of evaluations), and declining profits margins as a direct result of corporate clinics, hospitals, and physician owned practices encroaching on your territory?

You are probably lacking a system to ignite referrals from multiple sources, leaving you in the unenviable position of dependence on a handful of referral sources without which your stream of incoming patients will dry up immediately.

Even if you have multiple referral sources, you are probably lacking a system to motivate and train staff to "condition" patients for maximum retention and referral generation. (Just imagine if your staff could transform "regular patients" into "human billboards!" All you do is need to do is to give them the right scripts.)

Are you just plain *exhausted*… from the endless hours of trying to build your practice; spend quality time with your family; and build a stable financial future all at the same time?

That's exactly where I come in. I'm here to tell you that you are not alone and that it's not your fault. To tell you that the reason we struggle with this "business stuff" is simply because no one teaches us these things in PT school. Even though **it's not your fault**, the harsh reality is that over 43% of physical therapy private practices go out of business each year, according to research firm Bizminers.

Which is why I would like to extend a private invitation to a live "Strategy Phone Call" AT NO CHARGE where you will discover: **"4 Steps To Quickly Flood Your Practice With Patients … And How To Train Your Staff To Do This For You"**

Quite simply, I'd like to invite you to a **FREE** strategy phone call where you learn how to get more patients, train your staff and retain more patients so <u>you can have your best year ever in the next 12 months</u>… **and this will not cost you a single penny.**

Schedule Your Call Now: **www.strategycall.com**

In this call, we will identify exactly what you need to do to grow your clinic and streamline your existing processes. You'll become privy to the kinds of strategies that *43.38% of private practice owners did not have access to* (which is why they failed). These are my exact steps for success in your private practice!

During this call, you'll discover **CRITICAL IDEAS** and **PROVEN STRATEGIES** to grow your practice, including:

4 strategies to get new patients and trigger referrals from existing patients and the best part is you can implement these strategies within 24 hours.

How to track ROI with media (email, phone, text messaging, print advertising, mail) and determine the FASTEST way to ignite a flow of new patients

How to generate more revenue for every hour you spend in your practice (while actually working LESS)…

And MUCH more!

I will help you transform your business, just like I have transformed hundreds of private practice clinics over the years.

After you schedule your call, you'll be able to make informed and educated decisions to grow your practice. As a physical therapy private practice owner myself, I promise my team and I will be respectful of your time and present you with all the relevant facts about how to grow your practice.

Keep in mind that we only have a limited number of openings for these strategy calls, and once they are all taken, the website will be deactivated. You may have to wait a while before your call can be scheduled again.

Please head to your computer right now and schedule your call TODAY to grow your practice, before your competitor does.

Schedule Your Call Now: **www.strategycall.com**

7 HABITS OF HIGHLY SUCCESSFUL PRIVATE PRACTICE OWNERS

As a success minded private practice owner, it's important to identify trends and new drivers of profitability in your clinic. A successful business is in a state of constant innovation, looking for new ways to improve customer experience and streamline operations. In order to establish new standards in profitability for your business, you need to master a new set of skills. Becoming a business manager first and a clinician second is the only way to grow a private practice. After a lot of brainstorming with mastermind coaching clients and platinum clients, we realized that there were 7 attributes common to all successful private practitioners:

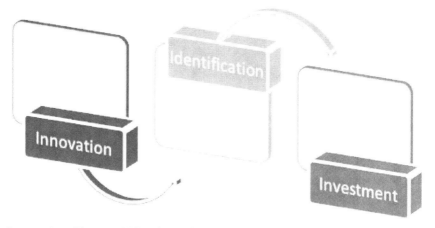

1. **Innovation**: They are NOT "know-it-alls" and are always open to new ideas, new ways of learning (especially from other industries and experts). They have the right mindset for growth and success, and are constantly adapting to a new economy, changing times and evolutions in standards of care and marketing. They are always looking for new materials and resources to grow. They are experts at physical therapy management and know how to leverage themselves for quick and explosive growth. They are in a state of constant innovation.

2. **Identification**. They know EXACTLY what type of patient they want to work with and have systems in place to attract the RIGHT patients from the RIGHT referral sources while weeding out the rest. They are able to precisely define the average patient and create a patient 'avatar'. They know the fears and frustrations, wants and aspirations, and are conscious about exactly what the patient (and referral source) needs from them. They are able to deliver this in a systematic manner, with the right people on board; and they are able to build successful, mutually beneficial, and long-lasting relationships.

3. **Investment**. They invest in their marketing education and are able to measure their return on investment. For example, they are able to track that an investment of 'x' gets a return of 'y' and only continue that particular strategy if 'y' is consistently greater than 'x'. They are able to outspend their competition not because they like overspending, but because they know their business metrics so well that they can afford to go the extra mile, since they have a predictable, measurable return on investment.

For example, if a new patient is worth $800 for your practice and you had to spend $200 to acquire that new patient (something your competitors would never think about), then you can outspend your competitors because you know your business metrics better than anyone else.

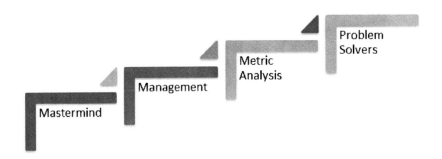

4. **Mastermind**. They create and nurture a successful group of mentors and associates whom they can count on to get answers to their most pressing questions. They are able to cultivate the right relationships with the right people, leading to SIGNIFICANT growth and new opportunities. These 'right people' are usually other successful private practice owners, experts in marketing and business development, employee productivity and billing/collections. They are able to approach such contacts (and colleagues) with a giving hand and are able to <u>add</u> value to the world instead of seeking to <u>extract</u> as much value as possible. In some cases, they may even seek to 'model' their mentors. They have no interest in 'reinventing the wheel' and are constantly looking to expand their circle of influence and interact with individuals who have better people and systems than they do, in an attempt to learn and get better themselves. They are a part of highly successful private practice mastermind group.

5. **Management**. They are MASTERS at time management and people management. They know EXACTLY how to manage their day and focus on the high value tasks (people management, business systems and relationship building) that lead to growth in the business. They tend to look past the minuscule, the day-to-day activities, and the frustrations that most people get bogged down with. Instead they have a firm, determined attitude with insight and long-term vision.

6. **Metric Analysis**. They can clearly define the lifetime value of a patient and tie it in with their business goals. Most practices have no idea what the lifetime value of a patient (LVP) means. The lifetime value of a patient is the amount of profit you make from your patient during the lifetime of your relationship with them. It is a measure of:

❖ How much you get paid for the average treatment.
❖ How many times a year the average patient schedules an appointment.
❖ How many of their friends they are likely to refer to you
❖ Your average net income per patient visit.

Most patients have a lifetime value of several thousand dollars. Successful private practice owners understand this and know that Repetition + Request = Referrals

7. **Problem Solvers**. They are not afraid to tackle difficult questions and seek solutions. A successful private practice owner has the ability to answer tough, insightful questions about his practice. He is able to answer questions like:

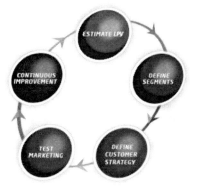

✓ What do I want to be known for / as?
✓ How much income would I like to make each year?
✓ How many patients do I need to see each week to reach that goal?
✓ How many therapists do I need to hire to reach that goal?
✓ Am I good or bad at employee management?
✓ How can I put systems in place to manage employees and achieve my goals?
✓ By which date should I achieve this goal?
✓ What additional products and services can I provide my patients so I can increase the lifetime value of each patient?

A couple of interesting observations about attributes and 'timeline'. These private practice owners know what to do, but in their early years, they also knew which mistakes to avoid. When you are just starting out, it's often the mistakes you don't make that are as important as the right actions you decide to take.

Here are some of the BIGGEST mistakes I see the 'little guys' / new physical therapy private practice owners make with their lives, businesses, income, and freedom. I'll go into a lot more detail on the next page, but these are worth mentioning at this point.

MAYBE YOU'RE MAKING THESE BIG MISTAKES TOO...

❖ PERSONALLY treating patients, day-in and day-out forcing them to work IN the practice and not ON it (Inevitably leading to total burn out).
❖ They were dependent on insurance companies and one or two physicians for ALL of their referrals (unpredictable income).

❖ They did not have any other source of revenue other than their own time (trading time for money).
❖ They used old unpredictable advertising like print ads, fliers, and websites that NEVER built patient lists and were invisible on the search engines.
❖ They had no script or system to convert a prospect into a patient.
❖ They had practically ZERO patient referrals coming in and no matter how hard they tried they could NOT get patients to refer.
❖ Blaming POPS, hospitals, vested interests, and insurance companies instead of seizing their own destiny (a mistake that I often made, I quickly realized it doesn't help to be a crybaby about things like this).

...and the list of "mess ups" goes on and on. If you don't know where to begin, start with 'education based marketing' and teach people about what physical therapy can do for them.

It all starts with the patient.

TOP 5 MISTAKES MADE BY PHYSICAL THERAPY BUSINESS OWNERS

The right strategies to market your practice can be powerful, but the wrong ones can be lethal. Sometimes, the things you do incorrectly can do more damage to your practice than what the other, less relevant things that you manage successfully can do (especially for new private practice owners). Here are five of the most common mistakes made by physical therapy business owners.

1) SPENDING SIGNIFICANT AMOUNTS OF TIME AND MONEY ON 'PAID' ADVERTISING

Since we are not taught about how to market a physical therapy business in school, it's easy to get seduced into thinking that effective marketing has to be expensive. Cutting edge marketing ideas can be no cost or low cost (have you considered a press release to the local media?) and get you results very quickly.

For example, sending surveys to and cold calling physicians is an old-school way of doing things. Using PURL (personalized URL) marketing campaigns, acquiring the right lists and identifying potential patients EVEN BEFORE they need physical therapy is the way to the future of physical therapy business. Forget the old ways of reaching patients; the way to market your practice is to reach your patients even before they are contemplating physical therapy. Imagine if a patient got a postcard in the mail with their name on it which said "Dear Jim, please visit our website at www.abcphysicaltherapy.com/jim for a special message JUST FOR YOU."

Do you think the patient, or the referral source is likely to sit up and take notice?

2) TRYING TO BE ALL THINGS TO ALL PEOPLE

It's the equivalent of being nothing to a lot of people. Do you have a program that will help you stand out from other providers? Have you perfected a method or treatment option that can be the 'flagship' offering in your practice? A service that is so viral that it becomes a talking point and automates your physical therapy marketing? Niche programs are undervalued by the therapist and overvalued by patients.

3) ENGAGING IN 'INTERRUPTION' REFERRAL REQUESTS INSTEAD OF 'RECIPROCITY' REFERRAL REQUESTS

Instead of telling (interrupting) physicians and referral sources with a "Here I am, and I am wonderful" message, offer them with a tempting, irresistible offer - "Here's something I would like to give you, no strings attached, whether you refer back to me or not". Instead of saying "We treat low back pain and we are nice people" in your brochures, write a short book on "Low Back Pain" and give it away to patients, physicians and anyone remotely interested in low back pain - but only if they request the information. The mode of delivery can be email or printed version. Now, you have helped them, have their contact information and are in a (unique) position to legitimately contact them again; this time with another relevant piece of content, which has your name, contact information and 'hook' all over it.

4) THE ABSENCE OF A 'PUNCH LINE IDENTIFIER'

What do you think of when you hear these words?
- ❖ Billions and billions served
- ❖ 15 minutes can save you 15% or more on your car insurance
- ❖ Fresh and hot pizza in 20 minutes or less. While the McDonalds [TM] punch line isn't as strong, the Geico [TM] and Dominos [TM'] identifiers are more benefit driven and allow you to instantly associate the benefit with the brand. Can your practice do this? Don't say boring things like "*We help you relieve pain.*" Use punch line identifiers like "*Our pain relief protocol will transform your life,*" or "*Who wants instant pain relief,*" or "*Imagine your life without pain… and we can get you there!*"

5) INABILITY TO CONSISTENTLY ENGAGE PATIENTS ON A SOCIAL LEVEL

Human beings are social animals. Find ways to introduce fun and education in a social environment. Don't conduct dull 'seminars' or 'workshops'; instead reposition the event as a 'patient appreciation day' or a theme based event with some refreshments thrown in. "Join us for a free seminar on 'Pain Relief 101' and an evening of friendship, conversation, and some of the best coffee and croissants in (name of your town). This is a limited-seating event (notice the use of the word 'event'). Come with a friend and join us in our clinic at (date and time). Call Amy now at (phone number) to RSVP today. We only have 31 seats remaining (odd numbers induce more scarcity) and anticipate a waiting list, so RSVP today!"

This idea does not have to be restricted to patients; it can be used for physicians too.

PATIENT COMMUNICATION 101:
THE BACKBONE OF THE 21ST CENTURY PRACTICE

The key to a successful practice is: Improve the patient's understanding of what physical therapy can do for them and in the process, you get recognized as an expert in your community.

By educating your patients, physicians, and local media to recognize your clinic as a local authority in your field/specialization of therapy, your clinic will instantly stand out. A successful private practice clinic should not depend on patient volume but rather on average income per patient, to maximize chances of financial success.

For example, you will generate more revenue by treating 70 patients a week with an average income of $90 per patient instead of 90 patients per week with an average income of $60 per patient.

So how do you make your clinic stand out and increase your potential to command cash-paying programs?

In order to make your clinic stand out as the first healthcare choice and to build a steady and predictable flow of high-value patients, a physical therapist must attach a very high value to his services. In the world of marketing, perception is reality. I have seen many health and fitness professionals charge upwards of $100 an hour and get it! As physical therapists we should overvalue, rather than undervalue our services and time. It's important to have the mindset of a successful provider to become one.

Your clinic must offer a broad range of services and 2-3 specific programs that enable you to stand out as a provider. Examples of such programs include "Fall Prevention for Seniors", "Pre and Post Pregnancy Physical Therapy", Injury Prevention for Athletes", "Fitness and Lifestyle Management Programs", etc.

A regular source of communication with the patient community is mandatory. Remember, out of sight is out of mind. You don't have to resign yourself to the imbalances of slow periods and physician referrals. If you can remain in the minds of patients, they will eventually come to you or refer someone they know. This happens all the time.

So how do you communicate with patients, physicians, and even the local media?

REGULAR COMMUNICATION HAS 4 MODES:
PHONE, MAIL, EMAIL, AND PERSONAL CONTACT

As I mentioned in the first chapter, there are 4 modes of communication. It can be in the form of a phone call (cold calling is not advisable), direct mail (post card), personal contact (door-to-door marketing) and e-mail contact (instant & cost effective). A separate public relation department that can establish your clinic as a leading name in your community performs all of these tasks in large corporate PT clinics. The truth is that you and I are small business owners and we do not have that kind of a budget. We must find the most cost-effective method of marketing and communication to maintain contact with patients.

Ideally, such a method should lead to a constant, reliable stream of patient referrals that grows each month. This will open up new possibilities for your clinic. It can allow the development and implementation of cash-pay programs that help you break free from the chains of insurance reimbursements.

The biggest mistake most physical therapists make while building a private practice is wasting time and energy in door-to-door marketing with physicians. The truth is that physicians, insurance carriers, and patients are going to work with you and respect your services, provided you have already established a compelling identity for your company.

The reason most physical therapy clinics fail is that these authorities do not know who you are, what you do, and how you can help them.

CAN YOU SET YOURSELF APART?

As a private practice owner, ask yourself this question, "Can you define the services of your clinic in a specific manner and in one sentence?"

Defining your services is the key that will make your clinic shine as a successful private practice. When you have a clear identity, you can attract more out-of-network patients and command cash for your services with more confidence than ever before. This is the hallmark of a successful private practice.

The behavioral psychology of a patient (and referral source) is intriguing! Ask yourself, "Why does a patient complain about a $20 co-pay, when the same patient gladly spends several hundred dollars on an iPad? What motivates a physician to overlook physical therapy as a viable option for patients and recommend surgery instead?"

The reason is a lack of awareness about the benefits of physical therapy. Most individuals do not know what physical therapy is and what it does.

As a private practice owner, you must educate these individuals about physical therapy and, more importantly, define your own brand of physical therapy in order to stand out as a well-known physical therapist. You must create an identity for yourself in order to succeed as a private practice physical therapist.

In today's market, the two biggest problems faced by physical therapists are declining reimbursements and increasing competition, especially from physician-owned private practices.

On the other hand, there are encouraging signs for private practice owners in today's climate. There is an increased demand for physical therapy amongst seniors, and there is an increased demand for health promotion and wellness-based physical therapy.

Consumers are being forced to spend more and more out of pocket.

Is this a bad thing? Not at all! If a patient is being conditioned to pay more out of pocket, they are more likely to pay you as well, as long as they know you, like you, and trust you.

TO SUCCEED, GET THE PATIENT TO
KNOW YOU, LIKE YOU, AND TRUST YOU

Direct access from patients is the best way to build a physical therapy private practice fast! Patients are the single biggest sources of referrals for the private practice of the 21st century

The majority of physical therapists depend on 4 to 5 physicians for patient referrals.

As we know, the patient has the right to approach the physical therapist directly. In most direct access cases, the PT can see the patient, complete an evaluation, and request a fax prescription from a physician.

In the unlikely event that the physician refuses to fax over the prescription and insists on seeing the patient, the patient can be asked to set up an appointment with the physician to obtain the prescription, provided the physician considers the physical therapy to be a medical necessity.

Other components of a successful private practice include:
- ✓ Improving patient responsibility collection systems.
- ✓ Requesting payment from the patient at the time of service.
- ✓ Increasing the number of patient referrals.
- ✓ Providing value-added services to physical therapy patients for cash reimbursements is another way to boost revenue.

For example, foot massage, laser therapy, and trigger-point massages on an electric chair are handy ways to boost revenue.

Communication is extremely important, but it has little value if you overlook the most important principle of business: if you can't measure it, you can't grow it.

Monitoring and measuring your practice is critical in today's economy, which is the subject of the next chapter.

RESOURCE

FREE WEBINAR:
4 Steps To Unlimited Referrals... &
How To Train Staff To Do ALL THE WORK For You

In this webinar, I will teach you:

- ✓ The 4 types of individuals that can make or break your practice (and it's not what you think)
- ✓ The 4 modes of communication that will trigger infinite growth (or dismal failure) in your marketing efforts
- ✓ Specific tips you can use IMMEDIATELY to identify prospects for your practice, boost referrals from existing patients, establish credibility and expert status with physicians and other referral sources and become an expert in your community using a done-for-you system that's so easy a high school kid could implement it.

This training will help you if:

- ✓ You are looking for more ways to get new patients and boost referrals from former patients to help you grow your practice.
- ✓ You are tired of the same old 'high priced' consultants that promise the world and leave you stranded with 'teaser' content
- ✓ You want to save time and money by using cutting edge technology for marketing, scripts that have been proven to work and cut-and-paste systems to constantly drive new patients to your practice, while your staff manages your practice on autopilot.
- ✓ You want to implement systems that will allow you to step away from the day-to-day operations of your clinic.

To reserve your seat, simply register for the webinar at the link below and click the "Register Now" button NOW. Hurry, because seats are limited!

www.foursteprefferrals.com

CHAPTER 2

Identifying Key Leverage Points

To Set The Stage For Explosive

Growth In Your Practice

NOT ALL PATIENTS ARE CREATED EQUAL

From a clinical point of view, every patient deserves the same high quality of service and attention. However, from a business point of view, some patients are more important than others because of their impact on your practice and its reputation.

You've probably worked with new patients that tend to be demanding, uncooperative, and very price sensitive despite all the value you provide. These patients can be a financial and emotional drain on your practice.

On the other hand, you have probably treated patients that were a pleasure to work with. These patients recognized the importance of physical therapy, remained compliant throughout the treatment process, and trusted you as the expert. Chances are that these patients never complained about price and service (or anything else for that matter) in your clinic.

There are a few characteristics that separate a high quality patient from a low quality one. These include:

THE ORIGIN OF THE PATIENT

When the patient first came to your clinic, what brought him/her to your clinic in the first place? What was their expectation from you as a clinician and your clinic as an organization? Did the patient hear your praises from another patient who was a raving fan? Did the referring physician give you the highest of recommendations and tell the patient *"this physical therapist will take good care of you"*. The "pre-frame" with which the patient enters your practice triggers a cascade of events that define the life cycle of that patient and his/her "patient quality score" for your practice.

As they say, the first impression is indeed the last one.

SOCIAL PROOF

As you demonstrate testimonials and success stories from other patients, you condition existing patients to become referral sources. There are several ways to do this; you can have wall frames and pictures of other patients all over the clinic, online videos and audios in which past patients affirm your expertise, and articles/newsletters featuring you as the expert. People tend to 'follow the herd'. If a patient notices that several individuals in the community have worked with you and have had great success, they will subconsciously start believing in the treatment process with you along with your authority and expertise as a provider. This facilitates the treatment process.

The patients that know you and like you the most are going to be the ones that will provide with the most social proof (i.e. strong testimonials). These are the patients with the highest patient quality score. These patients play a valuable role in raising the overall quality score of your entire patient population.

EVALUATING THE QUALITY SCORE OF YOUR PATIENT

Here is a simple test for you to evaluate the "*quality score*" of a patient. You can answer yes/maybe/no to each of these questions with a score of 2/1/0 respectively for each answer.

Any score between 8 and 10 is considered a high quality score. A score between 5 and 7 is an average quality score. Any score of 4 and below implies that the patient is unlikely to help you grow your practice.

1. Is the patient willing to give you a video or a written testimonial?
2. Has the patient referred at least 1 friend/family/coworker to your clinic?
3. Has the patient shown an active interest in utilizing other products / services offered at your clinic?
4. Has the patient been compliant with the treatment process and responded well to treatment?
5. Has the patient praised you publicly inside or outside the clinic and brought you unexpected gifts (cookies / cakes) as gesture of gratitude?

The patient quality score can be improved with a combination of high quality treatment and "future pacing" expectations. This involves the use of precise language to manage the patient's expectations from physical therapy, encourage responsibility and compliance in the treatment process, and condition the patient to refer friends and family to you. An example of a "future pacing" script would be:

> *"We look forward to providing you with the same high quality of care that we have provided to hundreds of other patients over the years. When you finally recover and get better, don't forget to continue with your home exercise program and follow the guidelines we have established for you. We appreciate the fact that you chose to work with us and we value the trust that you (and the entire community) has placed in us. We are never too busy for your referrals; in fact, a referral is the best way for you to thank us. Our goal is to improve the health of as many individuals as possible in our community."*

Understanding and improving the patient quality score is the single most important thing you can do to grow your practice. The high quality score patients are also the ones likely to give you the best testimonials, the subject of the next section.

THE ANATOMY OF A TESTIMONIAL

Speaking of patients, testimonials from them can play a powerful role in your practice, especially when you are trying to set yourself apart from the competition. The best way to get the patient's (limited) attention with advertising is to make him / her feel you have helped someone 'just like them'. This is the exact reason why ads on television show 'everyday' people reinforcing the benefits of a product or service.

If you are not collecting testimonials in your clinic, it's something you may want to consider. Please check your state guidelines to make sure the use of testimonials is allowed before implementing the strategies in this section.

THE CRITICAL VALUE OF THE TESTIMONIAL

A patient who is willing to give you a testimonial is the most valuable referral source for your clinic, outside of the referring physician. The harsh reality is that most private practice owners never ask for testimonials and even if they do, the patient is completely neglected after such a testimonial. Patients who give you a testimonial should be appreciated and treated as valuable business assets through regular, frequent contact using email, snail mail, text messaging and phone calls. You want to regularly polish your 'diamonds in the rough'

THE IMPORTANCE OF LIFE CHANGING 'EMOTION' IN YOUR TESTIMONIALS

For best results use strong, life-changing testimonials in your marketing. A testimonial like:

> *"Hi this is Amy from Maryland. I am blessed to work with John. My lower back improved so much after working with John that my life has improved significantly. I can go hiking with my family and am FINALLY able to do the things I could never enjoy before. Go to John's and Son's Physical Therapy if you want to change your life, just like I did."*

This is a lot better than most testimonials, which are along these lines:
"John is a good PT, I recommend him" (such testimonials have zero, sometimes negative impact since the reader feels you are like 'everyone else')

THE BEST TIME TO ASK FOR A TESTIMON]

Most private practice owners wait until discharge, which is a mistake. The patient is already thinking of 'life after physical therapy'. Do NOT wait until discharge. The best time is immediately after a 'good' treatment session, when the benefits of therapy are dominant in the patient's mind. The longer you wait, the less likely it is that you will get the testimonial. You could take this strategy one step further and ask the patient if they know anyone who might be a good candidate for your services. Once you have a name, phone number and email, you can initiate contact with the prospect.

Now that you've decided to ask for a testimonial and you know when to ask for it, the question arises:

"How do you ask for it without appearing desperate or making the patient feel uncomfortable?"

The best script to use to ask for a testimonial is the "*Patient Appreciation Formula*" script, which is:

---

*"Did you have a good treatment session? (*__Treatment Reinforcement__*) Do you realize how much better you are now compared to when you came in?*

*Great! The best way for you to thank us is by giving us a testimonial, so that other patients can learn more about our services through your experience. Is that fair? (*__Logical Affirmation__ *–wait for patient to say yes).*

*You see, as a small business, we do not spend money on advertising, but instead rely on word of mouth referrals from valued patients like yourself. This way, we can reduce marketing expenses and focus more on quality of treatment instead, don't you agree? (*Wait for patient to say yes*)*

*So all I'd like you to do is to step here, tell us about your experience and that's it! While you are at it, would you mind filling out this form listing a couple of people you know that might be good candidates for our programs? All it takes is a couple of minutes. (*Wait for a couple of minutes*)*

We'll offer them a no obligations trial consultation as a way of thanking you for taking the time to do this testimonial. Thank you.

We can grow because of the support from valued patients like you.
*You have come a long way (with us). I appreciate you.(*smile and a handshake - __Appreciation__*)"*

There are several subtle elements in the script above, and they include:
1. Reinforcement of treatment benefits
2. Constant affirmation triggers (get them to say yes)
3. Appreciation (everyone likes being appreciated)

THE BEST SCRIPT TO USE TO GET THE TESTIMONIAL

Simply ask the patient to say these three things.
1. Who you are
2. What benefit you got from physical therapy
3. Why the person watching / reading the testimonial should come to YOUR clinic

THE BEST WAYS TO COLLECT TESTIMONIALS

If possible, have a flip cam ready in your clinic and get testimonials on video ALWAYS, since the videos can be used on your website, on monitors in your clinic, and the actual words (and pictures) can be transcribed and re-purposed on your website or marketing brochures.

A hand written testimonial runs a close second, since it can be used in a picture frame, scanned for your website, or even inserted into a digital frame.

Always have the patient give you written consent to use their testimonials in:
✓ Audio / Video (website, DVDs to physicians)
✓ Typeset (website, brochures, ads)
✓ Handwritten (picture frames, photo frames, scanned letters on your website – very useful strategy, makes your website stand out immediately)

On a final note, pictures on your website and the patient's first name will boost response rate significantly, especially if the readers feel the patient is 'just like them'. As far as possible, use the patient's full name and city if possible, or first name and initials at the very least. Ask the patient to sign a written consent form authorizing you to use the testimonial in any media (website, print ads, letters, display signs etc).

EMBRACING CRITICISM AS A STEPPING STONE

The German poet, Heinrich Heine noted that a person "*only profits from praise*" when he "values criticism".

While testimonials from patients are always welcome, it is equally important for a successful practice to embrace criticism. This will enable your practice to identify new opportunities for growth and improvement.

We all know that word-of-mouth is a powerful source of referrals - *positive* word-of-mouth (which is directly correlated with testimonials). But what about *negative* word-of-mouth? In a web-based world where information travels quickly, every patient interaction matters. **As good as your clinical skills may be; negative interactions are inevitable.**

There is a right (and a wrong way) to handle criticism.

Instead of ignoring a negative opinion, try to value the patients who criticize and find "common ground" with them to improve the patient's experience. Use this as an opportunity to identify strengths, address weaknesses, and make improvements where needed.

Answer these questions to determine how you respond to criticism:

- ❖ When your practice has negative feedback from one or more patients, what is your immediate reaction?
- ❖ Do you have a forum (drop box, website) for patients to voice their concerns?
- ❖ Does your practice invite complaints?
- ❖ Do you have "ostrich syndrome"? Do you bury your head in the sand when faced with criticism?
- ❖ If patients have complaints, is it easy for them to communicate them to the owner of the clinic, or do they have to jump through multiple hoops?
- ❖ Do you give them the option to remain anonymous when they criticize you?
- ❖ Do you ask for feedback once a problem has been identified and solved?

Negative feedback is an excellent opportunity to actually strengthen that relationship. There are a few things to do here:

1. Listen to what they have to say. For some concerns, listening is all that is required.
2. Next, thank the patient for choosing you for their rehabilitation needs.

3. Recognize their complaints and apologize for their troubles if needed– you will be in a better position to keep that patient coming back and gain useful feedback to improve your practice.
4. If possible, say what you will do to rectify it immediately.
5. Surprise them with a "consolation gift". Certain gifts should always be kept in the clinic to basically say *"we goofed up, so here's a little gift from us to make it up to you."* Some examples of "goof-up gifts" include:
    a. Starbucks gift cards
    b. A certificate for 2 movie tickets
    c. Gift certificate to a local restaurant
    d. A nice box of chocolates
    e. A home shiatsu massager – a version that can help the area of pain they experience (i.e.- low back, neck / shoulders, foot)
    f. Massage certificate – either at your clinic if you have a massage therapist on staff or a neighborhood spa (a business that you cross-promote with)
6. End by saying this: *"Is there anything else we can do for you?"* Most people will be pacified (often impressed) when they hear these words.

When your employees see that management evaluates and responds to negative feedback with an effort to improve, *they are more likely to follow in your footsteps.*

Issues brought forth by patients should never be ignored. Whether it's the wait times prior to treatment, complaints about treatment or things like rising copays (which are beyond your control), always give patients a chance to voice their concerns.

When these complaints are shared with staff, seek collaboration to make things easier for patients. It is crucial that you involve the front desk staff in these efforts, as they are the ones that will interact with, listen to, and (hopefully) console the patients.

Patients have a long memory as far as mistakes as concerned and a very low limit of tolerance. Most patients are willing to forgive errors the first time around. What they don't tolerate is failure to take responsibility for mistakes or the unwillingness to correct them.

Strong leaders don't hide from difficult situations. Your approach to complex issues should represent a willingness to address concerns from patients. Be open to new ideas that might turn your practice around, as long as it is true to your company's mission statement.

Once you value criticism and align it with your core values, you will profit (and improve) each time you get negative feedback.

You will also transform dissatisfied patients into referral sources (and potentially raving fans, as discussed in the next section). Criticism (and the way you handle it) is critical to the growth of your practice. This helps you get real time feedback from your patients and establish a 'feedback loop' to improve your practice.

THE PATIENT FEEDBACK LOOP

Are the patients and physicians in your area talking about you as a primary physical therapy provider?

When a patient reads your brochure, can they see and feel your passion as a provider?

After reviewing your marketing material, does your patient:

- ❖ Think you have a cause, a mission statement?
- ❖ Respect your credentials and expertise?
- ❖ Consider your services?
- ❖ Discuss you with family and friends?

If the answer is no, your practice may be getting too conventional.

Being predictable has its advantages. It's safe to conform to expectations and provide a service that people have come to expect. For a business, staying within the default comfort zone is easy and pleasant.

It's also the best way to let a practice slide into oblivion.

Your staff, pricing, location, and service fit the 'norm' and everything you do is by the book. Sometimes the 'right' approach in every aspect can be the wrong thing to do from a marketing perspective. If you try to become everything to everybody, you will end up becoming a vague thing to most prospects. A successful practice overcomes the inherent defensive mindset and embraces change.

In a recession, it pays to be unique.

Being different requires an investment of time and effort. It necessitates an unwavering commitment against all odds. If your passion shines through, you will make an impact and establish yourself.

Remarkable is as remarkable does. Start looking for ways to offer services with improved speed, efficiency, and specialization to your community. Isolate the exact type of physical therapy your audience is asking for; conduct surveys and match their needs with your abilities and passion as a provider. The best way to collect this information and make informed practice decisions is through your website.

COLLECT FEEDBACK FROM YOUR PATIENTS TO TAILOR YOUR PASSION

Marketing material should be designed based on feedback from patients, not beautiful templates created by graphic designers or theoretical excellence by therapists. Understanding your patient's thought process and decision-making process; their emotions, logic, and trigger points is an invaluable tool to tailor your services. When patients review marketing material, they typically ask one or more of the following questions:

✓ What is the benefit this clinic can provide me?

✓   How can I contact them?
✓   How soon will they see me?
✓   Do they accept my insurance?

Does your marketing material and website answer these questions? Ideally, you want live feedback from individuals who actually visit your website and review your material.

For best results, put together two control groups of 4-5 patients at your clinic and have one group review your material in front of you. Observe what they read, if they seek more information about specific programs, and their tendency to go the next step; ask for more information. Ask them the following questions:

❖   What do you like about my website?
❖   Does the brochure provide you with useful information?
❖   Do my programs interest you?
❖   Is there anything specific you are looking for?
❖   What don't you like about this material?
❖   Does this material encourage you to contact us?

Wait for honest feedback and be prepared for constructive, perhaps even scathing criticism. At the end of this research, you will have a clear idea about the needs of a majority of your patients.

Now, make the changes to your marketing material and website. Retest with the 2nd control group for a fresh, new, unbiased perspective. Test and retest strategies while alternating between both control groups. Observe the feedback that the new audience gives you and feel free to test and retest. The single best way to improve patient communication from your marketing material is to constantly test and retest with your patient audience. Testing once a month for 20-30 minutes allows you to stay abreast of patient requirements and current events.

A mission statement and marketing material that is tested, improved, and retested based on patient feedback will always result in more referral generation than content that is untested and built solely on the opinion of the therapist or web designer.

Make the changes and let the visitors guide you to unravel your true passion.

Follow this system every month. This time, they *will* start talking about you.

IDENTIFYING YOUR RAVING FANS

As the owner of a physical therapy private practice, it is important to identify patients who ascend from 'regular patients' and become your biggest 'fans'. These patients can become 'human billboards' for your clinic and word of mouth referrals from these individuals can play a significant role in the growth of your practice.

Most private practice owners do not understand the difference between a satisfied patient and a raving fan. **Every clinic has satisfied patients, but only the most successful clinics have raving fans**. A single raving fan can have huge implications for your practice and is likely to:

a) Refer at least FIVE of their family or friends to your practice.
b) Write or sign a pre-written letter of appreciation and give you permission to send it to their physician
c) Give you a video or audio testimonial that you can use on your website, encouraging other patients to visit your clinic

Now that you understand the difference between a 'satisfied patient' and 'raving fan', you'll understand why these 'fans' are important for your clinic. They are so enthusiastic about your practice that they become walking, talking billboards eager to promote you to anyone who will listen.

This public endorsement spreads quickly in your community and is a FREE form of advertising that is infinitely more effective than any form of paid advertising (print, radio, TV, website ads, etc.).

The secret to turning your satisfied patients into raving fans for your practice is to develop a closer, more personal connection with each patient. People want to go to someone they know, like, and trust (patient relationship trifecta). Once you transcend an individual up the ascension ladder into a raving fan, you will help create a 'tribe' of patients with a high quality score.

This trifecta is easier to establish if the individual comes to you as a referral from someone they know. The patient is now 'pre-framed' to recognize you as an expert, which makes the ascension significantly easier.

In my experience, the best candidates for your raving fans tend to be female patients. They have a circle of friends with whom they share meaningful information and advice. Good (and bad) news tends to spread pretty quickly with female patients.

Chapter 2   49

Incidentally, most of the physician's offices have receptionists and office managers that are women, who can send you many referrals.

You should also identify the patients who are the biggest influencers in your community. Do you treat the mayor, an athlete, or a police officer? Are you treating a successful business owner or a baseball coach who could refer you to his entire team? You need to focus a majority of your marketing efforts on your biggest group of influencers.

To help you convert satisfied patients into raving fans, use the following strategies:

1) **Know your patient**. Become interested (don't just "act" it) in what they have to say. Many physicians run in and out of their exam rooms, leaving many of the patients' questions and concerns unanswered. They spend a lot more time with the physical therapist. Know what your patients' concerns are and help them understand what to expect on the road to recovery (with you). For some patients, you might be the only person they can talk to.

2) **Remember to smile**. There's nothing more contagious than a smile. If you feel tension, your patients will sense it. When you and your staff members are happy, the patient will want to be around you.

3) **Reiterate your patient's name as often as possible**. There's nothing sweeter to a person's ear than the sound of his or her own name. You must go a step beyond remembering the patients name and repeat it back to them multiple times in a conversation.

4) **Listen to your patients**. They need to be able to develop a relationship with you. Listening is a skill. People need someone to talk to, someone who can understand and help them in the recovery process.

5) **Become friends with them**. Be a trusted friend, advisor and mentor, not just 'that physical therapist'. For example, when a patient thanks you for making them feel better or mentions that they are now pain free; seize the opportunity and say,

> *"I'm glad you're feeling better. Can I ask you for a favor, to help me spread the word so I can help your family and friends as well? If you know anyone who might benefit, please write down their name, email address and phone number on this pad. I will make sure we offer them a no-cost evaluation to determine how we can assist them."*

This is a variation of the 'Patient Appreciation Formula' script mentioned earlier in the section on testimonials.

At the end of the day, patients will not remember what you said to them or how you treated them. However, **the one thing that people will never forget is how you made them feel**. What you need to do is to make each patient feel like a celebrity and help them ascend into a raving fan. This is part of the 'Private Practice Success Formula' explained in the next section.

THE PRIVATE PRACTICE SUCCESS

The reason \ and become phy ̣sts is usually because v ̣ut to impact and change peoples' lives and be compensated fairly well in the process. We are taught to be excellent clinicians (as we all are); but when it comes to running a business, our expertise can fall short.

The truth is there is a big difference between being a viable practitioner and a viable practice owner. Getting patients to walk in is one part of the equation. Treating them well (literally) and conditioning them to refer from day one will be a critical component of a successful practice in this new economy.

Post discharge follow up using a combination of email, text messaging on their mobile phones, direct mail, and phone call follow-ups is the differentiator between a clinic struggling for referrals and one that is overflowing with patients.

This isn't just about 'educating patients' and physicians about the benefits of physical therapy; this is about becoming an important part of the patient's day-to-day life.

This is called the "*Private Practice Success Formula*" and it can be summarized as

PS + VP + AF + PM = PRIVATE PRACTICE SUCCESS

The new economy practice will have the following components in place even before the practice opens its doors for the first time:

PS = PROSPECT STIMULATORS

A prospect stimulator is an educational tool (book, audio CD, DVD, online course) that helps educate patients and leads them back to the clinic for more information. For example, an audio program on "7 things you can do to overcome low back pain" which leads to an offer for an appointment in the clinic can function as a '*prospect stimulator*'. Every clinic should have at least 5, preferably 10 or more prospect stimulators that are constantly distributed using various channels in the community.

VP = VALUABLE PROSPECTS

A high school student without insurance and the means to pay for physical therapy may not be a good candidate for your services (from a business point of view) as compared to an executive with the right type of insurance, someone who will not hesitate to pay his copay and even an appointment cancellation fee (which should be mandatory in all practices). Your practice must maintain visibility in front of your most 'valued prospects' using a web presence (search engine optimization), social media (Facebook, Twitter, Linkedin), print (strategically placed advertisements), direct mail (postcards to a targeted mailing list) and personal phone call follow-ups (with selected patients) to drive them, their friends, and family back to your clinic. This should not be a 'once in a while' thing. It has to be done for 2-3 hours every week, since this activity will sustain your practice during tough times.

AF = ASCENSION FUNNEL

The biggest mistake made by most private practice owners is the wrong offer. Patients are completely desensitized at the prospect of a 'free consultation'. They don't even care for a 'complimentary evaluation' in an ad filled with nice images and pictures of the physical therapist. Every advertisement should have one purpose and one purpose only – to get the contact information of the prospect and introduce them to your marketing funnel. Once the prospect's information (name, email, phone number) is obtained, contact from someone in your office who is very experienced in 'closing' the patient so they NOW want to come in is important. Too many practices waste tens of thousands of dollars trying to 'close' the patient right away with an ad. This is a cardinal sin; it's like proposing on the first date. The chances of success are pretty slim.

The 'new economy' practice will patiently get the prospect to know, like, and trust the practice and/or practitioners with personal stories and testimonials that elicit emotion and 'human connection' as opposed to color pictures and beautiful equipment in an ad that patients will spend 15-30 seconds reading.

PM = PATIENT METRICS

Every strategic private practice owner must keep an eye on important business metrics that pertain to each patient.

The success of a 'new economy' practice is measured by the following 'patient metrics'

a) The 'LVP' or lifetime value of the patient. This can be increased significantly by offering more products and services. It can also be increased by raising your prices for such products and services, which are not price regulated and independent of insurance reimbursements.

b) The 'PL' or patient longevity. Is the patient coming back to you or referring their family and friends? How many of your patients are becoming your ambassadors and coming back to you or driving more people to your door? Increasing patient longevity through patient conditioning is the fastest way to grow a practice. It yields greater results and takes less time, money, and effort than trying to 'schmooze' physicians and build new referral relationships.

c) The '**TS**' or therapist status (in the patient's mind). It is the barometer of *how important physical therapy is for them*. Are you constantly (yet delicately) reminding patients about your expertise, authority, and the benefits of physical therapy? Patients lose enthusiasm for ANY service over a period of time and you need to build systems to keep them constantly engaged, enthused, and motivated to come in for treatment and become your ambassadors. You must promote the 'concept' of wellness and how physical therapy can help; NOT the 'brand' or the 'company' that provides it. Patients are interested in the process of treatment; but **this interest nosedives after the first few visits**. This leads to an inevitable decline of therapist status unless you take active, proactive efforts to maintain the importance of physical therapy for the patient.

d) The number of patient visits each week. This is directly related to '*volume*'. Most practices assume that increased volume equals increased profits. While this may be true, it's possible to increase net profits WITHOUT increasing patient volume by increasing LVP, PL, and TS

PATIENT PERCEPTION IS PRACTICE REALITY

A private practice that stands apart from its competition must be able to position itself differently from the competition. A successful practice dedicates a significant amount of energy to 3 components of growth:

✓ Patient acquisition
✓ Patient satisfaction
✓ Word of mouth referral generation

In order to acquire new patients, the practice needs a combination of strategies in addition to traditional patient referrals. These include press releases, radio announcements, timely advertisements (Thanksgiving specials, New Year specials, Valentine's Day special events), online advertising, and direct mail / phone call campaigns.

Patient satisfaction is determined by the patients experience from the moment they walk through the doors of your clinic and their first interaction with your office staff to the moment they are discharged.

Word of mouth referral generation is a natural consequence of good therapy and the 'indoctrination' of the importance of referral generation in the mind of the patient. Patients must be conditioned to refer from the moment they step into your clinic with a script like this (an abbreviated version of the 'Patient Appreciation Formula'):

> *"We appreciate you as a patient and want you to know that the #1 way we grow as a clinic is through word of mouth referrals from valued patients like yourself. We do not rely on advertising, but instead appreciate the goodwill and positive reinforcement from patients. If you have a moment, please take the time to tell your friends, family, and physicians about the positive experience you have had at our clinic."*

The importance of a script like this is:

❖ It gives patients a great deal of importance. People like to be appreciated and made to feel important

❖ It reminds patients to refer to you. Over a period of time, your existing and past patients tend to forget about the importance of referrals. It is your responsibility to remind them to refer back to you and tell their physicians about the quality of your services.

❖ It helps you 'cut through the clutter'. The average patient is so overwhelmed with information and misinformation that they are less likely to refer your services to their friends, unless the benefit is obvious and powerful. It takes the right language and medium (phone, email, snail mail, and one-on-one interactions) to move patients to take action.

Regardless of the medium, the message and the way it is structured is the defining factor in the success of your marketing. The words that are spoken and the precise language used in texts, emails, and letters can sway patients into action or turn them away from your practice.

These '*descriptors*' need to be well-balanced reflections o. overstatements. A well designed descriptor has 3 key compon.

    1.) What it is that you have to offer to the patient
    2.) Why it will help them
    3.) How they can get it

When formulated correctly, the 'hook' will appeal to emotiona. ...u propel the patient to pick up the phone to call you. Don't make this messa.. too technical; it should be easy to understand.

The goal is to make patients say to themselves:

> *"Yes, this therapist understands my pain and can help me recover from my injury"*
>
> *"This therapist is different from other provider and can genuinely help me"*
>
> *"I can easily get an appointment and will get better very quickly"*

Some examples of a good 'hook' in your practice include:

✓ The first and only _____.
✓ You are just one phone call away from _____.
✓ We are known for _____.
✓ This is the REAL secret about _____.
✓ Have you ever wondered? _____.
✓ Every single patient who has come to _____ knows about our record with _____.
✓ Discover the real truth about _____.
✓ Within a few weeks, expect a transformation of _____.
✓ Learn the truth about _____.
✓ Don't make these _____ mistakes when you _____.

Be factual and highlight the benefits associated with your practice and not necessarily its features. Use language that patients use – pain, stiffness, swelling etc. Patient centered language reinforces your clinical efforts and boosts patient compliance, enhancing the perception of the standard of care.

Improving patient perception should be part of your 'high priority' or 'high lifetime value tasks' which should become a part of your critical 20%, as explained in the next section.

THE 80/20 FORCE FACTOR

During our training in physical therapy school, we are taught to think analytically about cause and effect as it pertains to the human body. While this is certainly true in the clinical realm, it could not be further from the truth in the business world.

If you are a business owner trying to grow your private practice, the relative importance of some things far outweighs others. It's critical that you identify the 'high leverage' factors and focus the majority of your time on them. Everything else becomes secondary.

As clinicians, it's counter intuitive for us to embrace business activities that push us out of our comfort zone and we (naturally) gravitate towards the tasks we know best.

We spend 80% of our time doing the 20% of the things that come easily to us.

The question arises:

Are 80% of results coming from 20% of causes, specifically powerful forces that govern growth?

If you take a closer look, you'll find that the answer is an overwhelming yes. In fact, there are times when **5% of the things you do are more important than the other 95%.** The 80/20 force factor can, at times, become a 95/5 force factor.

Have you found that the key meeting with a group of physicians, which barely lasted 20 minutes, did more to generate referrals than all the marketing that preceded it? Have you found a handful of patients (representing 20% or less of your total patient population) resulted in a significant portion of internal referrals? All physicians and all patients don't have the same capability to grow your practice.

To be a truly successful private practice owner, you must identify and leverage the critical 20% force factor at work in the world and turn it to your advantage. This means that a majority of the things you do (four-fifths) has little or no relevance to the growth of your practice.

This unusual 'force factor' pattern was discovered in 1897 by Italian economist Vilfredo Pareto who observed that a majority of the wealth and income in early nineteenth century England was distributed amongst the 'elite' in society. He realized there was a consistent mathematical relationship between a section of society and the amount of wealth they enjoyed. He discovered that there was a predictable imbalance of wealth distribution in society.

As a private practice owner, understanding the 80/20 principle will allow you to identify the critical 20% of the tasks that drive 80% of the growth in your practice. These "*force factors*" include:

   a) Identifying the 20% of physicians and patients that are your grade 'A' referral sources

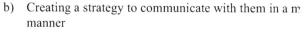

b) Creating a strategy to communicate with them in a m manner
c) Delegating the tasks in (b) above and managing employees effe.
d) Forming liaisons (syndicates) of local businesses with a mutually ben. referral relationship
e) Creating your own 'mastermind' network of successful individuals / mentors who can walk you through the highs and lows of running your practice
f) Negotiating with insurance companies for better reimbursements
g) Overseeing cash flow, plugging 'leaks' and unnecessary expenses

Every practice is different and you may need to come up with your own "*force factors.*" You may need to 'force' insight and introspection. Ask yourself the following questions to come up with your own list:

a) What are the activities that give you the most leverage in your practice?
b) What are the non-linear, strategic actions you can take to kick start exponential growth (instead of incremental improvements) in your business?
c) What are the key areas you can delegate to an assistant, eliminating the "80%" of activities that clutter your day? (think answering email, sending faxes, answering the phone, paying the bills)
d) What are the actions you need to complete to achieve a 'Zen like' state of ambition and authority while being relaxed and confident at the same time?

Identifying these '*force factors*' will dramatically increase your ability to run your practice instead of passively allowing your practice to run you. You will also realize that the 20% activities that result in the **highest leverage for your practice turn out to be the 'high lifetime value' activities** that were discussed in Chapter 1. You'll also be able to improve patient experience and increase revenue in your practice, while minimizing the downsides, including the cost of losing patients.

THE COST OF LOSING PATIENTS

Imagine having an army of patients singing your praises every single day! Envision a band of raving fans, walking, talking human billboards who promote your practice at every social occasion they attend. A social sales force that transforms the image of your business from obscurity to stardom.

The presence of such team members can transform your practice, while their absence can sink it.

A tribe of raving patients is possible and takes months of planning and effort. The results are worth their weight in gold.

The real asset of a physical therapy private practice is its relationship to past and present patients. The ability to engage, captivate, and influence the patients' healthcare decisions while email, phone, and regular mail contact is a priceless asset.

It is important to treat your patients as a gated community. Imagine yourself as a farmer guarding a herd of cows. As a therapist, never ever take your patients for granted and surround them with a wall of information and credibility describing your practice. In a competitive economy, coupled with declining reimbursement rates, many businesses and professionals are standing by to steer patients in a different direction away from your practice. A patient's attention should be treated as solid gold. Conversely, patients who are made to feel unimportant or under-appreciated may easily be lured away from your clinic.

Creating a sense of tremendous value with your patients begins with the personal contact and is reinforced with alternative modes of communication, spread strategically throughout the year. These '*communication points*' can consist of email, least desirable to a phone call (most desirable) during the period after discharge.

A word of caution; no more than one week should go by without a 'communication point' with each patient. You want the patient to subconsciously associate with you and begin to trust in your expertise. The regular communication points help foster quality of service, proximity of location, consumers' preferences, and the referral generation of that particular patient. The most preferable form of contact is a personal phone call from the therapist to the patient. This is ideal during birthdays, wedding anniversaries, and major holidays. An email/postcard can also be followed up with a phone call or vice versa.

Why not just use email? Isn't it free?

The problems with traditional email include bounced email addresses, low deliverability ratios (not all email recipients open their email), delay in checking emails, and the general non-personal content within the email. It is worth the investment to call the patient or send a hand-written postcard. This allows the patient to hear the words you speak and manually open the packages you send, creating a better social connection.

If you believe you cannot write or do not know what to say, think again. There are only four key pieces of information you need to provide your patients during each communication point.

1. Who you are (an introduction or a reminder)
2. What you can do to help them
3. Why they should listen to you
4. How they can be helped by you (contact information)

Here is a sample script:

> *"Hello this is Mark from ABC physical therapy. I have exciting news for you today. For a limited time, we are reopening our low-back pain prevention workshop to a handful of people. This will teach you some insider strategies to take care of your lower back. To register before spots fill up, please call 555-423-1234 or email support@abctherapy.com."*

When you set up a *patient-centric communication point* like this, the patient recognizes your sincerity, effort, and energy involved. Regardless of the mode of delivery (email, regular mail, phone call), patients will now look forward to receiving communication from you. Not only will they read the email (instead of deleting it), they will forward it to their friends and function as a human billboard for your private practice.

A successful physical therapy practice identifies, obtains, and nurtures its past and present patients. Once you can get the staff involved in this mission and establish a system to reward them based on performance, you will be able to improve the patient experience, unite your staff for a common vision and improve profitability at the same time.

TURBULENCE AHEAD: THE WHAT, WHY, AND HOW OF STAFF MANAGEMENT (AND COMMON MISTAKES TO AVOID)

> *"You can do what I cannot do. I can do what you cannot do.*
> *Together we can do great things"*
> *~ Mother Teresa ~*

Imagine that your practice is like a bus motoring along a highway on a warm, sunny day. The driver is the private practice owner who is responsible for direction and speed, while the staff represents the passengers. The passengers rely on the driver and simply do what they are told. They react occasionally when a bump comes along, shifting in their seats but are passively 'along for the ride' for the most part. This was the old management system.

That's not the world we live in any more. The emerging economy brings constant change and fierce competition. Imagine the same bus, now inching forward nervously in the middle of the night, impacted by torrential rain and 100 mph gusts of wind with no help in sight for miles. The road is treacherous and visibility is limited. The bus is in danger of tipping over. Now is the time for split second decisions and the passengers CANNOT wait for guidance. Everyone must take responsibility and make quick decisions to remain safe and calm and possibly assist the driver to get through this testing period.

We are in this TOGETHER

The business climate in 2011 necessitates a proactive approach to problem solving, systems improvement, and customer satisfaction; best forged by an employee ownership mentality (EOM). This helps your practice prepare for inevitable turbulence, allowing every staff member to step up and assume a managerial role if required. As the challenge escalates, the need for teamwork escalates.

On the other hand, role restriction of staff members can lead to erosion of morale, restricted progress, and loss of staff members to competitors. Encouraging the right person with a set of diverse skills and providing benchmarks for salary increases allows the EOM to grow gradually.

EOM facilitates teamwork, which is at the heart of all great achievements in business. A good way to facilitate EOM and hand out bonuses as a reward is to

conduct quarterly accountability (QA) meetings and to measure
(DB) that each staff member brings to your clinic.

WHAT IS DIRECT BENEFIT (DI

The sum total of all the actions by the staff member that measurably improve the
profitability in your clinic represents the *direct benefit* from that staff member. This
should be 'scored' using a points system. Notice that this does not include any
subjective elements of ego, temperament, and insecurity. Granted these are important,
but they are difficult to measure.

Depending upon the role delineation in your clinic, it's critical to identify the DB
tasks for each staff member and calculate a '*DB score*' every quarter. This will allow
each individual to clearly understand his/her expectations and allow you, as a practice
owner, to objectively measure their baseline performance. The DB of a therapist is
different from that of the front desk staff, for example. Knowing where they are will
enable them to visualize where then need to be (increase DB), which will lead to
employee bonuses (EB). This will facilitate EOM.

QA + DB = EB = EOM

For example, DB of a physical therapist includes number of patient visits each
week and average duration of each treatment. An advanced measure of DB for the
therapist would be the number of patients who completed their plan of treatment
without a single missed appointment.

On the other hand, DB of the front desk staff includes number of evaluations
scheduled, minimization of cancellation rate, copay collections and family/friend
referral generation.

For each staff member, there will be a list of actions that contribute to the DB. Each
of these actions should be assigned a point value and a 'scoring system' should be
clearly outlined in an employee handbook so that it is transparent enough that every
staff member can easily calculate and keep track of their own DB.

To take the DB concept one step further, a part of their compensation should
always be linked to DB. In other words, the staff member earns a salary PLUS
additional income (can be as low as 5% of salary or as high as 15% of salary) for
getting a certain DB score.

Broad examples include:
- John, the therapist sees less than 50 patient visits in week 1 = point value
zero (just an example)
- John sees 70-80 patient visits in week 2 = point value one
- Average treatment time by John in the first week of April is 75 minutes =
point value zero
- Average treatment time by Sarah in the first week of April is 40 minutes =
point value one
- In the first week of April, the number of patients who completed their plan
of treatment without a single missed appointment with John was 3 = point

value six (John gets two points for every patient who completed their entire plan of care) and so on…

The biggest mistake most practice owners make is relying on subjective measures to determine employee bonuses. For the staff member, bonuses should be objective and easy to understand, leaving no room for questioning or contemplation because of the transparency of the DB scoring system. It's best to put all this in an employee handbook, available for any staff member to review. The absence of such a handbook is another mistake made by clinics trying to set up an employee bonus program. This precise, simple scoring system also allows the business owner to separate the high performers (and transform them into managers) from the low performers (the strength of the team is impacted by its weakest link and some team members may need to be removed).

QUARTERLY ACCOUNTABILITY (QA)

A quarterly accountability meeting to review an individual's performance should become a part of your clinic's culture. The practice owner should discuss the DB score of that particular staff member over the past quarter, compare it with past scores, offer feedback and welcome questions. This is an ideal time to discuss subjective elements, analyze performance, and plan expectations for the next quarter. This meeting will reveal some interesting 'big picture' links between productivity and external factors unrelated to performance. For example, one of the conversations that arise from this QA meeting could go like this:

> *"John, I notice that your average treatment time increased by 10 minutes in the past quarter. Does this have something to do with the new billing system we have transitioned into and what can we do to make things easier for you, without compromising on patient care?"*

The right person in the right place leads to progress and multiplication. On the other hand, the wrong person in the wrong place leads to regression. Remember that not every staff member will, should, or can take the journey with the rest of the team. Such individuals won't see the big picture, accept responsibility, or fulfill their expectations. The ones that do will be the ones who accept and respond to the systems you have in place.

> *"There are no problems we cannot solve together and very few we can solve by ourselves."*
> ~ **Lyndon Johnson** ~

PHYSICAL THERAPY TREND
WE HEAD TOWARDS 2020

The physical the ...stry is constantly changing and will continue to do so as we head to 2020 and beyond. As more and more private practices open and compete for the same patient population, a practice that embraces new trends will see an instant surge in income, recognition, and influence among patients and referral sources.

Every private practice has hidden assets, untapped income opportunities, and overlooked possibilities that can transform the practice. As we look at the road ahead toward 2020, some emerging trends will shape the future of physical therapy and private practice.

TREND 1

A practice that can structure, market, and improve traditional physical therapy programs will improve credibility with the consumer and succeed in obtaining cash payments.

With declining reimbursements from providers and long delays in payments, a practice that functions independently and offers an exclusive brand of physical therapy for cash compensation will be the 'dream' business model. When a practice successfully employs the 3 critical elements of cash practice success, it will carve a unique niche for itself and stand out from the competition. The 3 elements of cash-for-treatment physical therapy are:

- ✓ The right message
- ✓ An understanding of the market
- ✓ The right kind of marketing

TREND 2

A practice that understands how to integrate 'social norms' for employees and patients will attract better staff and more patients.

A traditional practice serves patients with high quality physical therapy, but falls short of establishing that 'personal' connection with patients. Phone call and postcard reminders on birthdays, anniversaries, and holidays help to achieve this. Lasting value and friendships are built on social connections (enriching conversations, empathy, and gratitude) and not on the exchange of money (copays) and reimbursements. Exchanging gifts with a patient and demonstrating reciprocity is another way to integrate 'social norms' into the physical therapist / patient relationship.

TREND 3

The 'ascension ladder' will empower small practices to achieve an increased number of referrals per patient and referral source.

Closely linked to trends 1 and 2 mentioned above, a practice that uses the right message and marketing with the right market, transforms a stranger through the various stages of prospect, patients, referral source, and raving fan. Every element of your practice; personality of your staff, quality of physical therapy, documentation, and receptionist interaction should move patients up in the ascension ladder.

TREND 4

Practices that collect email lists and cell phone numbers of patients will save time, money, and resources on marketing.

Since email is fast, free, and simple collecting email addresses from patients on your intake form should be standard protocol. If you don't have it set up like this there is a simple way to contact past and present patients to obtain their email, but this has to be done in the right manner. Don't ask for the email without offering something in return. Instead, offer a free report / booklet / downloadable e-book and confirm contact information, asking for their email to update your records. Send them an email newsletter (explained in detail in Chapter 9).

Collect cellphone numbers of patients. This data can be used for appointment reminders, birthday greetings, mobile surveys, mobile voting, and mobile keyword opt-ins (text the word PATIENT to 77453 from your mobile phone to see how this works). The use of mobile marketing to grow your practice is explained in detail in Chapter 10.

TREND 5

Engaging in joint promotions with local businesses will skyrocket awareness and increase public perception.

Obtain a list of non-competing local businesses from the local chamber of commerce or the local library. Besides physicians, examples include hair salons, gyms, health clubs, attorneys, accountants, and even bank managers. Approach these businesses, telling them you can help their business by promoting them to your existing list of patients. Ask them to send out a letter (which you provide) to their clients telling them about your services and offer to do the same for them. You can even do a joint advertising campaign to their clients and split the cost of the advertising or mailing. The big advantage of local promotions (as opposed to traditional advertising) is that you are leveraging the reputation of the business with its existing customers. Remember, the business has invested its own time, money, and resources to cultivate its own client list and to have access to this list with a plug into the business is like taking an elevator to the top of the remote Himalaya Mountains.

TREND 6

The FREE OFFER – instant patient acquisition with attention grabbing marketing

Provide patients with an irresistible offer to get them to walk in. Examples include a free CD of DVD on injury prevention, a free booklet on low back pain, or an audio CD on pain relief at home. These resources can be created at a nominal cost, usually under $5 each, and then announced in newspapers, magazines, or radio ads in your geographical area. This will allow potential patients to raise their hand and identify themselves while attracting the right kind of people to your practice. Your cost to acquire a new patient can range anywhere from $4 to $8 for this type of marketing and the results are immediate, as long as the message, market, and marketing is a good match.

Don't wait, be the first to apply some of these emerging trends in your area. Some or a combination of all of these strategies will transform your marketing.

The concept of patient-financed marketing can be expanded significantly to 'partner financed marketing' where 'partner' implies referral source.

Before we elaborate, it's important to elaborate on the 3 types of individuals critical to the growth of your practice:

1. People whose lives can be changed by physical therapy (*Patients*).
2. People whose lives have been changed by physical therapy (*Past patients = Referral Sources*).
3. People / organizations related to physical therapy (Physicians, medical organizations, medical representatives, health clubs, spas, massage parlors, insurance providers, accountants, attorneys, manufacturers and retailers of exercise equipment = *Referral Sources)*

Partner financed marketing will serve all 3 categories mentioned above.

RESOURCE

...s The Same Technology Used By Thousands Of ...⌐ Companies, Hospitals, and Physician's Offices To Help YOU Get More Patients, Generate Referrals, Boost Compliance, and Skyrocket Patient Retention… Completely On Autopilot?

Benefits include:

- ❖ SMS text messaging to patients
- ❖ Email messaging (newsletters, broadcasts, and automatic sequences)
- ❖ FREE social marketing

Until now, marketing your private practice has been a manual, difficult process. Your front desk staff schedules the appointment, but following up with patients and maximizing compliance is a different story. With the "Clinical Contact" marketing package you can add your contacts manually or import all your contacts with the click of a button. Create segmented lists, send out your first text message campaign and see a response within MINUTES. Not only does this technology automatically communicate with patients and prospects, it allows you to store their contact information (cellphone, email) automatically into your database for future follow-ups via email, text messaging and voice broadcasting.

MOBILE MARKETING

Get ready to revolutionize your practice with Clinical Contact's cutting edge technology for text, voice and email marketing. With Clinical Contact, anyone with an Internet connection can take advantage of the power of text messaging (SMS), picture messaging (MMS), voice broadcasting, email marketing and social marketing including Facebook and Twitter, to reach an unlimited number of patients! All you need is an ordinary computer with access to the Internet and nothing more.

Get Started Now: **www.clinicalcontact.com**

EMAIL MARKETING

Email marketing is a fast and easy way to keep in touch with your patients. We help you take email marketing **to a higher level** by giving you **ready-to-use** scripts that can be used for interactive and personalized communication with your patients.

Built by private practice owners who understand your time constraints, this service was created to provide you with the tools that will help you grow your practice. We will not overwhelm you with several unnecessary features that can be difficult to manage. Clinical Contact provides you with ready-to-use scripts that compel patients to contact you, generating more referrals and dramatically boosting patient retention rate and compliance.

The scripts we provide have been tried and tested to help you maximize your return on investment. These scripts are an exclusive benefit that is reserved for Clinical Contact Members only.

SOCIAL MARKETING FEATURES

Clinical Contact's social media features make it easy to manage the conversations that are already taking place about your practice on Facebook, Twitter and over 30 other social media sites.

Use our platform to integrate your SMS and email campaigns into social media pages like your Facebook fan page. This increases visibility and helps increase engagement, loyalty, and ROI. Empower your patients to share your offers with trusted friends and contacts. Since social media has a strong viral component, Clinical

Contact makes it easy for your patients to share your message with friends. This will help increase awareness and grow your patient base.

VOICE BROADCASTING

Clinical Contact voice broadcasting capability allows your recorded voice to communicate with ALL of your patients within seconds with only a few clicks.

Add the personal touch of a human voice to digital technology and blast your voice message to as many patients as possible, all with the click of a button.

This is the fastest and easiest way to reactivate former patients, welcome new patients, introduce special promotions, announcements, send invitations or reminders to special events in your clinic, create new product or service announcements, pass on directions to your clinic and a whole lot more.

Get Started Now: **www.clinicalcontact.com**

Section I

CHAPTER 3

The Blueprint To Move Individuals

Up Your Ascension Ladder

E very individual will most likely fall into one of the following categories, as it pertains to your private practice:

- ➤ A stranger (unlikely to seek your services)
- ➤ A suspect (aware of, but unsure about your services)
- ➤ A prospect (considering your services)
- ➤ A patient (actively using your services)
- ➤ A referral source (recommends your services)
- ➤ A human billboard (has used your services and is a raving fan)

These stages form the *'patient ascension ladder'*.

With your clinical skills and business systems, your goal is to move an individual through the various stages of this ascension ladder by offering them the best possible experience every step of the way. This can increase awareness and interest about your practice. An understanding of the patient ascension ladder will allow you to build sustainable, long-term relationships with patients and referral sources.

Once the foundation of evidence based practice and advanced assessments, interventions and techniques are in place, consider a *'prospect stimulator'* to promote your practice. The best way to do this is to have a 'front end' product that gives the patient valuable information and leaves them wanting for more, which is why they seek out your services.

When a patient calls for information or visits your website, offer them a free 'front end' DVD or book filled with unique content relevant to them.

TRANSITION THE INDIVIDUAL UP THE ASCENSION LADDER

When a stranger or suspect accepts your gift / prospect stimulator, they have already made a small commitment to your practice. A small affirmation can lead to a larger one over a period of time. When a patient requests your prospect stimulator, you should make it mandatory for them to provide their mailing address, phone number, and email.

This helps you build a patient and prospect list. The next goal is to provide value to this list through regular phone, email, and snail mail communication so that they are responsive to your message. More importantly, the individuals on your list will naturally transition up the ascension ladder.

The best way to move patients up the ladder is to get them into the ladder in the first place. In order for a stranger or suspect to enter your 'funnel' and climb up the ladder, you use the *prospect stimulator'*. What you achieve with this tool is:

1. A mechanism for your practice to collect a list of qualified prospects for your practice
2. Instant differentiation - You are now the only practice 'giving away' a valuable educational tool
3. The ability to contact your prospects again and inform them about special offers, lead them back to your services, and finally bring them into your clinic

Once you've established a system to move patients up the ascension ladder, offer them new and improved services to improve their lifestyle and well-being.

The ascension ladder does not have to be restricted to patients alone, it can be applied to all kinds of referral sources.

Building relationships with local businesses and moving them up the ascension ladder is an important component of business and marketing. Imagine if you joined forces with a local accountant (there are several you can speak with right now) and jointly created a special offer like "Free DVD reveals 21 ways to save money, improving financial and physical health" and allowed the accountant to promote this to your patients. In exchange, the accountant finances the cost of the DVDs and also sends it to his entire list of clients.

Take a moment to think what just happened here. You have managed to:

- ❖ Position yourself as an expert for free
- ❖ Leverage the time, energy, and resources invested by the accountant to cultivate a list of clients; plus, you just got instant access to them
- ❖ Create a new referral source (you can mail to his list again in the future)
- ❖ Reach a new category of patients who would never have known you existed

Imagine doing this with local, enterprising physicians with successful, growing practices. Imagine if you created such a partnership each month and advertised this in the local newspaper.

Such marketing collaborations can build your practice from the ground up, in little or no time, as long as you can build the relationships with them and move individuals up the ascension ladder. I'll go into a lot more detail about the patient ascension ladder in the next section.

THE PATIENT ASCENSION LADDER

The biggest asset of a private practice is its list of prospects, patients, and referral sources.

In addition to collecting 'opt-ins' on your website in exchange for free reports, you can collect a list of 'prospects' with public speaking, postcard marketing to local communities, and joint venture relationships with local businesses.

Building a list is important, especially for a referral based business like physical therapy. A list may be less important to Burger King, but it is critical to "John's Physical Therapy."

As therapists, we are programmed to complete the service for one patient and then spending time and energy trying to get a new patient.

While there's nothing wrong with this strategy, it's important to understand the 'progression' of the patient relationship; the *'ascension ladder'*.

When an individual shows interest in something you are giving away (a free report), they are automatically identifying themselves as potential clients. Essentially, they are raising their hands and saying, *"Yes, I'm interested, tell me more."*

Once a 'stranger' gives you some information on your website (an email, a phone number) or responds to your ad requesting a free report, they have already starting moving up the ascension ladder. This individual has already demonstrated some trust in your practice and has recognized your expertise.

At this point, you should educate and empower the anonymous suspect; transforming him/her into a likely patient (i.e. prospect).

Let's define some of the stages in this ascension ladder:

- ❖ **Suspect** - someone who just found you, has yet to trust your expertise
- ❖ **Prospect** - someone who has learned about your services and is considering working with you (this will be explained in more detail in the next section)
- ❖ **Patient** - an individual committing their time, energy, and resources to get better while under your supervision
- ❖ **Referral Source** - an individual (a past patient, physician, etc.) who recognizes your expertise and refers you to other individuals
- ❖ **Raving Fan** - a one of a kind referral source who constantly sings your praises and refers your practice to everyone they know.

A *suspect* can be transformed into a *prospect* in 3 different ways:

1. They hear about you from more than one source: newspaper, physician, internet, radio, magazines
2. They are influenced by the testimonials on your website, which are powerful and inspirational
3. Their friends have been talking (raving) about you

Unlike patients, prospects will NOT come to you after immediately seeing your marketing. Therefore, you must identify your prospects so you can follow up with them to build and nurture a relationship through 'pull' marketing campaigns.

Patients require a different approach, one that involves more nurturing. The fastest way for you to follow up and build a relationship with patients is email. However, having said that, regular mail and phone calls tend to work better over a period of time.

Each communication is considered a '*contact*'. Each 'contact' adds up and has an exponential effect over several weeks and months.

It takes about 7 contacts with your marketing before a *suspect* is transformed into a *prospect*. They may then decide to call your clinic and schedule an appointment.

This is significant since they had no inclination to schedule an appointment at your clinic in the beginning, just a need for some free information (a need you were fulfilling with a strategic advertisement and a giveaway).

At the end of the day, provide quality information and you build trust and credibility.

This is only possible when you have a high quality list that <u>wants</u> to hear from you. If a sufficient number of individuals in your list have moved up the ascension ladder, you will find that they want to hear from you and are concerned when they don't. This is a 'true' connection with your patient list. On the other hand, if you have a list that doesn't 'miss' hearing from you, then it's likely that a majority of individuals have not yet moved up the 'ascension ladder' yet.

Chapter 3   73

PROSPECT GENERATION AND FILTERING

As a private practitioner, your clinic needs an ever-growing list of prospects who can become patients. With intelligent marketing, you want to drive as many prospects as possible into your 'marketing funnel' so that they move up the ascension ladder.

It's critical to define a prospect before you try to acquire one. A prospect for your private practice can be defined as *an individual who is pre-conditioned to become a patient and potentially refer friends and family to your practice*.

The success minded practitioner must drive as many qualified prospects to the clinic as possible. With carefully planned sequences, prospects can lead to a busy practice with a high patient caseload.

Word-of-mouth marketing and improving the brand recognition for your clinic generates more prospects. Patients referred from social or professional connections come to you because they trust someone they know. You do not have a relationship with them and until someone puts you in front of them, you never existed for them. However, the fact that the patient has been referred to you by someone already positions you atop the '*ascension scale*' of respect and recognition.

This positions the patient as a prospect and you as a qualified provider.

Ideally, a patient walks into your clinic with a degree of 'trust' in you even before they have had a chance to meet with you or benefit from your clinical expertise. The patient has a preconceived expectation about your expertise, before he or she meets you in person since you are already established as an authority. The buzz that never settles down and builds up your reputation as a physical therapist will keep people interested in physical therapy; the otherwise mundane task of visiting a clinic will suddenly become a new experience for them.

This is an outcome of viral marketing, the kind of marketing which results in patients wanting to work with you. With the correct 'pre-framing', people will relish the opportunity to work with you. In your case, patients can be motivated subconsciously to visit you. To plant that seed in every subconscious mind in your local area, you need to know how to build a list of prospects and keep it growing.

In order to attract patients to visit your clinic, you must offer incentives to patients to come in. Create a free product or an offer that is relevant, useful, and enticing in exchange for their time and consent to receive information from you in the form of a newsletter. This is explained in a lot more detail in the next section called the *"Free Product Principle"*.

Section I   74

As fulfilling as it would be to have a list of potential patients, the real business value can be seen when you start to identify and filter your prospects. Imagine an Italian restaurant on a busy street with plenty of individuals walking by, but not a single person walking in for a gourmet pasta meal.

To discern a potential prospect from a casual onlooker you have to make him take an action as soon as possible.

For example, a prospect signs up for your online newsletter. This is the right time to offer them an incentive to schedule an evaluation with your clinic – a free book or educational DVD for example.

An excellent way is to convince people of the exclusivity of the product, like a limited time offer. The incentive could be in the form of a free foot massage or any service that is comforting, exclusive, and desired. Create a members only area, where your patients can make personal reservations for public events. They are sent entertaining content from local events and updated of the new developments in treating physiological diseases. Offer such exclusive services for a free trial period and then charge them a small fee after their free trial ends.

Once you have funneled out a list of prospects from subscribers you are in a much better position to design your newsletters, events, and other marketing plans. This is the point where we get into the psyche of *subscribers* and *prospects* and come up with effective marketing plans. Drawing an analogy from a high street shop-front again, subscribers are your casual onlookers and prospects are your excited customers. Therefore, it is imperative that your strategies focus on ascending both groups from your list up the action ladder from their current position.

All the marketing communication should be tightly knit together and address these two groups individually. You want to convert *subscribers* into *prospects* and *prospects* into *human billboards*. No matter what medium is used, your communications must integrate a set of milestones within. These small milestones are desired actions that your audience, from the list, should take and prove their commitment to the relationship with you. It could be as small as calling your clinic for more information, referring a friend, turning up for a seminar, or as big as paying for your services.

When communicating with prospects using newsletters (which will be discussed in great detail in Chapter 9), you want to:

1. Keep the <u>content</u> short, readable, and fun to read.
2. Let the <u>community</u> be a focal point of your content.
3. Keep the list <u>alive</u> and ascend people from where they are: visitor → subscriber → prospect → patient → referral source.

The goal is to create constant buzz for your practice by positioning yourself as a strong brand. Always stir it up and never let it settle.

PATIENT FINANCED MARKETING – THE FREE PRODUCT PRINCIPLE

As explained in the previous sections, any effort at marketing must move patients up the ascension ladder of relationships, transforming them from *suspect* to *patient* to *referral source*.

With strategic planning, the marketing dollars to get new patients and move them up the ascension ladder can come from the patient.

It's possible to build a list of potential patients and move them up the ascension ladder with the "*Free Product Principle*" outlined here.

This can create a flood of interest in your practice and drive traffic to your website, allowing you to quickly accumulate a list of prospects and patients.

When a patient calls for information or visits your website, offer them a free 'front end' DVD or book filled with unique content relevant to them.

Don't charge anything for it, except a $7.95 fee to cover printing, shipping, and handling.

Something critical happens when they accept. You collect their name, address, phone number, and email address.

Before you mail this out, hire a printing company to take about 30 cents from the $7.95 to print a four page sales letter on standard A4 sized paper (much more effective than a traditional postcard or brochure) filled with the reasons why they should come to your practice and how you stand apart.

The combined cost of printing, shipping and handling (including the 4 page sales letter) will not exceed $7.95 in this model. Several fulfillment companies will take care of the entire process for you.

What you have just achieved is:

1. A mechanism for your practice to collect a list of qualified patients (who show interest in your DVD and pay for it)
2. Instant differentiation - You are now the only practice 'giving away' a valuable educational tool
3. The ability to contact your prospects again and inform them about special offers, lead them back to your website, and finally bring them into your clinic
4. Patient financed advertising – the patient paid for you to advertise to them
5. A potential joint venture opportunity with physicians and local referral sources

Once you create your patient financed marketing system, start offering as many services as you can to better serve the patients and improve the financial value of each patient. Offer patients with new and expanded versions of your original book / DVD. Sell products and provide additional services to compliment treatment.

THE TRUTH ABOUT PATIENT FLOW

Some private practices are faced with an abundance of referrals and have more patient flow than they can ever handle. Other private practice owners are always looking for the next shiny object and are (with an open wallet) ready to try anything to get the attention of elusive referral sources. This private practitioner often says,

> *"I don't have the time, money, and energy to market to physicians. I can't even get their attention to begin with."*

Of all the strategies for referral generation, these are some of the big breakthroughs that can result in a flood of new patients to your practice.

1. There is no one single answer.

Every private practice has its own set of diverse challenges and strengths. Ideally, this practice should leverage its strengths to create multiple systems; each of which can create a distinct and measurable patient flow. There is no one single strategy that will bring in 40 to 50 new patients to your clinic this month. Don't waste your time trying to find it, because it doesn't exist.

Instead, dedicate your time, energy, and resources to introduce multiple systems; each of which can bring in two to three new patients to your practice this month. In this manner, your marketing efforts will have a strong foundation. You will also be immune to the dangerous dependence on one or two referral sources that plagues most private practice owners. Classify your marketing efforts by return on investment. For example, delegate more time and energy towards the physician who sends you five new patients a month than a physician who has never referred to you before.

2. Priority in referral generation mechanisms

The more methods you have in place for referral generation, the more you are able to prioritize some of those systems and the less your dependence upon any single method; therefore, the better-off you will be in your private practice. There is a clear and unpredictable correlation between the number of tactics and the patient flow in a private practice. When looking for an idea, don't copy your competitors and past employers expecting to get the same results. The same mechanism that works well for one clinic may fail miserably for another clinic. Try to be innovative and find your own hidden gold mines of referrals. Once you find it, find a few more.

Many private practice owners look to advertising as a means of referral generation. While this can work with some practices, referrals from existent, enthusiastic patients should be the priority.

The single biggest factor that determines the long-term success of a private practice is the referral rate. The best way to increase the referral rate is to have multiple systems in place, with a varying degree of emphasis on each system.

3. Education and Empowerment

A bored patient is a lost patient. Keep the patient interested in everything about your clinic and the referrals will come. The design and hygiene in your clinic and the social interactions between patients and staff members play a role. Follow-up mechanisms (birthday, anniversary, holiday messages, phone calls, unannounced surprises like an invitation to a pain prevention seminar hosted by you) will educate and empower your patients. The goal is to provide a sense of value and benefit to your patients, the kind that extends beyond the treatment session and touches them on a subconscious level. As private practitioners we have an unmatched, sincere need to help patients; we just need to make sure the patients know it! When these steps are taken consistently, you are effectively building a fence around your patients. They will think twice (and feel bad) about going elsewhere the next time they need physical therapy. The best part is, they'll make their family members and physicians feel the same way.

A great way to prove this connection with patients is to take the time to explain their condition and answer any questions. If you are able to help a patient understand how their muscles and joints work, what is going wrong, how they can deal with it, and why they need physical therapy, the long-term impact is enormous. Many physicians don't take the time to spend the three to four minutes with the patient to explain what is going on, leaving the patient with anxiety and confusion.

The practitioners who provide the simplest, most relevant and comprehensive patient education programs always have the highest referral rates.

ЛALIZE FOR MAXIMUM IMPACT

...cians we live in a very busy world. We go above and beyond for patients and strive to deliver the best quality of care to every patient during the course of treatment. However, most patients enter the land of the forgotten post-discharge. For private practice owners, this is an important business loophole that must be plugged immediately.

Individual contact does not begin and end with the patient visit. It continues after the patient visit, with e-mail, regular mail, and phone contact. It should be fostered as a lifelong relationship. We tend to apply the same principles with referral sources and should do the same with patients.

Think of every patient walking around with a sign on his or her head that says *"I need to be appreciated."* When you acknowledge the patient's efforts during the patient visit and following the patient visit it creates a sense of trust and connection that is difficult to match, even with the most elaborate marketing campaigns.

The need to be appreciated is at the backbone of every referral relationship. If you ever had a referral relationship go sour, chances are that it had something to do with the level (lack?) of appreciation, an acknowledgement showered on the referral source. Something as simple as a thank you card, e-mail, or phone call is more than enough for individuals to continue referring to your practice.

Acknowledge your patients by printing their name on a plaque, featuring them in your newsletter, having the patient's cheer for them, or simply throwing a little get-together for them. Patients, not only love the sound of their own name, but the appreciation that comes from recognition and encouragement from other patients.

Even when you send an e-mail or a letter in the mail to a patient, make sure that you mention their name at least twice in each communication. The mere mention of a person's name adds a dimension of personalization to the message that the traditional marketing messages can never convey.

Personalization of messages creates a *'second level connection'* with patients. Most patients will think of a physical therapy service provider as just another physical therapist. This is called the *first level connection*, which is a default mental association. However, if the patient can clearly remember something about your practice, like the name of the therapist, his/her favorite movie, sports team, or hobby, the patient and the therapist are now like friends. This is called t¹ *connection*' which only a few therapists can establish.

When you sprinkle the patient's name throughout your communications ,. you don't want to do it randomly. When reading a marketing message, the recipient s attention span is usually focused at the very start and the end of the message. This means that your headline or opening statement should be right on the money. You simply cannot afford to get it wrong. Also, closing comments or 'P.S.' section in your e-mails or letters are always read. Remember, the very core of your marketing message may go unheard, but the first impression and the closing comments are always noticed.

Ideally, you want to personalize the headline or the opening comment, because it will really grab the subject's attention. For example, a salutation of "Dear Dave" is infinitely more valuable than "Dear Patient." If you can make the patient feel like they really got some extra attention and care from you and they were not simply a number or a statistic, you have truly personalized your marketing message.

Ironically, we spend our time designing and perfecting the 1% that really doesn't matter. Patients don't care about fancy brochures and expensive leather couches in your waiting room, they care about the human connection you establish with them and are in your clinic based on your reputation.

Understanding how the mind of your patient works and selecting the right trigger words to make them feel comfortable and foster trust, depends on a simple skill. The ability involves the presentation of information in a specific sequence designed to elicit a response loaded with trust. In addition, it makes the patient feel like you are communicating to them and not to a large audience. You can really create that coveted personal connection.

The easiest way to personalize a message and cement a relationship with the patient is by remembering a birthday and wedding anniversaries. Next in the list of important dates are Christmas, Thanksgiving, and the New Year. The patient's date of birth is available on his/her patient intake and is a valuable piece of information.

Implement these strategies and you will truly emerge as an outstanding therapist in more ways than one. Personalizing your communication with patients will be the key economic differentiator for private practices in the 21st century.

LIFETIME VALUE OF PATIENTS

From a clinical standpoint, we evaluate and treat patients as efficiently as possible. From a business standpoint, the lifetime value of a patient is a critical measure that should be monitored by every private practice owner.

Many private practice owners have no idea what the lifetime value of a patient (LVP) means. Even if they do, they don't know how to calculate this crucial figure.

The LVP is a crucial number and is important to the success of your practice. The definition of the lifetime value of a patient is this:

> *"The amount of profit you generate from your patient during the lifetime of your relationship with them."*

Now, let's calculate the LVP in your practice. Here's what you need to know:
- ✓ How much you get paid for the average treatment.
- ✓ How many times a year the average patient books a treatment.
- ✓ How many of their friends they are likely to refer to you.
- ✓ Your average profit margin.
- ✓ Multiply those four numbers together and you've got your LVP.

Don't worry if you don't have the exact numbers; it's okay to estimate numbers to begin with. Knowing the LVP is so important that even having a close estimate will give you a guideline to use.

So let's have a look at an example…

Let's say Martha is a patient in your clinic and your net profit is $60 per visit (after expenses)

Let's say she gets treatment three times a week for 4 weeks.

The revenue per treatment is $60 (after expenses).

This patient is now worth 60 x 3 x 4 = $720.

If Martha referred two of her friends for physical therapy (patients should be conditioned to refer) and assuming these friends were legitimate candidates for treatment with referrals from their physicians, then Martha is more than a $60 per visit patient.

She is worth $2,000 or more for your practice. Her LVP therefore, is a minimum of $2000.

If you had 3 Martha's each month, you are looking at over $70,000 in annual revenue from referrals alone. This could pay the salary of a full-time staff therapist. Keep in mind that this was a conservative estimate.

Imagine if you were able to offer additional products and services to Martha, which would help her get better faster.

Would her lifetime value go up?

Knowing the LVP is important because you know how much profit a patient can provide for you and therefore, you know how much money you can afford to spend to find the patient.

The LVP will help you determine the cost per patient acquisition (CPA).

Traditionally, sales and marketing techniques only look at the profit or loss on the first transaction (i.e the first visit). For your private practice, this is the wrong approach to follow. Unlike product-based businesses, where it's a one-time sale and then that's it, as a service business you sell repeatedly to your patients... over and over again. In other words, you conduct more than one treatment session.

So as a service provider, making a profit on the first transaction isn't important. In fact, it's ok to lose money on the first (or even a few) transactions since the LVP of a patient is significant.

Let's say you run an ad in a newspaper. It costs $500. You get 5 new patients from the ad.

Your income from this ad is well over $3,500.

That's a 500% return on investment.

This is a successful ad.

The knowledge of LVP leads to effective ad tracking. Also, you may realize that it's cheaper and more effective to spend less marketing dollars nurturing and conditioning existing patients to refer instead of looking for new patients. You may be able to actually increase your earnings several times without ever increasing your patient base.

HOW TO GET PATIENTS FROM GOOGLE AND YOUTUBE

Getting more patients to come to your clinic and providing them with great service is our primary goal as private practice owners.

As busy as we are, it's important to investigate every single possibility to get more patients walking in through the door.

The fact is, there are patients at this moment looking for a physical therapist (or fitness professional) in your town (and surrounding towns within driving distance) online.

Since Google is the number one website in the world for search terms, it's important for your website to appear when anyone searches phrases like "low back pain", "physical therapy", "physical therapist", "pain relief" and "pain management."

There is no need to hire expensive 'web optimization' experts to help you with website rankings. All it takes is a few simple strategies that can be implemented with programs that are available for free online.

There is a quick way to appear on page one of Google for some related keywords that patients are searching for in your community.

This is possible because of one big reason.

Google owns YouTube and reserves a spot (sometimes two) on page one for relevant YouTube results.

What I am about to reveal is the single fastest way for you to put yourself in front of potential patients in your community within days and not weeks of expensive, unnecessary website optimization strategies that may or may not work.

The way we do this is to use Google's own tools to find out exactly what your prospects and patients are searching for.

Just go to Google and search for "Google keyword tool".

The first result will show you a tool where you can type in search terms that patients may be looking for. For example, I would type out a search phrase like "physical therapy new jersey" or "pain relief new jersey".

The results will show you the volume of inquiries each month.

Now, use another free online tool called the "Google wonderwheel" which you can also look up on Google. This tool will tell you the RELATED keywords people are searching for also. So you may realize that someone looking for "pain relief" is also looking for "exercises for pain relief" and so on.

Now, make a list of 10 keywords you want to rank for.

Next, go to YouTube and create 10 different accounts, using each keyword or phrase as the username / channel name for each account.

So for example, I would set up accounts like

YouTube.com/painreliefnewjersey
YouTube.com/physicaltherapynewjersey
And so on…

Now, use your phone or a digital camera and create 10 short videos on pain relief, exercise, and general do's and don'ts for patients. You don't have to provide specific tips, but provide general, valuable, useful content. At the end of each video, give your patients a clear instruction on what to do next like:

> *"I hope you got a lot from these injury prevention and pain relief tips. Be sure to visit my website at _____ and get a free book on _____ to learn more."*

When you save these files on your computer, make sure you name each file the keyword you want to rank for. So I would name the files as
Painreliefnewjersey.mov
Physicaltherapynewjersey.mov
And so on…

Now, simply upload the right video to the corresponding YouTube account you created and when you title your video, make sure it has the keyword mentioned in the title. You will have an option to mention your website link in the 'description' box in YouTube and you want to mention your clinic website there.

That's all there is to it! When Google sees this YouTube video, they will recognize its relevance and chances are that you will be the only one using this strategy in your community. Before you know it, you may be able to see your own video on page 1 of Google. If you remember my comment from earlier in this section:

> *Google owns YouTube and reserves a spot (sometimes two) on page one for relevant YouTube results.*

Now that you have a relevant YouTube video, you appear on the first page of Google, giving you an abundance of free advertising and visibility with potential patients who are actually LOOKING for your services online!

Why does this work so well? Since Google cannot interpret video content, it must rely on the file name, video title, and video description to categorize (and rank the video) which you can leverage in your favor.

Here's the best part; as a consumer presented with the option of clicking on yet another article versus a video, (which appears as an image or thumbnail when you search Google), the natural tendency is to click on the video thumbnail.

RESOURCE

**Discover For FREE The Closely Guarded Secrets To
Magnetically Attract 21 New Patients, Increase Referrals From
Existing Patients, And Quadruple Your Referral Network
In The Next 30 Days With A Done-For-You Marketing Plan...**

✓ How to get DOUBLE the number of referral source to your practice in the next 60 days
✓ Techniques to get existing patients to refer their friends, family and co-workers
✓ The DONE-FOR-YOU '4 Step Marketing Plan' to get more referrals
✓ How you can avoid the single BIGGEST mistake when marketing your services as a private practice owner

Get the blueprint here: **www.addnewpatients.com**

CHAPTER 4

Build Additional Sources of Revenue in Your Private Practice

REVENUE MULTIPLICATION: THE ART OF BOOSTING INCOME PER PATIENT VISIT

I played babysitter for a day. When my good friend had to leave for a sudden business trip, he reached out to me to take care of his two kids for the day. Sarah and James are pretty noisy and each has a voracious appetite.

It's no surprise that we ended up at McDonalds™ to feed Sarah's never-ending sweet tooth. While fumbling in my pocket to pay for the two chocolate milk shakes, I was asked, "Would you like fries with that?" The bill went from $3.99 to $5.49. I just witnessed a 37% increase in revenue for McDonalds™ based on an unhealthy, yet simple sales strategy. This single phrase adds millions of dollars to McDonalds™' bottom-line each year.

That got me thinking. Why don't we, as physical therapists, up-sell our services and generate additional revenue like they do? After all, our services actually promote health and human function. Shouldn't <u>we</u> be the ones 'up-selling'?

In a competitive economy like this one, clinics have to find a way to get more patients or increase revenue per visit. Given the dual problem of declining reimbursements and fierce competition, it can get quite challenging to bring in more patients.

With some of the strategies mentioned in this section, you may decide that you do not need a high volume of patients to increase revenue. If a clinic can find ways to increase revenue by $10-$20 per patient, the jump in the bottom line can add up.

Traditionally, patients have been unwilling to spend anything beyond their co-pay. It's not because the patient's don't want to buy our value-added services, we just need to learn how to sell such services to them! In many cases, the patient is likely to invest about $10-$15, when presented with a cash-based service that has a high perceived value. The patients who come to you already have faith in you and your services. In fact, they are already in a buying mode. As a therapist, all you have to do is to provide them with what they need and at the right time.

1. Increase The Prices Of Your Cash Paying Programs

Just do it, add 10% to the prices of your cash paying programs today. A small percentage of patients will object, but the extra profit from other patients who are happy to pay the slight increase will more than cover this. It's very easy to raise the price of your cash-based program, as long as you create the perception of significant value. Spend some time explaining the benefits of your cash-based program to patients. **Explain to them how it differs from programs offered by other providers. Use phrases like, "access to our high quality of care", "powerful benefits of our program" and "the benefit for you in your day-to-day life".** Emphasize benefits, not features. Present your clinic in a comprehensive and positive manner while making it appear that your service is so unique that there is no other product or service that can compare to it.

2. Cross Sell and Up Sell Other Services

There are always other add-on products or services you can recommend to your patients, similar to the McDonalds™ approach of '*would you like fries with that?*'

Ideally, a successful clinic should have more than one source of revenue. Reimbursement from insurance companies should be a part of the revenue stream. Consider providing a 'membership' to your clinic for patients who would like to come in and exercise on their own. Request the patient to sign a release of liability form, since they will not have the direct supervision of the physical therapist during the course of their membership. Arrange for automatic billing of the patient's credit card. This can be as simple way of adding $20-$30 a month from each patient. Hire a nutritionist to visit your clinic two to three times a week and encourage your patients to consult with the nutritionist for healthy meal planning. This is an instant source of cash-based revenue for your clinic. You can also recommend over-the-counter nutritional supplements, if you feel comfortable. You might even form a strategic alliance from a massage therapist, who will function as your employee in your facility.

Cross selling is easier said than done. It's a simple and effective mechanism to boost revenue, but it is overlooked by most therapists. I suggest you make a checklist so you and your staff remember to offer the cross sells and up sells to patients early on in the treatment process.

3. Package Deals – Silver, Gold And Platinum Packages

Like McDonalds™, offering the cash paying patient a #1, #2, or #3 with different options of service can a be very successful strategy.

Once the patient is discharged, you can give them multiple options to keep coming back. You can offer a combination of fitness training, nutritional coaching, massage, and training journal – a complete package to guarantee the patient's continued success. If you can present the package well, the patient will find it irresistible. So much so, that they will buy it even if they don't see the immediate need for it.

The strategy can also work well when you're testing out new services, before you actually roll them out as full-fledged services.

4. Extended Payment Plan

If you are selling a cash-based program worth several hundred dollars or more, consider offering your patients a payment plan. Register your business with an online merchant like authorize.net, which gives your clinic the ability to accept credit card payments and direct debits from the patient's bank account. **Having payment terms to allow the patient to make bigger purchases can dramatically increase what a client is willing to spend.** Patients should be able to break their investment into monthly payments, just like their mortgage or car payment. With this approach, a patient that might not have been able to invest a lump sum of several thousand dollars can get the services and products they want and only have a monthly investment of a couple of hundred dollars.

5. Focus on 'A-Grade' Patients

'A-grade' patients are the ones that don't complain, pay full price, tell you how wonderful you are, give you great feedback, and then tell all their friends (who likely will be 'A-grade' clients as well) how great you are. Identify these patients and nurture them like your own family. Provide them with exceptional service and make sure they are the first to know about any new offers, programs, or any new deals... they will love it and purchase more often.

Just choose a couple of these suggestions and implement them in your practice. The next time you go to McDonalds™, you can tell the server how up-selling has increased your monthly revenue. Just skip the fries.

CASH BASED FITNESS PRO'
PHYSICAL THERAPIS

The United States, overweight nation in the Obesity rates continue to clim each state, every year. Preventive, cash based fitness programs represent the need of the hour and a tremendous opportunity for physical therapists in 2011 and beyond. A well-structured, cash based group fitness program has several benefits.

It can be:

- ❖ A low cost add-on for existing patients
- ❖ An incentive for new patient populations
- ❖ A maintenance program for past patients
- ❖ A value added service endorsed by physicians
- ❖ An extremely newsworthy service for the local media

Scott Ward, president of the American Physical Therapy Association stated in his December 2nd, 2008 blog post

> *"As much as half of the $2.3 trillion spent on health care in the United States today does absolutely nothing to improve health - and could be dangerous as well - according to chief executives of some of the nation's top health care institutions who were quoted in the Washington post. One possible solution? A culture shift away from pricey high tech procedures to more conservative approaches such as physical therapy."*

WALK THE WALK, TALK THE TALK

Before you consider a service like this improve your own fitness level and demonstrate health, vitality, energy, and motivation to patients. If you don't do so already, take charge of your own personal health and fitness. Start going to the gym 3-4 times a week and improve your own diet by consulting with a nutritionist, if necessary. My wife and I are both physical therapists. We go the gym together, 4-5 times a week. When physicians and patients see you as fit and healthy, it's easy to promote your fitness program. This is the single most important component of a cash based fitness program.

START OFFERING GROUP FITNESS CLASSES, ALSO CALLED 'GROUP FITNESS FACTOR PROGRAMS'

A group fitness class allows the therapist to generate more revenue by working fewer hours. It also allows the patient to pay less and get better results than a gym. There is a social support component in group training that is reinforced by accountability. When a patient is a part of a team, it is easier to adhere to an exercise and nutrition program. With the present condition of the economy, a low cost, high value program offered by a physical therapist is an ideal service. The easiest market for a group fitness factor program is to train women; since women seem to respond better to a group environment (the success of Curves, Lucille Roberts, and Weight Watchers reflects this trend). Start your own group fitness factor program for women. If your clinic name is ABC, call it the ABC fitness boot camp for women. Conduct classes 3 times a week, preferably early in the morning. An 8 am or a 9 am fitness group fitness factor program for busy moms works well, since this is a large, untapped market.

CONSIDER A CORPORATE WELLNESS PROGRAM

Companies across the United States are struggling to lower healthcare costs. A healthier employee is going to be more productive and will cost the system less than an employee plagued by injury. Go through your local phone directory and find local companies with 30 employees or more. When speaking with administration, tell them about the financial benefits of the program. When speaking with the staff, help them understand the benefits of the program in day-to-day life. Corporate fitness programs are an affordable, profitable service that physical therapists can duplicate. The staff trains at work and there is no overhead for the therapist. Two group fitness workshops a week for one corporation are sufficient. The therapist can charge a monthly fee, based on the number of employees the service is offered to. A general rule of thumb is to charge $15 per employee per class, regardless of how many show up for the session. You want to charge based on the number of staff members who have access to you, not on those who actually show up for the group class. Therefore, for a staff of 30 employees who get 2 ergonomics and general conditioning classes a week, charges should be approximately $3500-$4000 a month. Two contracts with corporations in your area could bring in $7000-$8000 a month for your clinic with no additional costs, other than stationary and handouts.

INITIATE A GROUP FITNESS PROGRAM FOR SENIORS

A cash-based program may be a profitable alternative to traditional Medicare grouping. Such a program educates and promotes health and fitness among seniors. It can be planned and marketed as a "Get Fit At Any Age" group exercise class. Educate the elderly about the benefits of exercise by making presentations at senior citizens homes, organizing community events at the local YMCA, and mailing flyers to retirement communities. Engage them in a light, enjoyable, and functional exercise program at a cost of under $10 per person per class and promote packages of 8 classes at a time, 2 times a week for 4 weeks. Word about such a program spreads fast in this community, since seniors are looking for ways to maintain activity, meet other seniors, and improve function; all of which can be served by a preventive fitness program provided by the physical therapist.

As physical therapists, we are in the best possible position to design and execute a fitness program. Many personal trainers offer similar services and charge high cash premiums based on the perception of results they can deliver. As physical therapists, we can go above and beyond, using our expertise to partner with fitness centers and local health clubs. It's time for us, as therapists, to be the pioneers of fitness and health; improving our own lives and the lives of our patients in the process.

AUTOMATED BILLING WITH MONTHLY WELLNESS MEMBERSHIPS

Despite our current economic woes, many believe things will get better because of the measures taken by the administration. It's interesting that the quest for the resolution of a crisis (not the resolution itself) is what gives people hope and encourages them to continue on the path to an end result.

A gym membership is an example of a health quest, which is rooted in the community. With the social acceptance associated with 'being a gym member', there is a smaller likelihood for complaints, regret, or dropouts. Many individuals are happy to join a gym but, at some point, begin to skip workouts. Despite this fact, most individuals stay on, in the hopes that they will 'use the gym' soon. In other words, there is a social need for wellness programs that we, as physical therapists, are best equipped to provide.

As a physical therapist, have you thought about a monthly membership program for patients post-discharge? Champion a cause for health in your community and initiate an exclusive 'wellness program'. Envision a scenario in which patients visit their 'friendly neighborhood physical therapist' for exercise and wellness needs. There are huge advantages in working with motivated patients who know you, like you, and trust you enough to buy a membership and come regularly. They reach their goals faster, while you can predict monthly income and create a sustainable source of recurring revenue that is unaffected by external forces like physician referrals and insurance companies. The way to structure and sell these programs is a vast, untapped, unique market in physical therapy.

With such a program, you are almost guaranteed to work with patients who are more committed, more likely to respond to treatment, appreciate your services, refer you to friends, and remain your patients for several months, sometimes years, to come.

Here is the new offering for leading edge physical therapy clinics: offer a one year "clinic wellness membership" program consisting of a package of 'mini treatment sessions and supervised physical exercise'. Only accept patients who are willing to make a commitment for the entire year and invite all patients for a 'selection process', informing them that 'not all will be selected'. Scarcity drives people to take action. Work with a group of 5-10 or 20 patients as a control group and gradually roll out the program to a larger audience. With this model, you are selling a high value, niche, cash-based program based on a recurring revenue model. Timings for members of this plan can be designed to be such that it is both suitable to the clinic and does not hinder treatment of patients in the clinic.

Consider this: we see patients for their physical therapy needs until they meet their goals. What happens next?

One option that you, as their physical therapist, can suggest is continuing with a 'supervised physical activity program' that facilitates the use of your clinic. With such a program, they have access to you, their therapist, with any questions regarding techniques and progression of exercises as it specifically pertains to their diagnosis and history of injury. If the patient has a great rapport with you, it is more likely that they will want a clinic membership under your supervision. After all, you brought them to a point of functional independence and they trust you to help them improve even further.

With traditional physical therapy, we see a patient and wait to get paid by the insurance company. With a cash-based model, you not only get paid cash for your services, but you can also collect cash in advance for your services before they are actually rendered (i.e. – a monthly membership plan). In addition, you can get your patients to commit to pay a certain amount, on a consistent basis, month after month by authorizing you to charge their credit card. This is called electronic funds transfer (EFT).

You may want to present your patients with simple options that make sense for them. After discharge, sit with your patient across the table and explain the benefits of your cash-for-therapy program. Practice the script below and develop your own if needed. If you can succeed in making them see the value of the program, the cards will fall into place.

Script:

> *"Mr. Anderson, let me help you understand the benefits of our physical therapy wellness maintenance program. It will help you live a relatively pain-free lifestyle, maintain the positive advancement we made with you in therapy, improve function, and enhance your ability to perform your daily activities. Can I show you the options available to you?"*

> *"Here are the three options. The first program is a two times a week physical therapist supervised exercise program with one of our leading staff therapists. For a one year commitment, this is just $45 a session. This is an amazing value and is a total of one hundred and four sessions (52 weeks in a year) and it's only $45 per session. We also have a three-time-a-week option with your therapist. It's a total of one hundred and fifty-six sessions and it's only $40 per session. Finally we have our most popular program, four-times-a-week with your therapist supervising the program. A total of two hundred and eight sessions and it's only $35 per session. This provides the absolute best value!"*

Then, hand your patient a rate card with the rates you just mentioned.
- ❖ 2x week = @ $45 per session
- ❖ 3x week = @ $40 per session
- ❖ 4x week = @ $35 per session

Pause and wait for them to ask you questions. This is a critical moment during the sales process, where you should hold back and wait for a response.

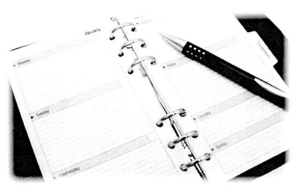

If they ask questions, you are close to the sale.

Guide them like an assistant and give them the resources to make a decision.

The statement that closes the sale is: "*My personal recommendation, Mr. Anderson is this plan (you recommend one of the plans). It provides you with the best value for money and is best suited for your goals. Which plan would you like to get started on today?*"

As long as the patient is made to see the value in the program, it's an easy decision for them. The patient signs an EFT agreement and provides you with their credit card number. Their card is charged monthly for the sessions coming up that month. In the above scenario:

- ❖ 2x week = @ $45 per session = Monthly charge is $360
- ❖ 3x week = @ $40 per session = Monthly charge is $480
- ❖ 4x week = @ $35 per session = Monthly charge is $560

If only 5 patients sign up for the 3x week program, the additional revenue for your clinic is $2,400 a month, which is $28,800 annually. If you can offer this program each month and add **5 more memberships per month, your annual revenue from this program alone could be well over $100,000** with no reimbursement hassles.

These strategies will set you apart from other clinics almost immediately and enable you to open new doors to increasing revenue.

Don't be intimidated. As with all new programs, early days can be trying; but the payout is worth the effort. It's not as hard as it seems, as long as you emphasize:

a) The significant value and benefits of the program

b) Expected goals and functional improvements

c) Billing will be 'monthly' and not all at once

d) Financing is an option and that discounts are provided for pay ahead cash payments

e) Encourage the patient to view the program as an investment in their future health

When structuring such a program, you can:

a) Ask the patient to pay for the first and last month in advance

b) Schedule them for monthly payments for the rest of the year

c) Introduce package variations; such as a 3 or 6 month option. Patients who are unwilling to commit for less than 3 months are unlikely to be good candidates for such a program.

d) Offer an incentive to the patient to join right away, like a $50 or $100 discount. Personally, I found a souvenir coffee mug with the words "ABC Physical Therapy's #1 Patient Award" is a simple take-action-now incentive that gets people to buy the program! It may sound childish, but it works!

e) Give the patient the option to cancel by providing you a written notice, usually with a 6 week advance notice. Patients should have the ability to terminate the plan, with advance notice, if they are not satisfied. This helps most patients overcome any inhibitions.

f) Think seriously about your market, their earning potential, and comfort level when instituting a cancellation fee. In affluent neighborhoods, a cancellation fee works. In less affluent locations, a cancellation fee can be counterproductive.

THE EXPONENTIAL VALUE OF A RECURRING MEMBERSHIP MODEL

The real value of a recurring membership model lies in its explosive growth when the model grows beyond a certain threshold. This threshold is usually 15-20% of your monthly gross income. When your recurring memberships start to generate more than 15-20% of your monthly gross revenue, your practice will never look back.

Let's say you are able to sell an annual membership package to 10 patients in January and each patient is working with you twice a week. If you charged $45 a session twice a week, that would be $360 per month in revenue. In January, you now make $3,600 from these patients.

Let's say you are able to sell an annual membership package to another 10 patients in January, and each patient is working with you twice a week. If you charged $45 a session twice a week, that would be an additional $360 per month in revenue for this patient. In February, you now make $3,600 from these new patients; but that's not all of the income. You continue to earn the income from January, which is $3,600. Your income from these recurring payments in February is now $7,200. The income in subsequent months is $10,800 (March), $14,400 (April), $18,000 (May) and so on.

These numbers are achievable with the right tools and planning.

This time around, your patient will not complain about the monthly membership fee. After all, they are being looked after by their 'friendly neighborhood physical therapist'. You will be the new 'health superhero' of your local community.

HOW TO LAUNCH A CASH PRACTICE

Here's an interesting story. I went to the supermarket to buy groceries and milk. On the way out, the cashier asked me – would our like to buy our new 'Power Lean Protein Bars', they just launched, taste outstanding, and are on sale for just 99 cents today ONLY.

She convinced me to buy some. So I asked her to wait, while I rushed back to the aisle to grab my discounted protein bars.

My bill went from $24.99 to $29.99.

Something interesting happened here.

The supermarket successfully increased their sales by 20% with one recommendation to a willing consumer, within seconds.

The question is: How would you like to add 20% to your bottom line by launching a cash program?

As physical therapists, it's wonderful to find new and innovative ways to boost income, especially cash based revenue. Getting payment from patients in a timely manner, as opposed to waiting weeks to get reimbursed automatically, adds to your bottom line. In this manner, cash based income is beneficial, because of the time value associated with instant income as opposed to delayed compensation.

Charging customers in cash can go hand in hand with a product launch that will benefit the patient, just like the supermarket sold a newly launched product to me.

So how do you structure a cash practice? More importantly, how do you launch a cash practice and get it off the ground running?

The mechanism to market a cash practice is entirely different from traditional physician marketing and involves a well planned, specific strategy that spans at least 3-4 months.

a) **Pre-launch Phase**. In the first few weeks, generate excitement and announce a 'launch date' for your cash program. This is the pre-launch phase. Give it a catchy title like "Low Back Protocol Training", "Pain Termination Project", "Instant Motion Method", "Active Super-Stretch Therapy" and so on. Build the 'buzz' for your program by announcing the name and releasing details in bits and pieces as the launch date approaches. Announce it to patients, physicians, local media, and influencers in the community. The more confident you are about your program and the greater the potential, the longer this stage can be. I have personally seen a program in pre-launch phase for 6 months and it was sold out before it even started. (Suggested duration = 2 weeks to 6 months).

Section I   98

b) **Beta-test Phase**. Enlist a select number of individuals for a discounted price to 'beta test' the program leading up to your launch. Your program is pre-structured and you are accepting patients, to work with them in small or large groups. You can also work with patients individually. Give them outstanding results, measure subjective and objective outcomes, and get permission in writing to use their pictures and names in written, audio, and video testimonials. This single step will enable you to surpass your expectations with a cash based program. (Suggested duration = length of your pre-structured program = 4-8 weeks)

c) **Social Proof Stockpiling:** A collection of testimonials is critical, you only work with patients who will enthusiastically provide testimonials (after you provide them with results) and give you signed consent to use their testimonials. A prospective patient must know that they can get incredible results with your program. Show the patients tremendous value in what they are getting. Over deliver and exceed their expectations. Make them feel like they have to break down doors to work with you.(Executed during your beta test phase)

d) **Line Up Platinum Promoters:** Influential physicians, business owners, social figures, media members, and 'Grade A patients' should be requested to promote the program to their friends and family. People have to be conditioned and constantly reminded to make referrals. They can literally act as 'talking billboards' for your practice and enhance the excitement leading up to your launch. They can hand out 'invitation cards' to friends and family inviting them to participate in your program. Ideally, a 'platinum promoter' is someone who has tried and benefited from your program. The town senator / health news journalist / highly respected veteran, all who have beta-tested the program with you can emerge as unusually strong referral sources because they start talking about you with their physician, friends, and family. Use a strong referral script (below) to get these platinum promoters on board.(Executed during your beta test phase)

e) **Strong Referral Script:** Also executed during your beta test phase, each individual has between 40-50 people they know and can recommend your services to. The essential components of a referral generating mechanism are positioning, honesty, 'buzz' and clear direction. Instead of asking a patient to refer, use a script like this:

> *"Dear XYZ, did you know that a majority of our patients come from referrals (awareness)? We don't believe in wasting money on advertising (positioning) and recognize that valued patients, like yourself, are the best referral sources for our business (honesty and sincerity). Can I ask you, as an influential resource, to go that extra mile for me (importance) and help spread the word about this exciting new program (buzz) by handing out these cards to your friends and talking to your physician about this (direction)?"*

f) Low Resistance Front Funnel: Instead of charging a high amount upfront, you can structure a cash program by charging nothing or next to nothing for a trial session. For example, a 1 week trial period, costing $10 (registration fee) and $199 a month following the trial period (if the program is ongoing). Get a majority of patients to come in and try the program. When everything is in place and they see the value, many trial members will become paid members.

g) Outstanding Website: A website entirely dedicated to your cash based program will allow you to effectively promote the program, otherwise it will get lost in translation as patients visit your website and discover the other services you offer. The cash program is a separate entity in itself and deserves its own web presence. A one page website with a strong, benefit driven headline, list of program features, patient benefits, social proof and the ability for patients to register with one click and a credit card will act as a 24/7 salesman for your practice. Do not give the patients too many options and pages to click. Just give them one page with all the information pertaining to the program and the choice to register, not register, or call to register, nothing more.

h) Launch Date and Scarcity: Announce the launch date and time (example, doors open on Monday, November 16th 2009 at 9 am). Send out emails, postcards, and reminders in the last 2 weeks leading up to the launch. Accept a limited number of people into the program. Don't accept everyone who wants to participate and build a sense of exclusivity into the program (perhaps you will only accept 10 participants in each phase). When a selected group of individuals, first come first served are accepted, you create an unparalleled sense of momentum, raising public perception to a new level. Human beings, as social animals, will want to be a part of your program. With the right planning and execution you may, unfortunately, have people who are upset they could not join the program.

A strong offer, good promotion, integrated referral scripts, outstanding service, low resistance to entry, and scarcity will create a cash program that can transform your practice.

SECURE Your Area Exclusive License NOW: Own a VIABLE Practice and Effortlessly Expand To Multiple Locations, Before Your Competitor LOCKS You Out Forever!

✓ Charge CASH – Don't be a prisoner to insurance companies anymore
✓ State-of-the-art CUSTOM DESIGNED website built for you (completely customizable)
✓ Easily delegated system to help grow your business
✓ Duplicate yourself and expand to multiple locations run by other professionals
✓ Members-only resource portal, exclusive networking and platinum coaching
✓ Automate, systematize & delegate your nationally recognized GFF business
✓ Multiple DONE-FOR-YOU marketing templates to drive MORE clients to your program
✓ INSTANT recognition in your community; get physicians to sit up and take notice
✓ STAND OUT from your competitors immediately!

www.groupfitnessfactor.com

HERE'S WHAT GFF™ CAN DO FOR YOUR PRIVATE PRACTICE... TAKE A LOOK AND JUDGE FOR YOURSELF...

❖ THE FIRST EVER GROUP BUSINESS MODEL

It doesn't matter if you are trying to funnel new clients into your program or work with clients post discharge, the Group Fitness Factor™ model allows you to implement a proven cash-paying avenue to provide group exercise therapy classes on "low back pain," "fall prevention," "post natal care," "rehab for athletes," "core stabilization," "weight loss," "body toning," and much more. This is not a replacement for, but a valuable adjunct to traditional physical therapy. It allows you to provide a valuable service to the community, gain INSTANT recognition in the process and reach out to physicians, positioning you as an instant expert.

❖ TURN KEY APPLICATION

We've done the hard work for you! The creators of the GFF business model are successful private practice owners who know what it takes to create a sustainable cash practice. We've been perfecting this system for over 8 years and have decoded the blueprint that allows you to hit the ground running from the beginning!

You'll have at your fingertips proven operational and marketing systems, live support via coaching tele-seminars, and state-of-the-art business solutions in the exclusive, password protected members-only website.

> ❖ **MULTIPLE DONE-FOR-YOU LOW COST AND NO COST MARKETING SYSTEMS**

As a licensed member, you get access to the regular updates in our members-only site with the latest strategies to drive more clients to your program. You can reap the benefits of plug-and-play templates without having to do any additional work. You get done for you forms, templates, scripts, live feedback in our member community and ongoing support from the entire GFF program so you get real time feedback about what's working and what's not.

> ❖ **AUTOMATICALLY BILL YOUR CLIENTS WITH ONLINE SYSTEMS**

Your Group Fitness Factor™ website comes fully equipped to accept payments and enroll clients automatically for ongoing service. You will now have a reliable and predictable revenue stream with all of the "bill collecting" work done for you automatically by your website.

> ❖ **LOCK DOWN YOUR TERRITORY – LEAVE YOUR COMPETITORS IN THE DUST...**

Once you are accepted into the program, your specific location is secured and cannot be invaded by other GFF™ owners. Therefore you will be the only PT in your area to take advantage of and implement the dynamic marketing systems and offer this precision engineered program in your community.

> ❖ **ONGOING SUPPORT FROM THE GFF™ FACULTY AND MEMBER COMMUNITY**

Members-Only access to cutting edge business tools, systems and marketing giving you plug-and-play options that minimize time, effort, and investment. Open forum and networking with other successful Group Fitness Factor™ owners.

> ❖ FORGET INSURANCE REIMBURSEMENTS – GENERATE AN AUTOMATED, CASH PAYING INCOME STREAM

Insurance reimbursements are diminishing every year and chasing down physicians for referrals is time consuming and exhausting. There's no need to restrict yourself to the old school way of running a private practice any more! Take control of your profits by offering a cash paying system that gives you a predictable and reliable income stream month after month.

At this precise moment, clients are searching for a low cost, high quality solution to their wellness needs (pain relief, strengthening, athletic performance, weight loss). GFF^{TM} is a cash paying program that allows you to stop trading time for dollars, and start leveraging your time for exponential returns. You can enjoy more freedom and enjoy the lifestyle you have always wanted.

❖ TRIGGER EXPONENTIAL GROWTH WITH
MULTIPLE PROGRAMS IN MULTIPLE LOCATIONS

Discover the EXACT blueprint to have other professionals manage additional locations of your already successful Group Fitness Factor^{TM} program. We map out the exact process to duplicate yourself and grow your GFF^{TM} business.

Once you have created a successful GFF^{TM} program, you can sit back and enjoy the exponential growth of your company without putting in additional time and effort.

❖ STOP TRADING TREATMENT SESSIONS
FOR DELAYED PAYMENTS

Working 10-12 hours a day IN your practice as opposed to 3 hours a day ON your practice is a dead end lifestyle. Leverage your time by hiring other professionals to do the work for you while you enjoy the FREEDOM and peace of mind you have always wanted.

We have engineered the Group Fitness Factor™ model with a precise road map that guarantees your success. Join successful PTs from all over the country who have implemented this cash paying program – secure your license today.

www.groupfitnessfactor.com

THE THREE NEW DRIVERS OF PRIVATE PRACTICE PROFITABILITY

As we start a new year in our clinics, it's important to identify trends and new drivers of profitability in your clinic. A successful business is in a state of constant innovation, looking for new ways to improve customer experience and streamline operations. The following methods will help you establish new standards in profitability for your business:

LEVERAGE LIFETIME PATIENT VALUE (LVP) TO INCREASE PROFITABILITY

In most cases, clinicians rarely think beyond the $70 to $100 generated in revenue from a patient visit. The truth is that the actual income (AI) generated from this patient is the average income for that visit multiplied by the total number of visits. So if a patient with an $80 per visit revenue is seen 10 times on average, the average income for that patient is 80 times 10, which is $800. This is the average income (AI) for that patient. This number is significantly different from another benchmark, called the lifetime value of the patient (LVP).

This number is significantly higher, sometimes as high as 3 times the AI of that particular patient, since the patient is a valuable connection to their own physician (a new referral source), can refer family and friends to you (a happy patient is a PRIME referral source), and most importantly the patient is a candidate for post rehab programs; group physical therapy programs and fitness/wellness programs post discharge. In other words, this patient is worth $2,400 for your practice during the course of their relationship with you.

Understanding the lifetime value of your patient and creating a plan to extract that value (by over delivering clinically, exceeding expectations with outstanding customer service, and strategically providing more products and services during the course of their lifetime) will be the driving force for a successful practice in 2012.

LOCAL BUSINESS TSUNAMI - COMMUNITY INVOLVEMENT WILL GROW YOUR PRACTICE

As private practices, we need to look beyond traditional referral sources like patients and physicians. Local businesses (those located within a 5 mile radius or your clinic) are valuable allies and strategic partners for your practice. In particular, local businesses with large lists of clients are (strategically) better allies than new businesses that lack a presence (and goodwill) within your community. Make sure you identify and forge mutually beneficial referral relationships with providers you trust and have utilized in the past. Otherwise, negative experiences that your customers have with other businesses that you recommend will creep back to you and affect your reputation.

With a combination of a well-planned endorsement strategies combined with an offer fueled by scarcity and urgency, you should be able to drive more patients and dramatically improve awareness about your practice and its services.

Each local business has its own set of clients and customer relationships which can be leveraged in your favor with endorsements. Once you can identify local businesses that serve your ideal patient, you want to start building mutually beneficial referral relationships with them. You can do the same for other businesses. The big benefit with local endorsements is your ability to 'piggyback' on the reputation of other businesses, establish instant credibility with residents in your community, reach a new patient population and minimize your new patient acquisition costs.

PATIENT REACTIVATION WILL BE
THE NEW "WEALTH ATTRACTION" MANTRA

Getting new patients is not always about getting more physicians to refer. This feeds the old school 'work more to get more patients' limited belief that we are conditioned to accept. This reinforces the notion that new patients come through extreme difficulty and constantly feeding physician's offices and schmoozing physicians, hoping that they will bless you with referral(s) one day.

Physicians are just one way to get new patients in your practice. If you think physicians are the only way, you are creating a subconscious barrier to abundant wealth. Your expectations about your profitability will be automatically downgraded. If you manage to get lots of referrals, a feeling of guilt sets in, preventing you from reaching new goals and exploding revenue potential in your practice.

It's important to understand that patients are everywhere. There are plenty of patients to go around (unlimited, in fact), when you master the art of reactivation and referral generation from existing patients. Until you believe this and master the skill, your ability to generate new patients will be slow, deliberate, painstaking, weak, and pessimistic. You will be modulating your wealth attraction potential and limiting your ability to achieve unlimited wealth and freedom in your practice.

There are more patients to be had than you can possibly imagine, once you start to condition your existing patients to refer their friends and family. Word of mouth referrals are the fastest way to grow a practice.

HOW TO USE VARIOUS HOLIDAYS AS YOUR NEW MARKETING WEAPONS

Every season has some type of "holiday" involved; winter, spring, summer or fall. During the holiday seasons, stores are buzzing with activity. Such sales usually involve weeks, sometimes months of planning.

Speaking of planning, it's important to think several weeks (or months) ahead if you want a steady and predictable stream of patients coming to your practice.

Holidays are an excellent time to connect with patients and physicians because a holiday is a timely reason to share your message.

Holiday promotions can be unifying and entertaining, since they get a lot of people involved and help raise awareness about your practice in the community. It's always easier to engage someone when you enter a conversation that is already going on in their minds. People respond better to special occasions since the mind is in 'hyper-drive' mode and there are positive feelings and mental associations with certain times of the year.

Chapter 4

*events that you can use to communicate with patients and a
below. Each holiday is opportunity for a strategic,
ting campaign to a section of your contact list.*

January

- ❖ 1st – New Year's Day
- ❖ 17th – Martin Luther King day (3rd Monday of January, traditionally January 15th)

January is National:

- • Bath Safety Month – hand out small rubber duckies with temperature gauges on them or just plain rubber duckies.
- • Hot Tea Month – hand out a packet of an herbal tea for relaxation or stress relief
- • International Quality of Life Month – hand out free copies of "Living Wills" for your state

February

- ❖ 6th – Super Bowl Sunday (currently the first Sunday of February)
- ❖ 14th – Valentine's Day
- ❖ 18th – Presidents' Day (traditionally the third Monday of February)

February is National:

- • Time Management Month – hand out pocket calendars or pens
- • Mend a Broken Heart Month – hand out heart awareness pamphlets (perhaps cross promoting a local cardiologist's office for heart healthcare)
- • Library Lovers Month – hold a promotion for your local library (take up a collection or collect gently used or new books) or offer a special one time discount to anyone who shows their library card

March

- ❖ 9th – Employee Appreciation Day
- ❖ 17th – St. Patrick's Day
- ❖ 21st – Good Friday

March is National:

- • National Multiple Sclerosis Education & Awareness Month – promote with your local MS Chapter, contact them for free give-away items & cross promote with free massages to anyone involved with the MS Chapter

- • National Craft Month – hand out small craft kits (cross stitch, beads, etc.) or highlight a client who does a particular craft like quilting and one of their quilts or knitting projects

- National Umbrella Month – hand out an umbrella to each visitor this month with your clinic name on it
- International Women's Month – Promote a female staff, local physician, or female client

April
- ❖ 1st – April Fools Day
- ❖ 18th – Patriot's Day (traditionally 3rd Monday in April)
- ❖ 20th – Passover (variable based on Jewish calendar)

April is National:
- Couple Appreciation Month – Promote a buy 1 get 1 free massage for couples
- Autism Awareness Month – Promote with your local Autism Chapter
- Defeat Diabetes Month – Promote your nutritionist to schedule free or discounted nutritional counseling to prevent or handle your dietary needs for diabetes

May
- ❖ 5th – Cinco De Mayo (Mexican)
- ❖ May 8th – Mother's day (second Sunday in May)
- ❖ May 30th – Memorial day (last Monday in May)

May is National:
- Better Hearing & Speech Month – Cross promote with a local hearing aid company for free hearing tests in return you provide their customer listing with free massage or complimentary item
- Arthritis Awareness Month – Promote water therapy and/or massage therapy for those suffering from arthritis
- Skin Cancer Awareness Month – Cross promote with a local dermatologist; offer sample tubes of sun block or free cards with how to keep safe in the sun

June
- ❖ 10th – Ice Tea Day
- ❖ 12th – Father's day (third Sunday in June)
- ❖ 14th – World Blood Donor Day (Sponsor a blood drive with your local blood bank)

June is National:
- Audio Book Appreciation Month – offer your own audio book or an audio book that has to do with something that would be of interest to clients for ½ price this month only
- Perennial Gardening Month – hand out packets of perennial seeds with your clinic name on them or offer a gardening basket to one lucky winner this month (each time they visit they can put their name in for a drawing)

Chapter 4

- National Rose Month – Pick one day and give every visitor a free rose to say thank you for being our customer during National Rose Month

July

- ❖ 4th – Independence Day
- ❖ 20th – Neil Armstrong becomes the first man to walk on the moon in 1969

July is National:

- Herbal Awareness Month – this is a great time to promote herbal remedies and homeopathies you may be selling in your office as part of your up-sell products
- Ice Cream Month – print out a free ice cream maze for customers to share with their kids and grandkids, just to celebrate Ice Cream Month! See about cross promoting with a local ice cream parlor, coupons for buy 1 get 1 free ice cream for your customers and a buy 1 get 1 free massage or up-sell item (vitamin D for when they can't get ice cream?) from your business.
- Tour de France Month – Promote bike safety awareness & enter clients for a bike helmet or cross promote with a local bike shop giving your customers a discount on any bike safety item and their customers a discount on leg/feet massages

August

- ❖ 1st – Francis Scott Key's birthday (author of the National Anthem)
- ❖ 13th – International Left-Hander's Day (special discount for anyone left handed?)
- ❖ 15th – Best Friends Day
- ❖ 19th – National Aviation Day
- ❖ 21st – Senior Citizens' Day

August is National:

- Golf Month – have visitors sign up for a golf related give away (free game of golf or pack of golf balls) or even a ½ price "Golfer's Massage" for sore shoulders/arms
- Cactus Month – Give miniature cactuses out to customers during a certain time period
- Water Quality Month – Give out a bottle of water with your Clinic Logo printed on it with a sheet of how important it is to drink plenty of water

September

- ❖ 2nd – First day of Ramadan (Islamic, based on lunar calendar)
- ❖ 11th – Patriot's Day
- ❖ 30th – Rosh Hashanah (variable based on Jewish calendar)

September is National:

- Baby Safety Month – Visitors can enter for a chance to win a baby safety basket with special safety products such as electrical outlet covers, cupboard locks and Mr. Yuck stickers

- National Coupon Month – Hand out coupons for $ off any service you want to promote for the month – good for September only!
- Whole Grains Month – pass out information about how important whole grains are to your diet, sign up to win a bread machine to make your own whole grain breads, hand out whole grain cereal bars with your company Logo/sticker on it.

October

- ❖ 9th – Yum Kippur (Jewish, variable start day, nine days)
- ❖ 13th – Columbus Day
- ❖ 31st - Halloween

October is National:

- Apple Month – have a basket of Fresh Apples (see if you can't get a great deal from a local farmer if you promote his farm) and have them sitting out at the registration desk for clients as they leave from their appointments
- Halloween Safety Month – Hand out fluorescent Halloween Bags with your clinic logo on them or glow sticks
- National Physical Therapy Month – Have a promotion giving anyone who brings in a referral gets a special gift, free session or discounted product from your office

November

- ❖ 4th – Election Day (Tuesday after first Monday in November)
- ❖ 11th – Veteran's Day
- ❖ 27th – Thanksgiving (4th Thursday in November)
- ❖ 28th – Black Friday (Friday after Thanksgiving Day)

November is National:

- Military Family Appreciation Month – offer a free service or service upgrade to anyone who is in the military, has a family member in the military, or has served in the military. Encourage them to share their military stories (especially older veterans love to tell about their days in the service)
- Family Stories Month – Entice clients to share their family history and put a display up, especially with generational pictures to enhance their stories to share with others or highlight one particular family and share their story. Everyone has a story, even if they don't think they do.
- AIDS Awareness Month – Have a campaign to raise money for a local AIDS chapter, or sell AIDS ribbons, or sell AIDS gel bracelets

December

- ❖ 22nd – First day of Hanukkah (variable, based on the Jewish Calendar)
- ❖ 24th – Christmas Eve

Chapter 4

❖ 25th – Christmas Day
❖ 31st – New Years Eve

Christmas, for example, is the time to get and give presents. Go to a bookstore, find books that you believe will be beneficial to patients and have them shipped directly to your patients (with a note from you) as a gesture of goodwill.

The personal note is the key. A lot of businesses do the same old stuff and send patients customized gifts (calendars, notepads, etc.) with a company logo on it. This is old school and people have now become immune to the subconscious marketing messages embedded in these freebies.

Here's the best part – it does not matter to the patient whether you wrote the book or not. What matters is that it's coming as a gift from you and was sent by you as a thoughtful gesture.

Include a personal note that says something like "*I read this book on pain relief and I thought you'd really benefit from it etc.*" This has a tremendous perceived value with the patient. The book will probably cost you $10-12 plus shipping but the goodwill generated will be significant.

This gift giving strategy during the holidays can be applied to physicians as well. Can you imagine sending a book to a physician that you feel might be beneficial for them and following up with a phone call? Even if you spend $1,000 or more sending these books, a single referral will pay for the cost of your campaign.

In case you are wondering, "*What happens if they never read the book?*" the fact is, it doesn't matter if they read it. What matters is that you sent it.

Even if the patient or the physician NEVER reads the book, they will remember this as a thoughtful and unconventional gesture (no one else does things like this).

Start using holidays in your favor and create a strategic holiday plan for the coming year.

11 WAYS TO BOOST P

The following tips will help increase the production an⌐ any clinic instantly.

1) Up-sell patients on related services that will add value to the treatment session. For example, would you like to purchase these exercise bands today? They will enable you to carry out your exercises at home with gradual, controlled resistance.

2) Regular activation campaigns - Do regular chart audits and conduct e-mail, phone call, and letter follow-ups to keep lost patients and appointment cancellations to a minimum.

3) Patient retention should be in place. It is far easier to keep an existing patient and seek referrals from that patient, than it is to get a new patient. An existing patient is like the low hanging fruit in your private practice. Minimizing patient attrition is the least expensive method to grow a practice. Patient retention can include newsletters, seminars, special offers and unannounced 'thank you' gifts.

4) Accept multiple modes of payment, including credit cards. Besides physical credit card terminals that can be swiped in your clinic, have a virtual credit card terminal (accepting payments online). Consider accepting e-checks and installments for payments, charged periodically to the patient's credit card (like a recurring gym membership).

5) Offer a pay by phone option, where patients can pay with a check or credit card over the phone. Introduce pay by SMS choices.

6) Don't compromise on your payment policies. All costs associated with a treatment should be paid for in advance. Always have a credit card on file for each patient as standard policy. Make credit card information part of the patient intake form. When you conditioned the patients this way from the beginning, you will not be questioned. The patients who resist can be politely told that the card will not be charged without prior warning and is a backup funding source in case of past due balances. Align your policies so you cut a refund check to the patient, as opposed to chasing them around like a bill collector.

7) Follow up with insurance companies on a bi-weekly or if possible, weekly manner. Do not wait until the bill is 30 days past due to initiate contact. Always find the right person to contact, preferably someone high up in the corporate

ier, with each insurance company. Your follow-up has even more impact if iu represent a group of independent private practice owners, who follow-up collectively. Strength in numbers is something that providers cannot ignore. Critically evaluate the effectiveness and the return on investment of an advertisement. Consider the average value of a new patient. Let's assume this is $800. If an advertisement that costs you $800 brings in two new patients, you have doubled your return on investment. Don't try to reinvent the wheel with advertisements. Rerun past advertisements that have been effective. Rinse and repeat.

9) Find online services to clean and purge old patient lists electronically. Update all patient addresses, phone numbers, and if possible e-mail addresses. Begin contact with the patients and reintroduce yourself with step (3) mentioned above.

10) Set up a payment collection system. Call the patient and gently remind them about the past due balance. You want to use a concise, well-planned phone script. An insider strategy that works well to boost the responsiveness of your collection efforts is to tell the patient that a letter reminding them about the past due balance is also on its way. This acts like a 'double reminder' and proves to the patient that you are firm in your collection efforts. The timing of this phone call should be on or a day before the delivery of the letter. With the right timing, phone script, and the letter, the patient will feel obliged to make their payment as opposed to ignoring the letter or regarding it as a nuisance.

11) Finally, if you offering a cash-paying program announce that you are raising your prices. Nothing works more effectively to create urgency and cash flow than the prospect of a looming price hike. You can offer existing and past patients the alternative to lock in their low 'current' prices, forever by signing up for a long-term, cash-paying program (wellness of preventive) in your clinic. Think of the last time you went to a gym. If the gym normally charged $50 a month membership, but offered you an annual plan for $359 (bringing your monthly costs down to $30) are you likely to take it?

BILLING AUTOMATION FOR PHYSICAL THERAPISTS

Although most physical therapy practices are alien to it, the strategy of automation is used by most successful businesses. Automation is the incorporation of a streamlined process that allows businesses to save time, increase productivity, and slash unnecessary costs. It is a mechanism that allows the physical therapist to sleep comfortably at night, knowing that the procedures inherent to running a practice can continue in a seamless, consistent fashion in the relative absence of human intervention.

Automation is convenient and necessary tool today. We live in a world that increasingly resists manual labor and the investment of time. Automation of business practices allows the incorporation of consistent, predictable processes that add value to the patients, providers, and third parties.

RECURRING CREDIT CARD CHARGES –AUTOMATION BILLING

If your practice is not already accepting credit cards, then the time to start is now. Another mechanism of automated billing is called electronic funds transfer, abbreviated as EFT. Your practice automatically debits the patient's credit card or checking account a preset amount every visit. The basic principle behind the automation of billing in a physical therapy private practice is consistency of income. Most major businesses adopt the strategy and are extremely successful. Think about your cell phone, Internet, or cable TV bill. Imagine for a moment that these companies were attempting to bill your card manually each month, or requesting your authorization each time. These companies know better and require you to authorize automated billing as soon as you do business with them. As a consumer, you are conditioned to agree and don't think twice about it. If these companies had to bill you and wait for payment each and every month, they would soon be out of business. If they can do it, why can't we? As a profession, we are light years behind automated billing. In fact physical therapists languish at the other end of the spectrum. We treat, complete paperwork, and then wait weeks to get paid; while other products and services of a lesser value bill in advance without a hint of discord from clients.

The incorporation of automatic credit card billing will transform your practice. As far as possible, encourage patients to keep their credit card information on file with your clinic. The patient's credit card is charged for the co-pay. The patient can be charged a cancellation fee of $10-$15 for no shows or last-minute cancellations. In this manner, the physical therapist or the receptionist no longer has to function as a 'bill collector.' The responsibility to settle the bill now rests with the patient. Another advantage of automatic billing is the opportunity to provide memberships to a monthly wellness program at your clinic.

The principle behind successful automated billing is the involvement of patients in systems of therapy not sessions of therapy. Enroll the patient in an open-ended wellness program as an extension of a close end, finite physical therapy program. With the right amount of skill and salesmanship, you can bridge the gap between the physical therapy covered by insurance and the wellness program that the patient truly needs by presenting the option of an affordable cash-based exercise program. Offer a unique, monthly physical therapy coaching program which includes, in addition to physical therapy sessions, unlimited e-mail and phone consulting with you. Most patients who purchase this program are unlikely to take advantage of the unlimited coaching component, but will be glad to know that they have unlimited access to their physical therapist. You can transform yourself from a physical therapy provider into a complete wellness provider; providing general information on health, fitness, and lifestyle management.

The use of automated billing in cash-based fitness programs boosts compliance and guarantees that you will work with high-quality patients. It's time for practices to evaluate, incorporate, and embrace automated billing to ensure a successful, stable, and growing practice.

BUILD YOUR PATIENT LIST

When someone visits your website or calls you for the first time, they are *prospects* searching for information. The success of a marketing system lies in transforming the *prospect* into a *patient* and a *patient* into a *referral source*.

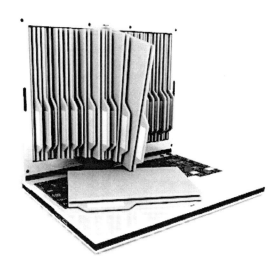

It is possible to drive patients through an initial funnel where they visit your website or call you to a productive patient relationship that can be worth several thousand dollars over the course of a lifetime. Think of it this way, how much is the patient worth to you over the course of his or lifetime? Chances are that the single patient relationship can be worth $500 minimum. In some cases, repeat visits from the patient and/or referrals initiated by the patient can increase the lifetime value of the patient to several thousand dollars.

Keeping this in mind, ask yourself *"How much am I willing to pay to acquire a new patient?"*

Keep in mind that buying or acquiring a list of names and e-mail addresses of individuals (even if they happen to be local residents interested in physical therapy) is unlikely to yield results. Most people respond to individuals whom they have a prior business or personal connection with. Besides, sending unsolicited e-mails to individuals with a marketing intent is considered spamming.

With the advent of pay per click advertising and lead generation pages on the internet, it is possible to drive specific, targeted visitors to your website and start collecting names and e-mail addresses of prospects within hours. In many cases, you may pay less than two dollars a prospect and accumulate a high quality list of patients fairly quickly.

Pay per click advertising is offered by most major online search providers like Google, Yahoo, and MSN. The way it works is that you sign up for an account and 'bid' for certain key words that your patients are searching for.

Depending upon your practice niche and your location, the "keywords" may look something like this:

❖ Low back pain New York City
❖ Shoulder pain New Jersey
❖ Boston physical therapist
❖ Pain relief in Denver

Chapter 4

Based on these keywords, you can set up an advertising account. Depending on the amount of competition for your keywords and your bid amount, your ad can show up on page 1 of all major search engines within hours, allowing you to position yourself in front of your target audience quickly.

Each time someone clicks on your advertisement, your account gets charged. You can set daily limits for your account, so that you ads turned off once your account threshold is reached.

The big advantage with this kind of advertising is the ability to track results. You can check exactly how many people clicked on your advertisement and measure your cost per click.

THE OTHER SIDE OF THE STORY – THE OPT-IN

Getting a patient to visit your website is only half the battle. Your website must be designed in such a way that it provides the patient with such a significant amount of valuable information that you are able to extract their name and e-mail address in order to deliver them even more targeted information.

For example, a patient looking for information on low back pain arrives at your website. You provide them with a free downloadable book on "Low back pain prevention 101".

However, in order to get access to this information, the patient must 'jump through a hoop' and enter some data in a sign up form.

This is called a successful '*opt-in*'

With a very well designed and crafted website, your opt-in ratio should exceed 30% of your total website visitors. If you spent two dollars per click and three out of every 10 patients to visit your website becomes a prospect, you could be spending between six and seven dollars per prospect.

The patient has to enter their name and e-mail address in a form and click 'submit'. At this point you have successfully captured the name and e-mail address of the patient and can follow up with them in the future.

Why get the patient to 'jump through the hoop'? The goal is to 'pre-qualify' legitimate prospects and separate them from the rest of the pack; namely the individuals seeking free information only, but unlikely to be a patient or referral source.

At the very least, your sign up form should ask for an e-mail address. The more information you ask for in your sign up form, the less likely it is that people will opt in.

The good news is that this strategy will increase the quality of the list significantly. Patients who take the trouble to enter all of their contact information on your website (name, address, e-mail, and phone) in order to get access to your content are the best, most reliable leads for your private practice.

The quality of the list and your relationship with them is infinitely more important than its size. A small list of 200 patients who know you, like you, and trust you will do more for your practice than a list of two thousand patients who do not remember you or perceive your practice as a profit driven corporate identity that probably does not care about them.

When you combine a strong pay per click strategy designed to drive patients to your website and an irresistible offer of a patient to opt-in, you will build a high-quality, reliable list of prospects and patients.

SECTION II

NO NONSENSE CLINIC
Grow Your Practice

CHAPTER 5

Undercover Techniques To Structure

Your Website To Attract More Patients

TOP 5 WEBSITE CONVERSION SECRETS FOR PRIVATE PRACTICES

As busy private practice owners, we understand the importance of a website but don't have the time to go back and forth with website designers who don't understand our requirements.

Even if a majority of your patients don't use the Internet, a good website presence establishes you as a professional practice dedicated to quality and visibility. Your website must be structured to elicit a PRECISE outcome from each visitor. Every word, every image, and even the color of your website can play an important role in its eventual function. When someone visits your website, they have a maximum of 5, maybe 6, seconds before they form an opinion.

How is your current website structured? Does it control the experience of the user? If someone were to visit your website, would they:

a) See an attention-grabbing headline?

b) Want to provide you with their name and email address and other contact information?

c) Want to schedule an appointment with your clinic?

Or would they:

a) Get tons of information

b) Lack a clearly defined goal (sign up for our free book, schedule your free appointment, etc.)

c) Leave your website with the intention to '*come back later*' (which never happens)

The ideal private practice site controls the experience of the visitor; transforming them from visitor to prospect and then prospect to patient.

The visitor is not allowed to 'sway' away from the "most wanted response."

Online behavior is predictable. Companies like Google and MSN have spent billions of dollars testing 'eyeball movements', 'click tracking', and 'heatmaps.' They have discovered that it takes a few seconds before a visitor becomes 'hooked' or is lost forever.

This is called '*web analytics*'. Wikipedia defines web analytics as "… the measurement, collection, analysis, and reporting of Internet data for purposes of understanding and optimizing web usage". Google, now a $100 billion dolla company, is an expert at providing visitors with exactly what they want.

These strategies will help you get the most out of your website.

A) WHAT ARE YOU TRYING TO ACHIEVE?

You HAVE to provide your visitor with the right information immediately. Therefore, it is important to identify the main focus of your site. Is your main focus to collect a list of prospects and patients, or is it to get patients to make appointments? Your website should have a clearly defined goal (referred to the "*most wanted response*" earlier in the section), preferably lead generation. Everything else, including resumes about your staff, equipment in your clinic, and libraries filled with information will only detract from your main focus. Most websites that I review lack a main focus. They are a mish-mash of many different things blended together.

B) ARE YOU GIVING THEM PRACTICAL INFORMATION?

Give them what they want. Always provide the patients with the information they immediately want – 'How To Relieve Pain.' Every website should have a section on "How To Relieve Pain" Include "*Prospect Stimulators*" in your website marketing. Provide visitors with a valuable tool (a downloadable e-book, audio interview, or a video) that gives them practical information that they can use immediately).

C) ARE YOU ASKING THEM FOR CONTACT INFORMATION?

Make it easy for visitors to give you their contact information. Include the 'sign up' box for your *prospect stimulator* on the top right hand side of each page. If you're not building an email list of local prospects, patients, media contacts, local businesses, and potential referral sources and actively emailing them high quality, practical information, you are overlooking the simplest and most effective way to remain visible to current and previous patients. You MUST build your own list and cultivate it.

D) ARE YOU EMPHASIZING THE BENEFITS FOR THE PATIENT?

Always have a strong, confident, benefit driven headline on each page; one that resonates with the needs of your patients. A sample headline is "*All You Ever Needed To Know About Pain. The Complete Pain Relief Solution. Period.*" Many websites waste this 'prime online real estate' by simply announcing the name of their clinic.

E) DOES THE PATIENT HAVE AN INCENTIVE TO CONTACT YOU IMMEDIATELY?

Make it easy for your visitor to contact you. Provide your contact information (phone number on the top right hand side of each page, close to the top margin). As simple as this may sound ask yourself, "*is it easy to find our phone number on every page of our website?*"

Promote a FREE consultation where you invite patients to come into your clinic. This does NOT have to be an objective evaluation, but a simple medical history followed by an explanation about the possible benefits of physical therapy. The purpose is NOT to give away your services for free, but to get the prospect to walk through the door. Once they're in it allows your in-house process to kick in and explain the benefits of physical therapy to the client.

The truth is that our mental models of website development are, for the most part, incorrect. Many websites are an unrecognizable mix of information and self-promotion that do not lead the patient to the "*most wanted response.*"

Getting your users to take the "*most wanted response*" on your website is a science; a result of years of testing, NOT a game of chance.

YOUR WEBSITE: YOUR 24/7 MARKETING EXPERT

Your website is a window to the world. Patients who are considering coming to you make an instant decision about your practice based on your website and the initial phone call they make to your clinic.

A successful website has several components that work seamlessly; chiefly, content and tracking tools.

Take 10 minutes to analyze your website today. A few changes can make a huge impact on your image, referral capabilities, and profitability.

SOME IMPORTANT QUESTIONS TO ASK ARE:

- Do you provide relevant, patient friendly information to your visitors?
- Do you have a system in place to track visitor information and communicate with patients after they have visited your website?

Some therapists manage their own website while others outsource the task. In both cases, the emphasis is usually on design, good looking logos, expensive equipment, and other factors which the patient finds mostly irrelevant.

The big question you need to ask, if you currently own a website, is: "*How do I improve the potential of my website to attract new patients?*"

The two steps to a successful website are content and visitor tracking.

DO'S AND DON'TS OF CONTENT

Your website must have excellent information that is relevant to patients and a conversion process that transforms them from website visitors into actual patients and even potential referral sources. Good content begins with an overview of information that is relevant to the patient and appears precise and reader-friendly. Adhere to your area of expertise and give patients tips on what they can use. Good content enables you to connect with your audience and includes an action-oriented message, combined with a sense of urgency. A simple, clear message that encourages visitors to pick up the phone and call your clinic is the single most important parameter of success. Patient testimonials are another big part of the success of a website.

The patient must be able to contact the office or schedule an appointment online at any time. The easier you make the initial contact, the more profitable your site will be. Your goal is to get the visitor who comes to your site to call or email you requesting further information about your services.

The last thing you want is for the reader to leave your site without initiating contact with you. In most cases, you have less than 30 seconds to make an impression with your site. Even if the visitor leaves your site without contacting you, you want an "*email stimulator*" box on your site that encourages the visitor to provide you with their name and email address. This should be a simple form asking for the visitor's name, email address, and phone number. It should be placed prominently and attractively on your website. Offer your visitor an eBook, a newsletter, or some incentive to provide you with their contact information when they visit your site. It is critical that contact information should be easily viewable on all pages of the website, perhaps as a part of the website banner. Make it easy for your visitors to contact you and leave their contact information behind. Your website should help you build a patient database, since hundreds or potentially thousands of patients could be visiting your website each month.

Most sites seem like encyclopedias and information that may make sense to the therapist and staff, but not the patient. Don't be verbose with the therapists' resumes, achievements, and the mission of the clinic unless it relates directly to patient care.

DO'S AND DON'TS OF VISITOR TRACKING

Tracking involves the science of analyzing your website traffic, listening to the customer by observing behavior, and improving your site. Google provides an outstanding, free analytical tool called '*Google Analytics*'. It can be implemented instantly and provides you with information such as:

- The number of visitors to your site each day, time of visit, and navigation path through your site
- Who referred the visitors; how they found your site
- '*Goal tracking*' – what percentage of visitors clicked through to your contact page
- At which page did a majority of visitors 'exit' the site (your weakest link)
- Amount of time spent by visitors on individual pages and number of pages viewed
- Ratio of new visits vs. visits from repeat individuals
- Historical data, trend analysis, and page to page / website comparison
- Comparison of the performance of your emails, ad performance
- Industry wide benchmarking, ecommerce analysis, and much more.

This will give you a clear idea of what visitors are expecting from your product or service, allow you to focus more on pages that work, and modify pages that don't. Too many therapists waste time, money, and resources on <u>what they think</u>; instead of focusing on <u>what they need</u>. Ask yourself, "*How can I make this easier for my customers and help them make sense of this information?*"

Your website can now become your most powerful marketing tool. It's your window to the world, so put your best content forward and track visitor behavior. The results will open new doors of communication with your patients.

21st CENTURY PHYSICAL THERAPY BRANDING / USING TECHNOLOGY TO BRAND YOUR CLINIC

In a competitive economy, practitioners must think outside of the box. A successful private practice is as much about marketing and relationship building as it is clinical excellence.

Patients today can find you in a number of ways; the physician is just one example of a referral source. Patients can look you up on the Internet, in the yellow pages, obtain referrals from other patients, or even read about you in the newspaper.

In a world driven by increased technology and decreased human interaction, the private practitioner is faced with a new challenge; a limited attention span from patients. This also presents numerous options to reach a target audience, all of which are technology driven. The following strategies leverage the latest online and offline methods to promote your practice, build a brand, and reach a newer, larger patient population.

1)   Consistent, relevant communication with referral sources

How consistent should you be? You want to strike a fine balance and be consistent, but not be overbearing. On the other hand, you don't want to 'fall off the map' and be forgotten by referral sources. These referral sources can generate thousands of dollars in revenue over the course of a lifetime. The most common mistake is to communicate too little. You need a plan to communicate on a regular, timely basis. Not once in 3 months or once in 6 months, but once every week or every other week is acceptable, especially with patients.

What should the communication consist of? For patients, the communication should be an informational, patient friendly handout, flyer, or newsletter that provides

the patient with valuable take-home lessons on health and physical therapy. For physicians, a faxed version of a newsletter is helpful. Physicians can provide this information as a resource to their patients.

Communication is best when performed face to face, because the patient is able to associate a human face, voice, and personality to the message. This is best

Chapter 5

achieved with public speaking; conducting a workshop once a month on-site is the best option. Recent innovations have also made it possible for you to conduct live video broadcasts, where patients can see you and provide comments by phone / within a text-based chat box while you are speaking with them live. All these efforts will bring the patient one step closer to knowing you, liking you, and trusting you as a leading physical therapy provider. Resources like ustream.tv allow this kind of video interaction at no cost.

The next option is voice, without a face-to-face meeting. Offer a free teleclass (which is easier to market than 'conference call') on different topics like low back pain, posture, biomechanics, deep breathing, etc. once a month. Several services on the internet provide free teleconferencing services and also provide the added benefit of recording your phone calls, which can be archived or re-mastered to create patient education audio CDs.

2)   **An interactive approach, online and offline, to obtain visitor contact information**

If a patient searches for *"physical therapy (your town name)"*, does your clinic show up on page one? If it does, the patient will start viewing your clinic with a positive impression.

To achieve this, make sure your pages are optimized for your main keywords. Your keyword *"physical therapy (town name)"* and its variations like *"(town name) physical therapist"* should be present naturally throughout the content and in the title tag of your web page. You should also strive to obtain links from other sites/pages on the internet related to your site. Display several pictures and include video testimonials of satisfied patients.

Any discrepancies in the site can lead to a negative perception. Pages like 'under construction' or 'not found' are unacceptable for a private practice. Your phone number should be present on each and every page; patients should be able to read articles that add value, skim over your resume, and be able to easily pick up the phone to call you.

A website rich with video testimonials, audio messages, and live chat boxes also encourages the visitor to interact with you. Engaging a stranger (in this case, the website visitor) is step one of the website marketing process. Your goals, through a series of steps, is to convert the 'stranger' into a prospective patient. A prospect, in turn, can be converted to a patient using the technique explained in step 1 – consistent communication over time. You need to, ideally, create a series of emails that go out to

Section II   130 the patient over a period of time in order to establish a reputation of consistency and quality.

Your website is not the only marketing tool on the web. Various social networking sites, like Twitter and Facebook, also allow you to connect with individuals in your area. The goal should be to communicate with several individuals at one time, and several physicians (physicians; meetings) if possible as well. Public speaking and communicating with local chambers of commerce to set up such meetings, is invaluable.

All these methods are based on time and technology leveraging; the essence of 21st century physical therapy marketing. Think outside the box and watch your practice flourish.

TOP 10 WEBSITE DESIGN STRATEGIES FOR PRIVATE PRACTICE OWNERS

1. **Identify the main focus of your site.** Is it to collect a list of prospects and patients, or is it to get patients to make appointments? Your website should have **a clearly defined goal,** preferably lead generation. Everything else, including resumes about your staff, equipment 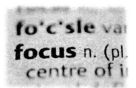 in your clinic, and libraries filled with information only detract from your main focus. **Most websites that I review lack a main focus.** They are a mish-mash of lots of different things blended together.

2. **Give them what they want.** Always provide the patients with the information they immediately want – How To Relieve Pain. Every website should have a section on *"How To Relieve Pain"*

3. **Include "Prospect Stimulators" in your website marketing.** Provide visitors with a valuable tool (a downloadable e-book, audio interview or a video) that gives them practical information they can use right away.

4. **Make it easy for visitors to give you their contact information.** Include the 'sign up' box for your prospect stimulator on the top right hand side of each page. To be perfectly honest, if you're not building an email list of local prospects, patients, media contacts, local businesses, and potential referral sources and actively emailing them high quality, practical information; then you are leaving a lot of money on the table and holding yourself back from achieving optimum success. You MUST build your own list and cultivate it.

5. **Always have a strong, confident, benefit driven headline** on each page, one that resonates with the needs of your patients. A sample headline is *"All You Ever Needed To Know About Pain. The Complete Pain Relief Solution. Period."* I see a lot of practices wasting this space just announcing the name of their clinic.

6. **Make it easy for them to contact you.** Provide your contact information (phone number on the top right hand side of each page, close to the top margin). As simple as this may sound, ask yourself if it's easy to find your phone number on every page of your website.

7. **Promote a FREE evaluation / consultation** where you invite patients to come into your clinic. This does NOT have to be an objective evaluation, but a simple medical history followed by an explanation about the possible benefits of physical therapy.

8. **Leveraging video.** Put up a video of yourself explaining the benefits of physical therapy. All the marketing in the world means nothing if you can't convert that website visitor into a patient. You HAVE to get good at creating videos, putting them up on your website, and working closely with a web designer who can assist you with making your website more interactive

9. **Integration of social media like Facebook.** Link your Facebook profile to your website and mention your website in your Facebook wall posts, to drive traffic to and fro between your site and Facebook.

10. **Use a template that works.** The fastest, easiest and most direct way to a successful website is modeling a formula that works. Don't try to create a custom website and recreate the wheel.

Chapter 5

IS YOUR WEBSITE CHOCKING YOUR ABILITY TO GET NEW PATIENTS?

We've been brainwashed by people around us who insist it's CRITICAL to have a nice website with tons of information; that the website should be optimized for all the search engines, and that we should 'be on Facebook' to market ourselves. On top of that, it seems we should start selling things on our websites and make a commission on products sold through our 'online store'. However, all this 'website stuff' that we are sold on and told to do… it's not logical persuasion about the what and the why of websites, but rather a constant drilling and reinforcement of the benefits of 'online marketing'.

The mission is to make you 'compliant' with the internet era; to make you believe that a website is the answer to all your prayers. You are gently nudged into a sense of belief that 'a nice website' is a safe and easy way for you to get noticed and bring in a flood of new patients.

Now, it's entirely possible that your website ALONE can be the source of referrals for your clinic and that your website may be the single best marketing decision you ever make. But I don't believe it.

Don't get me wrong, everything I just mentioned has a place somewhere deep down the ladder of priorities for a busy private practice owner.

HERE'S WHAT MOST ONLINE MARKETING EXPERTS WON'T TELL YOU:

• A 'static' website, that just sits on the internet, will RARELY rank in the search engines unless there are regular, original content updates posted to the site (which you are responsible for)

• 'Original' content updates imply that the content should NOT be duplicated elsewhere on the Internet, which is frowned upon by the search engines. (Beware when you are sold another 'encyclopedia' website with tons of articles for patients). Besides the fact that most patients won't read the dry, boring articles, the duplicate content on your website can be damaging to your search engine rankings. **Search engines like Google can penalize your website for 'duplicate content'.** If you have a website that has the same content as

numerous other sites, the search engines perceive this as 'content dupli
and will punish your website with poor search engine rankings.

- Most of your patients have a Facebook account but demographically it's likely
they spend very little time (if any at all) reading your updates on Facebook,
contrary to what you are led to believe. Even if they are interested in your
updates, Facebook is primarily a non-business platform. People are on
Facebook to interact with others, not be marketed too. It's easy to goof up
Facebook marketing unless you are posting messages frequently, sharing
things about your life, constantly engaging your audience with attractive offers,
and being 'out there'. You may or may not feel comfortable doing this.

- You do not need to rank at the top of all the search engines. Google is the only
one that really matters since it gathers over 70% of all search traffic. On top of
that, Google Local is the only listing that matters to brick and mortar
businesses and I provide FREE training on how to get your clinic to rank at the
top of Google Local here.

- Selling things on your website is like picking up pennies while neglecting the
gold coins sitting right under your nose. Why make a few dollars asking
patients to visit your website to buy stuff, when you could use the same
(limited) attention span from patients to generate more referrals, convert them
into cash paying program clients or create connections with their physicians
(which is invaluable). It's a matter of priorities.

If you are going to do all that, why not do it with email, print, phone, and text
messaging directly with your patients since you have their contact information? Why
waste time on Facebook?

It's like the wild, wild west out there and as private practice owners the common
questions are:

- How much information (and what kind of
information) should be on my website?
- Should I optimize my website for the
search engines?
- Should I market my practice on
Facebook?

When someone asks me these questions
during a strategy call, the response from my
business advisers is:

*"I appreciate your enthusiasm, but
these are the wrong questions to
ask, because online marketing is
ONE TYPE of marketing. It should
be lower down on your to-do list. It
should, in fact, be number three or
four in the list of priorities for most
private practices".*

Chapter 5

ebsite providers' prey upon the uninformed, who spend
ands of dollars on websites; when that effort could have been
rs to BIGGER questions that can make or break a practice.

❖ *Which modes of communication should I use to contact patients and physicians?*
❖ *Do I have systems in place to follow-up with my patients?*
❖ *Am I doing everything I can to squeeze that last referral out of my existing sources?*

If you don't have the answers to these questions dialed in (which is exactly what I help my clients with during a strategy call) then spending time and money on a website is like buying icing for your home made cake. The problem is… no one ever showed you how to bake.

As private practice owners, we tend to look for the 'magic pill' that will bring us a flood of referrals and recognition. Having a website seems like a quick and easy way to make yourself visible. Don't get me wrong, a patient-action oriented website is important, but if it exists as a crutch for a fractured system then it's doing more harm than good. It prevents you from addressing the IMPORTANT issues that can help you grow your clinic.

✓ The ability to leverage different modes of communication – email, direct mail, text messaging, and phone work best for patients. Faxes and phone call follow-ups work best with physicians.
✓ Systems to communicate with past, present, and prospective patients on a consistent basis. A regular, content rich physical therapy newsletter for physicians and patients in print, email, video, and faxed format will do more for your clinic than a boring, static website ever will. A 'done-for-you' program like "Therapy Newsletter™" is the most advanced patient generation technology on the planet and should be your PRIMARY marketing weapon. This is a very different approach from half-baked copycat online packages, outdated 'encyclopedia' and websites. This is an approach that differs from a 'me too' newsletter that is poorly written and lacks a 'call to action.'

Instead, with Therapy Newsletter™ you have a better way to market your clinic with multi-mode delivery, 99% email delivery rate, customizable content, done-for-you eBooks that you can brand with your clinic name, birthday reminders, and email auto responder sequences. In fact, at Therapy Newsletter™, we offer a FREE website design upgrade for newsletter clients; because a website should be an adjunct to a terrific newsletter, not the other way around. (At my company, we put our money where our mouth is. Plus, I don't believe our clients should have to waste any money or continue to pay expensive monthly hosting fees on their existing websites).

✓ Maximum leverage of existing referral sources with strategic conditioning campaigns.

✓ Once all this is dialed in, it's then and only then that you want to hire a top notch physical therapy website designer who provides you a fast turnaround time, low rates, and a money back guarantee. If you are designing your website from scratch, then I strongly recommend Instant Private Practice Site since they have built excellent websites for most of my clients.

Let's focus on the things that really matter and put website marketing at number three or four in our list, after the CRITICAL systems are dialed in.

ANATOMY OF A PERFECT WEBSITE

What does it take to have the PERFECT website for your practice?

Consumers are dictating today's digital media environment.

Consumers have less patience than ever before. Without an understanding of the emotional triggers and the factors that drive them to visit your website, most websites, including the best-designed ones (especially those with an encyclopedia of information) are bound to get lost in the sea of the Internet.

THE 30 SECOND FORMULA – DO OR DIE FOR YOUR WEBSITE

You have less than 30 seconds to get a patient's attention when they visit your website.

They will be gone forever if:

* ❖ They get confused
* ❖ They are overwhelmed with information
* ❖ They are not given a clear 'call to action'

"According to a recent survey, 64% of consumers make a buying decision based on their initial digital experience with a brand...."

(2009 Survey, Razorfish Digital Media Experience)

Imagine if a patient comes to your site and sees:

* ✓ A simple, clean interface
* ✓ Short, concise, easy to understand information
* ✓ A precise 'call to action' (Do this, get that: enter your name and email address, get a free report)

THE BIG SOLUTION – A WORDPRESS WEBSITE

The world's simplest website platform is called '*WordPress*' and if you own a website, make sure it is 'WordPress based'. This should give you a username and password that enables YOU to change ANY page at

ANY time. WordPress blogs can be easily optimized for the search engines, allowing

you to rank quickly in the search engines for keywords like "*physical therapy (your town name)*"

Let's face it. We DON'T have the time to get bogged down with the techy stuff. As busy private practice owners and clinicians, we want the content pre-written, the ability to edit all content, add an unlimited number of pages… something that works RIGHT OUT OF THE GATE.

IS YOUR WEBSITE REALLY WORKING FOR YOUR PRACTICE?

If your website is set up to DO WHAT IT'S SUPPOSED TO DO; drive more patients to your practice, you must:

1. Give patients the option to download, print, and complete relevant forms so that they can bring these in before the initial evaluation. This saves you time and money.
2. Display your address and contact information on EVERY PAGE.
3. Display a clear call to action with an "email stimulator" box on the main page.
4. Demonstrate video, audio, and written testimonials from patients and endorsements from other referral sources.
5. Include an 'integrated blog' function where you can post regular updates for patients and website visitors.
6. Provide visitors with useful information on what physical therapy is, where pain comes from, healthy lifestyle tips, etc.

GOOGLE CHANGES PHYSICAL THERAPY BUSINESS

Google has changed the way people use the Internet and it is now changing the way a physical therapy business markets itself. Now, with the advent of Google Local, they are doing it again.

Did you know that a well-structured Google Local listing can have your private practice website on page one of Google within days, if not hours?

Imagine a patient searching for "physical therapy (name of your town)" or "physical therapist (name of your town)". If this patient was to arrive at your site and you were able to get their contact information, follow up with them, and build a lifelong relationship; what would that mean for your practice?

If you are serious about growing your physical therapy business, this is something that you cannot ignore.

Observe the first ranking. Now observe the last ranking. Since a Chiropractor clearly knows what he is doing, he is ranking for the search term "physical therapist new york city"

Here's the bottom line… Every private practice must have a website that appears on page one of Google and that page must convert visitors into prospects. The strength of a website lies in its ability to convert cold traffic to warm traffic. A website is like your 24/7 salesman on the Internet. It is your physical therapy business ally.

There is a flip side to the coin. It is frustrating to find a good web designer who meets your needs and delivers on time. You definitely don't want to spend several weeks or several thousand dollars designing a website that is a mish-mash of information and benefits, because that leaves patients confused and frustrated.

I can speak of this from my own experience. I've spent thousands of dollars on websites that took months to complete, looked horrible, and most importantly could not be found anywhere on search engines.

The truth is that, most web designers have NO IDEA how to get visitors OR convert them into prospects and patients. You see, a good website for your practice is NOT about how pretty it looks and how much information you give the patient.

It's about one thing and one thing only.

CONVERSIONS

Conversions

Can you get the visitor to contact you? This instantly identifies the visitor as a prospective patient. If your website does anything else but identify the visitor as a prospective patient then it's missing the point.

Here's an example of a good conversion: For every 100 visitors that come to your site, at least 5 of them contact you to request more information.

Imagine if your practice had a clean, professional website that was a patient generation machine, NOT a glorified brochure without a strategic intent.

WITH EVERY AMBITIOUS GOAL COMES A CREATIVE CHALLENGE

The challenge for me was finding a team that could understand marketing, provide quality designs, and integrate my "Referral Ignition" methods at a low cost with a quick turnaround time. Ideally, I wanted this done in 4-5 business days.

That's why when I finally found a team who delivered quality search-engine-optimized websites at a great price with a good turn around time I was ECSTATIC!

It's been one of the single biggest factors of my success today… I just let them create my websites while I focus on the critical tasks that I am good at. This team consists of sophisticated web design professionals who use the latest eye catching designs (did you know light blue and light green colors are pleasing and elicit trust from visitors?)

Web design is a science and an art; one that this team understands inside out. They understand how Google works and are on the cutting edge of all search engine optimization strategies.

They do the thinking, so you and I don't have to stress over websites.

After some arm-twisting, I decided to convince them to offer their services to my readers and to make things significantly easier for you. I wrote ALL THE CONTENT for the website.

The result? You get a done-for-you website, within 4-5 business days, and it's possible to appear on page one of Google Local.

Here are some of the things you should consider about Google and the way they can change your physical therapy business.

- ♦ There are 12,000 + searches a month for "physical therapists new york" on Google alone
- ♦ There are 6,600 + searches a month for "physical therapy new jersey" on Google alone
- ♦ There are 18,100 searches a month for 'physical therapist ca' on Google alone

The chart below will show you the rising trend on Google for the search terms physical therapy and physical therapist. Remember, these are actual patients looking for physical therapy services on Google.

Are they finding you?

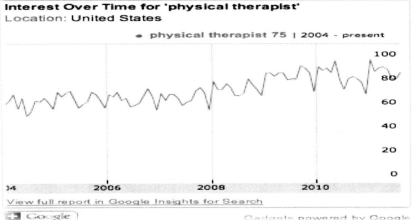

WEBSITE CONTENT DO'S AND DON'TS

Your website must have excellent information that is relevant to patients and a conversion process that transforms them from website visitors into actual patients; even potential referral sources.

Good content begins with an overview of information that is relevant to the patient, appears precise, and reader-friendly. Adhere to your area of expertise and give patients tips on what they can use.

Good content enables you to connect with your audience and includes an action-oriented message, combined with a sense of urgency. A simple, clear message that encourages visitors to pick up the phone and call your clinic is the single most important parameter of success. Patient and client testimonials are another big part of the success of a website.

The patient must be able to contact the office, or schedule an appointment online at any time. The easier you make the initial contact, the more profitable your site will be. Your goal is to get the visitor who comes to your site to call or email you requesting further information about your services.

The last thing you want is for the reader to leave your site without initiating contact with you. In most cases, you have less than 30 seconds to make an impression with your site.

Even if the visitor leaves your site without contacting you, you want an "email stimulator" box on your site that encourages the visitor to provide you with their name and email address. This should be a simple form, asking for the visitor's name, email address, and phone number placed prominently and attractively on your website.

Offer your visitor an eBook, a newsletter, or some incentive to provide you with their contact information when they visit your site. It is critical that your contact information should be easily viewable on all pages of the website; perhaps as a part of the website banner.

Make it easy for them to contact you and leave their contact information behind. Your website should help you build a patient database since hundreds, or potentially thousands, of patients could be visiting your website each month. Track your website traffic using tools, such as the powerful Google Analytics in your personal training marketing.

Most sites seem like encyclopedias and make sense to the therapist and staff, but not the patient. Don't be verbose with the therapists' resumes, achievements, and the mission of the clinic unless it relates directly to patient care.

RESOURCE

The Real Truth Your Website Designer Is Hiding From You... Revealing The All New Private Practice Website Blueprint

If You Want To Structure Your Website To Help You Get New Patients And Rank #1 In Google Local, Then This Is The Most Important FREE Training You Will Ever Attend And Here's Why...

I will teach you the BIG REASONS why MOST private practice websites FAIL MISERABLY at converting website visitors to patients and WHAT YOU CAN DO to become part of the ELITE 1% who own an automated, patient generation website...

Making the right decision about the website provider you work with can be the difference between a lifeless, dull website with the occasional person trickling in and a dramatic, turn-key solution that attracts patients, helps you build a prospect list and markets your clinic on autopilot. In this new course, I will teach you:

✓ How to get to page 1 of Google local to attract the maximum number of local leads to your practice...
✓ A unique online lead generation strategy to monetize your visitors and the only website success factor formula you will ever need to convert suspects to patients from your website
✓ How to get your site noticed in the infinite sea of the internet... these simple changes can generate new patients for your practice by recognizing their "emotional triggers" and delivering exactly what they are looking for...
✓ How to structure your website to help you convert 'suspects' to patients paying TOP DOLLAR for your services
✓ The BIG reasons why most private practice websites fail MISERABLY at converting visitors to patients
✓ What you can do to become a part of the elite, 1% who own an automated website that literally sends you new patients 24/7

Go To: **www.privatepracticewebsite.com**

CHAPTER 6

How To Win Patients And Influence Them To

Trigger An Avalanche Of Internal Referrals

THE PATIENT REFERRAL FORMULA

When it comes to the art of patient referrals, most physical therapy private practice owners tend to prospect physicians using cold-call methods. Sometimes the physical therapist waits for patients almost like a fisherman sitting on a lake. The ideal physical therapy private practice should be able to grow from multiple referrals from former patients. The dependence on physician referrals should be minimized as much as possible. The reason why many private practice owners flounder in their practice is because they fall into the trap of dependence on 3 or 4 physicians. Once a single physician stops referring, a crisis with patient flow happens almost immediately.

That's not the only problem.

Most patient relationships are inadvertently based on the ***principle of linear discharge***. This means that the relationship with the patients can be summarized in 3 words.

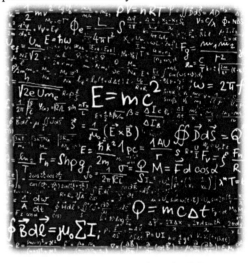

- ❖ Evaluation
- ❖ Treatment
- ❖ Discharge

The ***linear discharge approach*** forces the private practice owner to spend most of his energy hunting for the next patient or referral source. When he gets a patient, the only objective is to transition the patient from evaluation to treatment and finally to discharge.

The clinician becomes so preoccupied trying to find the next patient, he / she neglects to stay in contact and build a relationship with the patient who was just treated.

If your private practice runs in this manner, every single day involves the start of a new relationship as opposed to the nurturing an existing relationship. The amount of energy involved in creating a new relationship is significant and can be compared to the tremendous thrust that an airplane requires just as it is about to fight the earth's gravity and take off.

On the other hand, the energy required to maintain a relationship can be compared to an airplane cruising at a set altitude and potentially flying higher. It is critical for a private practice owner to have a system in place to communicate with patients using a combination of e-mail marketing, text messaging, voice broadcasting, and regular mail to build relationships.

The biggest myth about relationship marketing is that it takes several years to master. You don't need to be in practice for several years before you build a trustworthy relationship with patients and physicians.

In the new world driven by social media and technology, it's easier than ever before to build relationships using different forms of media. The fact is that various individuals like communicating with different forms of contact. The elderly population prefers regular mail. The younger population prefers emails and text messaging. Most individuals, regardless of age, respond to voice broadcasting especially if they get a phone call from the office of a trusted provider.

Relationship marketing is a strategic marketing approach for your practice. Once you shift your thinking and embrace this approach, you'll never feel the need for cold-calling, door knocking, and advertising again.

The old school ways of trying to get new patients are inefficient, stressful, and expensive. To some extent, these outdated methods are still prevalent in the marketing agenda of most private practice owners.

If you have a website that functions as a fancy brochure instead of trying to build a relationship with the patient using email capture and newsletter marketing, you are losing an opportunity to implement relationship marketing.

Here's another example. If you are collecting cell numbers of your patients, you should be sending them appointment reminders, birthday greetings, and engage them with mobile voting, polling, contests, and other special offers to come back to your clinic. If you're not doing this, then you need to ask yourself if you aren't losing out on an opportunity to nurture a connection with your patients using their cell phones.

Relationship marketing doesn't just apply to patients. It can be used to build meaningful connections with referral sources. If you have the fax numbers of physicians in your area, you can communicate with them in several different ways. Send one of your newsletters to the physician and offer to feature the physician as a preferred provider in your next newsletter. People like to see their name in print. You can also extend this to patients and feature patient success stories or "a patient of the month" feature in your next newsletter.

Take advantage of as many chances as you can to build a relationship with patients and referral sources. Use different forms of communication. Keep working on and refining your scripts and involve every staff member in the relationship building process. The goal is to get as many individuals as possible to know you, like you, and trust you. Once you are successful with your relationship building efforts, people will expect to hear from you on a regular basis.

At the end of the day, frequent, relevant contact is the backbone of relationship marketing. When done correctly, relationship marketing will enable your practice to function on autopilot. You'll be able to enjoy the benefits of cruise control, instead of having to try to expend a tremendous amount of energy in the 'initial take off' phase.

5 TIPS FOR 'WORD OF MOUTH' REFERRALS

Internal referrals represent one of the fastest ways to grow a private practice. As a practice owner, your biggest asset is your list of patients and prospective patients. The following strategies will help you get more referrals from your existing patient database.

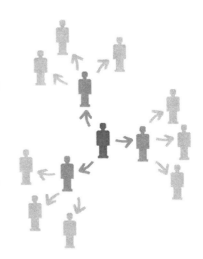

a) Communicate often and provide relevant, useful information.

You've probably heard the saying, "out of sight, out of mind." Keeping in touch keeps you in the minds of those on your mailing list. People may not need your services right now; however, they may need them later. By keeping in touch and staying on peoples' minds, you'll be the first person they call when they do need your services. Regular contact with your list doesn't necessarily mean selling your treatments every time. It could be as simple as a quick "thank you" note, a brief email to see how they are, or some article or resource you came across that they might find interesting. Small gestures like these can go a long way to developing a lasting relationship and patient loyalty.

b) Occasionally promote your treatments and services.

Finding new patients can be expensive and time consuming; however, patients who have already worked with you, are familiar with your practice and services. In most cases they already know you, like you, and trust you personally. This is significant. You've already established trust and credibility with them.

c) Promote "Patient Only" special offers.

This gives the patient recognition and makes them feel like a "VIP." Everyone likes to feel like they're getting a *'special offer.'* When you offer them special deals, make sure that these deals are not normally available to the general public. This is a legitimate and convincing way to show people on your list that you care about them.

d) Promote other businesses, even other therapists.

This may seem counter-intuitive but you have the ability, with your patient list, to promote services and products from other businesses (even if they are competing). You can arrange special discounts and offers not normally available to the general public and let your list know about them. Perhaps they are competitors but offer a different service or product that you can help them promote to your clients or perhaps you're booked full for a particular time and know that your client absolutely needs immediate attention. They'll value you more because you're bringing extra value to the relationship. Your competitor will remember the favor and return it someday.

As you can see, there are many good reasons why you must have your own database. This makes it faster and cheaper to get patients and appointments.

e) **Grow the database by giving away FREE 'products' of high perceived value on a regular basis.**

How long will it take you to create a quick PowerPoint presentation or booklet on low back pain? Better yet, you can purchase pre-written, copyright free content that can be customized to your clinic. This is the fastest way for you to build your own database. In general, patients will not give you permission to contact them (let alone give you their attention) unless you entice them with high quality information that is valuable to them. People are concerned about one thing and one thing only, *"How is this going to help me?"* Simply saying, *"Sign up for my free newsletter"* or *"Please give us your email address"* is not going to work anymore. Something to realize when asking for information is that the more information you ask for, the less chance you'll get it. If you were to ask for their name, home address, and home phone number, the response will dwindle significantly.

People who don't know you (prospects) are less willing to give out their contact information on your website unless there is *'something in it for them.'* When you get permission from people to communicate with them, it is called *'permission-based marketing.'* On the Internet it's called 'opt-in' to an email list. You need to give people who are interested in being on your list an option to sign on to join your mailing list and to opt-out of being on your list once they are on it. Give them an incentive, an ethical bribe. This *'product'* should have a high perceived value.

Offer something free, such as *"Give us your name and email address and we'll send you a free chapter of our new e-book on 3 Tips To Overcome Low Back Pain"* Interestingly, one of the most popular searches on Google for several years has always been the word 'free.' People have been conditioned to expect free stuff online, especially when it comes to information. They always want something for free.

Drive patients to your website and provide them with a free downloadable eBook for referring a friend, stay in touch with them, and make them feel special. This will help ignite word of mouth referrals in your practice.

REFERRAL SOURCE ANALYSIS

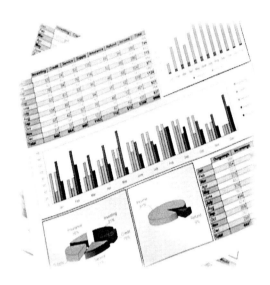

As a private practitioner, how much do you really know about your referral sources?

If you were asked to briefly describe one of your key referral sources, what would you say and how descriptive could you be?

A precise working knowledge of preferences, specialties, and intricacies of the business practices of your referral sources is the single most valuable piece of information in your referral generation strategy.

It's important to know why a referral is generated for your practice. If you take a closer look at the actual reason behind the referral, it may have less to do with your clinical skills as a physical therapist and more to do with factors like convenience, proximity, prior relationships, and patient preference.

In addition to determining, the reason for the initial referral, it's important to identify factors that lead to a consistent stream of referrals from one or two key referral sources. Nurturing these relationships to maximize referrals is the backbone of a successful private practice. A successful practice is based on a few key relationships with strong referral sources. Over a period of time, it is the quality and not the quantity of relationships that determines the long-term feasibility of a successful practice.

Now that you have identified your key referral sources, ask yourself these simple questions:

> *"How can you identify with them on a deeper level and connect with them in a manner that allows you to stand apart from your competition?"*
>
> *"How can you express your sincere gratitude, acquire their attention, and make them gravitate to you on a regular basis, so that you remain at the top of their mind as a resource?"*

The best referral relationships made dilute to over a period of time in the absence of reinforcement, consistency, and quality of contact. Your goal is to avoid this is a private practice with a well-planned strategy of communication; which includes e-mail, snail mail, fax, and phone calls.

Another factor to identify with your existing referral sources is the existence of comment traits and characteristics that exist with these referral sources.

For example, say a surgeon specializing in knee injuries refers a patient to you and another physician specializing in low back pain also refers a patient to you in the same week. What could be the common link, if at all? Is it likely that these physicians heard about your practice thanks to a recent marketing initiative? On the other hand, did the patients request you as their physical therapy provider of choice? Did they happen to be relatives or friends of a former or current patient and heard about you from them?

The main thrust of your marketing should be geared towards an analysis of likes and dislikes of key referral sources.

Your understanding of the physician and his patients must be so finely tuned that you should be able to surprise the physician, or his staff, by providing them with exact solutions that their patients need. Making them feel as if you've been working with their practice for many years.

Make the physician wonder, even somewhat fear how you know their practice so well. Have them asking:

> *Has this therapist been hiding out in my office? How does the therapist understand exactly what I am looking for and what my patients need?*

When you able to elicit this "you are right" feeling, all you have to do is nurture it with regular communication to earn your first referral.

Approaching the physician or a referral source after having done your research instantly separates you from other private practitioners who are treated like cold callers.

Just make sure your research is on target and get in touch with the decision maker at the clinic. Visit your local library to get access to information databases that can provide you with relevant contact details of local physicians. When you initiate contact with potential referral sources, approach them with a giving hand. Suggest cross-promotional strategies that can leverage your existing relationships to promote the physician and his practice. This kind of an attitude reflects your standing as an expert and distinguishes you as a welcome guest to the physician's practice; as opposed to just another practitioner seeking referrals. This is only possible when you have a full understanding of the physician's practice.

THE COST OF A NEW PATIENT

There is a cost associated with the acquisition of a new patient, called the *"Patient Acquisition Cost"* (PAC). Once you know what PAC you are comfortable with, you can reverse engineer your marketing to drive more patients in your practice.

When you are trying to drive more patients to your clinic, it's important to determine which channels bring you new patients at the lowest possible patient acquisition cost.

There are four main channels:

- Email
- Print
- SMS/mobile
- Direct mail

Many practices buy lunches for physicians' offices to build a referral relationship. Ironically, this may result in a higher patient acquisition cost than other, less traditional methods. Let me explain.

A lot of private practices run ads in local newspapers to drive more patients to their practice. When you're creating an ad in a local newspaper, it's important to pay attention to the initial experience that the prospective patient has with your clinic (their first impression). This can increase or decrease your PAC substantially.

In order to fine-tune this initial experience, you need to strategically test different marketing methods. The better you are at being able to establish that initial, meaningful contact with patients, the better your results will be and the greater your return on investment with your marketing.

Now, when you're testing the marketing method that works best for you, you want to test high-priced and low-priced methods. You want to test online and offline methods to determine the single, best way to attract new patients to your clinic.

Here's the important part, only change one variable at a time so you know what's working and what's not. Not only should you be testing single variables at one time, you should also be doing multiple tests simultaneously.

For example, let's say you're running an advertisement in a local newspaper offering a free consultation for lower back pain (this is called your offer).

You want to change one variable to see if it's working.

Let's say you change the offer.

Now, instead of the free consultation for low back pain, you test either one of the following:

❖ A free 'pain relief' consultation (a more generic offer)
❖ A free book on "Lower Back Pain"

Your prospective patient can call and request a specific offer. This helps you generate leads and you will know which offer seems to be attracting the most response.

In this way you're changing the main offer of the actual advertisement and you're changing one variable at a time.

What's important is that you should be testing these individual variables simultaneously by running three separate advertisements; using three different media (for instance try utilizing a magazine advertisement, letters, and a website special).

The reason you do this is because if you were to test only one variable at a time and one test at a time, it would take you a long time before you figure out what's working and what's not. So testing one variable and doing multiple tests, running multiple advertisements at one time, is the best way for you to determine which ad is working and which is not. You can test any one of the following:

- ❖ Headline ("What you always wanted to know about low back pain… revealed by your physical therapist)
- ❖ Offer (which can be a free consultation or a discount for your services)
- ❖ Advertising Medium (letter, postcard, ad, website, etc.)

You definitely want to test in multiple media, both online and offline. Avoid the mistake and temptation of testing the least expensive media.

Remember, whatever happens with one media is indicative, but not always predictive, of what will happen in another media. So you can test an ad with a newspaper, a magazine article, local Val-Pack, and perhaps even a door hanger or a car magnet.

Your best investment in your private practice is going to be testing what brings you new patients in a predictable, measurable manner. At the end of the day, you want to test over and over until you find a method that delivers new patients at a patient acquisition cost that is acceptable for your clinic.

IPI + UO = Patient Referrals

Every private practice needs a clearly defined identity; one that patients and physicians can easily associate with and remember. You can call it an "*Instant Practice Identifier*" or **IPI**.

When you're trying to market your clinic and get more patients, personalization is considered more elite than generalization. Precise targeting of your audience (with clearly defined expertise) has more value than broadcasting a 'me too' approach. Patients want to believe that the services that they're being offered are individualized and specifically engineered, custom created just for them.

Put yourself in the mind of a patient 'shopping' for the right physical therapist. Imagine that a

patient says to himself "*Yes, this is the right therapist for me.*" If the patient does indeed feel this way, there is a very high probability that they will end up coming to your clinic for physical therapy.

When this happens, price (cash pay) and proximity (driving distance) become less relevant. So the question you need to ask yourself is: "Does a patient look at your clinic and say to themselves, '*that's the right place for me*'?"

IPI CREATION - USE YOUR OWN PROPRIETARY LANGUAGE

When you're coming up with your own IPI don't hesitate to use your own terminology, your own language, in order to be able to define the specialization of your clinic or what makes your practice unique. Come up with your own "unique" language, something along the lines of:

Ultimate Low Back Pain Protocol
"*All you ever needed to know to treat low back pain*"
The Hidden Truth About Pain Relief
"*We've taken great pains to put together the ONLY pain relief solution you will EVER need.*"
Instant Motion Method
"*Permanent relief from stiffness, pain, and discomfort*"

IPI CREATION – WHY SHOULD THEY CHOOSE YOUR CLINIC?

When trying to create your own IPI, there is one question that you need to be able to answer quickly and effectively: *"Why should the patient (or the physician) choose your clinic versus any other clinic down the street?"* You should be able to answer this question immediately and with conviction. If you struggle, chances are you're more than likely getting patients strictly because of price, referral relationships, the convenience of your location, your personality, 'winging it' or just plain good luck.

You can certainly get away with all of this, but fair warning – this is not the most stable way to build a private practice. A reliance on these factors leaves you in a very, very delicate situation since a new competitor with a unique IPI could easily take your place. You need an IPI as quickly as possible.

IPI REINFORCEMENT WITH UNBELIEVABLE OFFER (UO)

You can boost the effectiveness of the IPI with an *unbelievable offer* (UO). This is an irresistible 'call to action' that encourages a person to take action. This action can be a prospect calling to schedule an appointment at your clinic or it can also be a physician's office calling for more information about your clinic and its services.

IPI + UO = Referrals (did you notice the use of proprietary language in the title and the body of this section so far?)

Notice that the UO must be exciting and intriguing. The cardinal sign by most clinics is that the offer is boring. The UO reinforces the IPI and encourages people to take action; action that they would not have taken under normal circumstances.

PREVALENCE OF UO IN DAILY LIFE

When I was on a limited budget during my college days, I'd wait for five dollar coupons in the local newspapers that allowed me to go to my favorite all you can eat buffet in one of the local restaurants nearby. Sometimes I would wait several weeks for the coupons, cut them out, and stand in line to be able to get my chance at the five dollar meal which was normally priced at $12.95.

This is the impact of an unbelievable offer. It motivated me to take action. I would not have done that under normal circumstances.

Next time you get a coupon in the mail that affords you a meal at an unbelievably discounted rate or some other product or service at a steeply discounted rate and you decide to do business with that establishment, you'll recognize the importance of the unbelievable offer. Most physical therapy practices lack a clearly defined UO or unbelievable offer. Keep in mind that the UO doesn't have to be a free evaluation in your clinic. The following are examples of a UO:

- ♦ A free book, DVD, or audio CD to a patient who schedules an evaluation.
- ♦ A free ticket to an educational seminar for a patient who successfully completes his course of treatment.

♦ A one-month membership to a fitness center or a wellness center that you have connected with for a discharged patient (you can even have something in house).

Combine the effectiveness of the IPI and the UO to drive more patients to your clinic. Every successful practice has a clear identity and a precise '*call to action*' tied in with the offer.

The big question is… **What is your IPI and UO?**

CUSTOMER SERVICE 101:
THE IMPORTANCE OF THE RECEPTIONIST

On my way to work I stopped by at an upscale café for a soy latte. I also ordered some biscotti to go with it and the bill was $7.95. I asked for some extra soymilk in my latte.

There was a new attendant behind the counter. I was informed, rather curtly, that they could only use a certain amount of soymilk for each cup and that no extra soymilk could be added. I asked her if there was any way they could charge me for it, in an effort to contribute to their already substantial profit margins. I also mentioned that the attendant prior to her gladly added to my latte all the time. The newbie shrugged, adding that the company was simply reinforcing their policies before she brushed me aside by quickly announcing, "*Next!*"

It was embarrassing; there were 5 people in line behind me. I was made to lose some of my dignity. The café just lost a customer over a drip of soymilk.

In an economy that is getting more and more competitive, the interaction between staff and customer is as important as the one between therapist and patient. A clinic must focus on what the patient wants, not what is best for the clinic.

The right kind of communication between staff and patient can set the tone for your clinic. Just as bedside manners are important for physicians, communication skills, combined with a vibrant personality are core competencies for a receptionist.

The general qualities that the therapist seeks, from various interviews with candidates, is the ability to multitask, be able to schedule, and manage paperwork. While these are important prerequisites for a receptionist, the most important quality is the skill of communication.

The receptionist should be warm, friendly, patient, and supportive to all patients who call or walk in. He or she should make an effort to look the patient in the eye, smile, and say "*Thank you for coming in, how can I help you?*" When answering the phone, a good way to start is, "*Thank you for calling ABC physical therapy, how may I assist you?*" The employee should also communicate with patients after they come into the clinic, while they are waiting for the therapist by engaging in polite conversation. Something as simple as: "*How was your day today?*" and "*Are you feeling better since your last visit?*" can do wonders in making a patient feel as though your office truly cares about them personally. A phone call once a week to the patient simply following up by asking, "*How was your experience with physical therapy this week?*" and "*I'm just confirming your appointment for next week*" in a concerned and compassionate tone should be another task assigned to the receptionist.

Additional things that the receptionist can do to add value to the patient's experience and boost revenue include:

❖ Assisting the patient to understand the potential value and importance of physical therapy.

❖ Drawing the patient's attention to various programs that may interest them, including cash-based options.

❖ Providing the patient with a brochure on such programs and following up with them by phone / in person when the patient visits.

❖ Requesting patients to complete a feedback form at discharge; such forms describe the patients' experiences – positive and negative – and can be anonymous.

When the patient may present with some conflicts with scheduling, the correct response is, "*I understand your situation. Please wait for a moment while I do everything I can to assist you.*"

Combining these strategies over a period of time will allow your receptionist to build patient loyalty and foster long-term relationships with your patients. There is a big difference between customer dissatisfaction and satisfaction and loyalty. Going back to my experience at the café for some soy latte;

❖ Since the extra soymilk was not provided to me, I was dissatisfied. Worse, I decided not to take my business there anymore.

❖ If the attendant had obliged me, I would have been satisfied.

❖ If the attendant obliged me and added with a smile "*I love my latte with extra soymilk too, doesn't it taste great?*" then I would have been transformed into a loyal customer.

Customer service is sometimes overlooked in busy practices. In most cases, the first thing the receptionist asks is "*What type of insurance do you have?*" This is the wrong question, since it immediately classifies the patient as a statistic based on their insurance provider instead of a living, breathing human being.

All it takes for patient goodwill is an appearance of courtesy and a perception of kindness and caring. A patient likes to be appreciated as a person, not treated like a number. Most patients will not experience an instant benefit from physical therapy, but will derive a significant degree of perceived value from a clinic with friendly staff and a supportive environment.

THE VIRAL PHYSICAL THERAPIST

What does the word '*viral*' mean?

It refers to an idea that spreads rapidly, improves awareness amongst patients, and opens up new doors of emotional and social enlightenment.

If your patients knew you were offering a medically sound exercise program, complete with body fat analysis, blood sugar testing, blood pressure measurements, and provided the services of a nutritionist, would they be interested and tell others?

If your patients found out you were offering a one-time seminar on "*The 5 minute self-help low back massage*" in your clinic next weekend, would they spread the word and become walking billboards for your practice? Perhaps they may even "bring a friend."

For an idea to be viral in the real sense, it should help the patient's condition and the service provider's profitability. The concept should be beneficial and commercially viable at the same time. A viral product empowers the patient to tell your story for you and become your own marketing representative. In addition, viral marketing is social proof, which carries the stamp of credibility. A patient is very likely to pay attention to the success story of another patient who has worked with you in the past.

Let's assume you conduct a seminar on low back massage (as mentioned above). The word spreads and many attendees manage to show up for the seminar. This makes the seminar 'somewhat' viral. But the therapist delivers a dry, tedious presentation. Unfortunately, the attendees don't enjoy the seminar. They walk away confused and dazed; they don't recommend the clinic to a single soul. They never become your patients.

The viral intent is crushed.

On the other hand, you conduct a great seminar filled with energy and passion. The patients understand, enjoy, and apply the techniques they have learnt. You now have a winner. You provide a ton of patient-friendly information, 'pre-written' notes, practical tips, 'refer-a-friend' cards, and ready to use appointment cards that patients can fill out on the spot. The therapist can offer incentives to prospects by offering free eBooks (which require a patient's email address). This allows the therapist to accumulate a list of emails, which can be used to provide timely, relevant information to patients.

Your seminar is transformed into a viral, patient-stimulating phenomenon ready to increase your referrals.

Chapter 6   159

The seminar helped both sides. It increased awareness about physical therapy, the existence of your clinic, your positioning as a primary provider, and most importantly it opened new doors of communication between therapist and patient.

It's important to differentiate between viral and traditional marketing.

Traditional marketing like advertising in the newspaper, radio, and TV is not viral in nature, unless it includes a 'call to action'; an incentive for the patient to tell friends and a reason to schedule an appointment. Keep in mind, not everything can become 'viral' in nature. It doesn't matter if hundreds or thousands of people know about your service; it's the right people that matter, not the volume of individuals you market to.

The essence of viral marketing is that the service or product should be 'reproducible'. The more people use the product or technology, the more they like it, the more people they tell, which in turn means more people use the product.

As physical therapists we provide a <u>service</u> (physical therapy), not a <u>product</u>. A service, especially one such as skilled as physical therapy, is less viral than a product. It requires personal time and attention from the therapist, is not easy to reproduce, benefits one patient at a time, and the patient (generally) lacks the incentive to tell others about the service.

In order to introduce a component of viral marketing into your practice, consider the introduction of a product to complement your service. Tip the scales in your favor by creating your own or promoting someone else's exercise DVD or a book on health and physical therapy. Creating a 'ready to use' home exercise DVD is extremely easy; all you need is a camcorder, a DVD editing software like Ulead, and a DVD duplication service in your vicinity. You can also provide patients with a regular, patient-friendly informational newsletter that provides relevant, timely information on health and physical therapy.

Such measures will boost the public image of your clinic significantly. Your patients become your marketing representatives and tell their friends, helping you spread the word. Your reputation grows.

In essence, you can duplicate your marketing efforts with viral marketing.

Thankfully, our clinical skills remain our own.

THE IMPORTANCE OF CONSISTENT PATIENT CONTACT: THE ART OF NURTURE

❖ Clinical skills are the foundation for success in a physical therapy practice.
❖ In a competitive, patient driven environment it is imperative to improve a patient's knowledge of what physical therapy can do.
❖ A therapist should educate the patient consistently within and outside of the clinic.

As therapists, we have been highly educated and heavily armed with the right tools to treat and heal patients. At the end of the treatment process the patient is usually grateful and brings a homemade cake, a gift, or a hand-written card, which we proudly display in our office.

In most cases, the relationship ends at this point with patient discharge.

For a savvy private practice owner, discharge represents a foundation for building a relationship that flourishes with time. It is an ideal opportunity for the therapist to get the patient's permission to provide valuable, relevant information in a consistent manner. To be successful, a clinic must educate and empower the patient and the best way to achieve this is to communicate with the patient post-discharge using a consistent, information driven mechanism.

An empowered patient is a well-treated patient. Consistency of communication and the quality of information disseminated to the patient set the foundation for a long-standing patient relationship. This relationship can be worth several thousands of dollars in revenue per year for the clinic.

Consistency of contact begins with personal communication during the visit and phone / postcard / email follow up after the visit. By educating your patients and local physicians with precise, relevant, patient friendly information, you will differentiate yourself as the local authority in your field/specialization of therapy. Your clinic will instantly set itself apart from competitors. This will also increase your potential to command cash-paying programs!

In order to establish and consolidate the position of your clinic as the primary provider and to build a steady and predictable flow of high-value patients, **your clinic must offer a broad range of services and 2-3 specific programs that differentiate**

you from your competitors. Examples of such programs include vestibular training and fall prevention for seniors, pre- and post-pregnancy physical therapy, injury prevention for athletes, fitness and lifestyle management programs, etc.

A regular source of communication with the patient community is mandatory. If you don't make an effort to stay in the patient's mind, they will gradually forget about you and may even visit another therapist. A good practice not only retains patients, but also enables them to refer other patients. Communicating with patients and physicians can be done via phone calls (time consuming, but effective) or personal contact (door-to-door marketing is extremely effective, but labor intensive). Some therapists use direct mail options like postcards (expensive and targeted, with variable response rates). In the 21st century, more and more therapists are using email and the internet as a form of marketing. This is instant, measurable, and generally free. As a clinic owner, **it is important to find the single most cost-effective method of marketing and communication to maintain in contact with the patient post discharge.** The intent is to transform the individual **from a patient to an ardent fan and a powerful referral source.**

Ideally, such a method should lead to a constant, reliable stream of patient referrals that grows each month. This will allow the development and execution of cash-based niche programs that are independent of insurance reimbursements that continue to decline with the economic crisis.

Old school marketing, the kind that involves the therapist going door-to-door soliciting physicians has now been replaced by therapist-to-patient marketing. As a clinic owner, your goal is to be first and foremost in the minds of patients and be considered a leader in your community. When patients perceive you as the provider of choice, they will directly ask their physicians for a referral to you. In the new age of physical therapy marketing, patients are the primary referral sources. A patient should know your clinic, like what it has to offer, and trust the staff enough to ask for a direct referral. The way to achieve this is to give them information about your clinic and your brand of physical therapy. As a private practice owner, you must create a unique identity for yourself in order to stand out as a respected physical therapist and community leader.

Sending a mailed, faxed, or e-mailed newsletter is the quickest, easiest, and least expensive way to establish yourself as the local expert. You get an opportunity to brand your clinic's identity and conclusively establish yourself as the expert therapy provider in your local community. You should write a fresh newsletter to your patients, friends, family, physicians, and any other referral sources every other week for best results. Whether it is standard care or a niche program, the public will look to you as a source of meaningful information and seek your services for physical ailments.

TRANSFORM YOUR PHYSICAL THERAPY PRACTICE WITH THE RIGHT WORDS

To be a truly successful physical therapy practice, you must set yourself apart. Without the right marketing, most of your patients won't hear about you and your clinic will be resigned to oblivion. In the age of consumerism, every patient is bombarded daily with marketing messages from using different forms of media. This has reached a saturation point. Consumers are more likely to ignore your message, especially when it does not seem important to them.

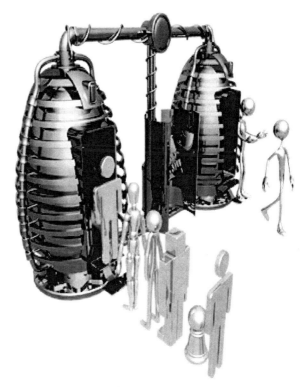

Your existing and past patients value your messages less and less over a period of time. The problem is compounded when your messages do not solve the current problem faced by the patient. Even when your message cuts through the noise, patients are less likely to take action. The average patient is so overwhelmed with information and misinformation, that they are less likely to refer your services to their friends unless the benefit is obvious and powerful. It takes a lot of effort and more importantly the right words to move patients to take action. In this new age of physical therapy marketing, you must be able to create a unique brand of physical therapy and convey the message with the right words to a precisely targeted audience. With the right words, your phones will never stop ringing.

The "headline" or, "attention" grabbers draw your patients toward your practice. This is a specific comment designed to promote your practice and stimulate curiosity. An ideal headline is a glorified truth, not any empty overstatement. It should appeal to the emotion triggers and propel the patient to pick up the phone to call you. Don't make this message too intellectual, because you want the patient to take action as opposed to simply nod in agreement. With The right headline, the reaction you want to illicit is "I *have* to call them". Some examples of a strong headline include:

- A major breakthrough in _____.
- You owe yourself a _____.
- Not just another _____.
- They don't call us _____ for nothing.
- What they never tell you about _____.
- How many times have you said to yourself_____?
- Anyone who knows _____ will tell you _____.
- Discover the real truth about _____.
- In the next six weeks, you could be_____.
- Get all the facts about_____.
- Don't make these _____ mistakes when you _____.
- The best kept secret in _____.

Use precise language to outline the benefits of your services and convey the most important advantages for the patient. It's important here to use language that patients understand and identify with. Avoid the temptation to describe or praise your own practice. Patients hear less than 5% of what is important to you and 95% of what is important to them. You must be able to convey, in less than 10 seconds, how you will relieve pain and improve function for them. Always speak with the patient's perspective in mind. Patient centered language reinforces your clinical efforts and boosts patient compliance, enhancing the standard of care.

Some examples of descriptions and benefits include:

- We were the first to _____ in our community.
- _____ is just a partial list of our services for you.
- Everything you have always wanted in a _____.
- We have rewritten the rules with_____.
- The States most respected _____.
- Discover how easy it is to _____.
- _____ is what we have always done better than any other provider.
- The kind of_____ you have only dreamed about.
- We have taken great pains to _____.
- We give you the power to _____.
- You are in control.
- The choice is yours, _____ or _____.

Once you can understand your audience, cater to their specific needs and desires with the right phrases. With the right words, you can position yourself as a leading physical therapy provider in the community. Strike a balance between "marginal hype" and statements of fact. In an effort to avoid an excessively dry and boring tone, don't overcompensate by using strong words like excellent and instant relief, which can impact you creditability. With the right expressions, you function as a gentle, but persuasive coach and proponent of your service. You are steering the patients toward your services without creating unnecessary hype. With the right combination of clinical skills and patient centric terminology, your patients will become referral machines and generate the hype for you. Comments like *"they are excellent"*, *"they can give you instant pain relief"* and *"I had an outstanding experience with my physical therapist"* are the powerful closing statements that clinch public opinion in your favor.

The words you use can turn strangers into patients and patients into referral sources. The words used by these patients to describe your practice can build you an army of raving fans.

MULTI-STAGE MARKETING

Is your practice the kind in which any patient can walk in and get an appointment?

Does your practice seem 'universal' or non-exclusive to the average patient?

It's human nature to want what we cannot have. You can use this principle to great advantage in your private practice.

Perception is reality, so if your clinic is perceived as an 'exclusive' facility that accepts a limited number of clients, you will find patients lining up at your door to 'get in' as your local reputation precedes you. This air of 'importance' is grounded in a

multi-stage marketing strategy in which your prospect is asked to jump through certain hoops before they can 'be selected' to become patients.

The intention is not to deny patients the physical therapy they need, but to better 'qualify' patients and influencers in your community to boost your reputation. Your goal is to drive patients to your practice, particularly the patients most applicable to your practice.

For example, a traditional pull advertising ad would ask the patients to enlist themselves for a seminar on low back pain. The patient is asked to take the proactive steps of either calling your clinic or registering on your website in order to be able to attend the lower back pain clinic.

This automatically pre-qualifies the prospect and eliminates individuals who are unlikely to be interested in that particular seminar, or your services. Once patients or clients register for such a workshop, the ones who actually take the time to show up for this clinic or this seminar are extremely likely to take you up on your services.

Typically between 50-80% of those who register over the phone or online should show up in person to take advantage of your particular 'pull' or 'lead generation' advertising mechanism. A lower response rate implies that your offer was not strong enough to elicit a response and that the offer needs to be strengthened with a reinforced sense of value.

In a successful physical therapy private practice, productivity is achieved with a well-defined selling mechanism. This requires testing, measuring, and tweaking the responsiveness of your advertisements and programs. With a powerful pull lead generation mechanism; your primary goal becomes to drive patients to that particular mechanism.

For example, if you have a low back pain seminar that seems to be pulling your audience to the tune of 70-80% (very common for such seminars), your primary goal becomes to drive more patients to your website or direct more patients to your particular offer.

For every 100 patients that are made aware of this offer, 80 patients are likely to take you up on this offer; which is an outstanding response rate. When the patient takes advantage of this offer, they are automatically transformed from a suspect to a prospect.

In order to register for the low back pain webinar mentioned above, tell patients they need to register on your website using the convenient form provided. You can also acquire the patient's information yourself and manually enter it into the system. This allows you to acquire the names and email addresses, in addition to phone numbers and mailing addresses, of these patients who have shown an interest in your services.

This is a list that's worth its weight in gold for your practice. All these patients should receive a follow-up email, phone call, or snail mail letter reminding them about your workshop and thanking them for showing an interest in your services.

Despite the most rigorous follow-up and reminders about such an event, the fact is that a 50% show ratio is very common. Out of the 80 who are likely to be registered, about 40-60 will actually show up for your seminar in your clinic. However, this provides you with an excellent opportunity to pre-sell them on your services. The simplest way to do this is to deliver outstanding value with a presentation that is patient friendly and benefit driven. It's a great idea to provide handouts and light refreshments during such meetings, when they are conducted in person.

At the end of the day successful physical therapy marketing comes down to a series of questions, all of which point to one big question:

HOW WELL DO YOU KNOW YOUR PATIENTS?

Once you can identify what drives them to contact you and what their emotional trigger is, you are already in a position to serve them better. How can you provide them exactly what you want?

Just surprise your patients with outstanding value and encourage them to initiate and maintain contact with you.

RESOURCE

FREE WEBINAR:
Discover How To Add $40,000 in Annual Revenue For Your Practice
Using a Simple, Easy-To-Use Newsletter

Inside this complimentary, ground-breaking webinar, I will reveal:

✓ The 3 giant mistakes that are KILLING private practice owners (like YOU!) using outdated newsletter marketing strategies...and how you can PARTNER with local physicians and referral sources to GROW your practice. (Yep, if you can't beat 'em it's best just to join 'em...)

✓ Why traditional source of referrals (i.e. advertising and word of mouth referrals) have all but dried up, and the "Distribution Trifecta" strategy that will help you add $40,000 in annual revenue for your practice

✓ The "3 Types of Content" and why the transition from Clinical Content to Bonding / Authority content is critical for your practice over the next 12 - 18 months...

✓ How you can follow my lead, build a relationship with every patient and referral source to be at the center of the largest wealth transfer that private practice has ever known...

✓ Why most marketing methods are killing traditional private practice, and why tactics like free evaluations and 'traditional referrals' may be gone forever. (There is a solution to this mess, but you have to watch the webinar to discover what it is...)

To reserve your seat, simply register for the webinar at the link below and click the "Register Now" button NOW. Hurry, because seats are limited!

www.newslettercode.com

CHAPTER 7

How To Get Physicians (and Other Referral Sources) To Approach You With Patients

SNAIL MAIL TO IGNITE PHYSICIAN REFERRALS

As a private practice owner, it is critical to be very efficient with the dollars spent on marketing and advertising. This requires a great deal of thought and planning about your patients and referral sources. The truth is that physicians and patients are part of an ever expanding breed of busy, overwhelmed beings growing increasingly resistant to any message that is irrelevant, common, and unessential. If you have had little success trying to get the attention of referral sources, then you may want to ask yourself the following questions:

a) Do I have something new to say to them that will get their attention?
b) How can I deliver the message to them, without obstruction from the gatekeepers?
c) How can I follow up with them, so the relationship is finally established?

Once you find the answers to the 3 questions above, the rest falls into place because your standards of care and patient results will speak for themselves.

For most private practice owners, these steps are simple when you have a one-to-one meeting with the physician. We know we can show them what we have to offer and get them to refer yet, having said that, it's tough to get such meetings with physicians. More often than not, a private practice owner is regarded as an unwelcome pest and unable to 'get past the gatekeeper'.

Another sticking point emerges, when the time-strapped private practice owner tries to take this one-to-one approach and apply it to one-to-many. If you do this successfully, you can reach MANY referral sources with the same amount of effort (albeit significantly more planning), identify the physicians who WANT to refer to you, build relationships with them, and spend less time worrying about the ones who will NEVER refer.

The best referral relationship is built one-on-one. The best systems are built one-on-many. You can do this with the help of a carefully written letter (and phone call follow-ups) to groups of physicians (and other referral sources) in your area. This letter is called the *'initial introduction letter'* and serves to break the ice with physicians by offering their patients something of value (a free book, report, or consultation) to help patients reach their goals. Do NOT ask for the referral right away, in the initial introduction letter. You need to treat referrals as a two-step process, using snail mail as a way to facilitate Step 1; the initial contact.

There are distinct advantages to using letters / packages (snail mail) mailed to potential referral sources in your community. When done correctly, this allows you to get physicians to pay attention to your practice. You graduate from an unwelcome pest to a welcome guest.

The primary advantage is the involvement from the reader. The more time you can get from the reader (2-3 minutes reading a letter), the greater the chances are that you can engage the reader into thinking about a referral. To get your letter past the gatekeeper, you can consider hand addressed envelopes (so they appear to be personal mail, which they are), hand written fonts and name personalization in the body of the letter, envelopes with the word 'confidential' written on them, unusual envelopes that appear to be 'priority mail', mailing the physicians at their home addresses instead of the office, and phone calls prior to the envelope delivery indicating that 'an important letter is on the way'.

Also, you can provide a physical, tactile experience to the reader. If you send different paper sizes and textures, folders, objects in the mail, lumpy mail, it's easier to get the attention of the recipient. When an individual can touch and handle a package that is sent to them, you 'break through the clutter' and have a significant chance of entering their conscious thought process.

This method of 'initial contact' with physicians can be systematized with snail mail. Let's say you spend $4 on a snail mail package consisting of a plastic pill bottle with a letter inside it that describes your services and how they can be an adjunct to traditional medicine for pain relief (example). It's easy to hire a company to send this out to 100 physicians in your area and your cost is $400. If you can get the attention of a single physician and ignite that 'first referral' with a phone call follow-up to the physician 2-3 days after this package was delivered to them, your return on investment was significant, since the net income from first patient will cover the cost of your mail campaign.

In the above example, we have assumed a response rate of 1% (since 1 physician out of 100 recipients will take notice). This ratio can be improved significantly with micro targeting and research prior to the delivery of your mail campaign. If you can identify subgroups of physicians in your community, understand their patients' needs and communicate with them about the individual goals of their patients and how YOU can help their patients get there faster, you will stand out.

There is no 'one size fits all' approach anymore. You should be able to take a list of all the physicians in your community, carve them up into slivers of potential referral sources, and send them variations of your *'initial introduction letter'* customized to their practice, their patients, and their needs to get the best impact from this snail mail system.

Make the effort to create a relevant message with the right amount of personalization and mail it to the right physicians in your community to see a surge of new activity in your practice.

Chapter 7   171

THE PHYSICIAN AND PATIENT PROFILING PRINCIPLE

The referral relationships of the future will be based more on reciprocity than the credibility and quality of the referral source and the benefactor.

Every human being is programmed with a fixed action pattern. This involves intricate sequences of behavior, ranging from a simple act of kindness to complex relationships like courtships and mating rituals. A fundamental characteristic of human reciprocity is that the behaviors that compose them occur in a predictable sequence every single time.

For example, you hold open the door for an individual in a crowded restaurant. In most cases, the individual (a complete stranger) will thank you and greet you with a smile. At any other time, it's likely that the same individual would not have made eye contact.

Human behavior is, in many ways, a sequence. It's like a film playing in the background of the same scenes following each other in a (somewhat) predictable pattern. It's almost like the same videotape is playing over and over again.

You just need to know when to push the play button.

When the situation calls for referral relationships between the physician and a physical therapist, certain patterns of action will work every single time. The quality of the physical therapy provider becomes less relevant than the actual trigger factor; which, in this case is an act of kindness / a well planned attempt to add value and provide recognition.

When a physical therapist attempts to build a referral relationship with a physician the relationship begins with an act of significant value which exceeds the expectations of all parties concerned. The goal should be to add value and not to extract it.

When you begin a relationship with the physician or any other referral source with a giving hand, you position in yourself as a provider with significant credibility. This creates the foundation for a significantly greater number of referrals during the life of the relationship. You also leverage the power of the most basic of human behavioral traits; reciprocity.

When you do someone a small favor, they feel indebted. The feeling of indebtedness carries with it a certain degree of discomfort. Most of us do not want to feel obligated to another individual. It tends to weigh on us until we do something about it. Reciprocal arrangements form the backbone of most relationships, both business and professional.

The simplest way to trigger reciprocity in a referral relationship with the physician is to feature the physician as a provider of choice in front of your own patients. If you published a newsletter, send e-mails, circulars, or communicate with patients on a regular basis (an important strategy), you can approach a local physician and 'offer' to feature him as a provider of choice in your next newsletter. This is called the *'physician profiling'* principle. Even though some physicians will not take you up on this offer, the ones who do are likely to be important referral sources for you in the future.

Here's how you would position this 'opportunity' to the physician:

"Dear Dr. Smith. I have great news for you. We have a newsletter that reaches hundreds of patients in the community. We would be honored to feature you as a provider of choice in our next newsletter so our patients can learn more about you and your services. We are open to the possibility of including a picture and a brief biography (80-100 words) which will be included in our next e-mail/print communication with our patients. If you are interested, the next deadline for our upcoming newsletter is this Friday."

When you explain the proposal in this manner, the physician perceives importance, opportunity, and urgency.

The good news is that these three emotions can trigger the most wanted response for you; the need for reciprocity.

At this point, you can leverage the principle of reciprocity by saying:

> *"By the way Dr. Smith, would you mind if we provided you with full-color copies of this newsletter (featuring you) for your waiting room, so your patients can read your feature story and learn more about our services?"*

It is very difficult for the 'featured' physician to turn you down.

Use this principle with multiple physicians in your area (as long as they are not right next door to each other).

You can use the same principle of reciprocity with patients. Feature patients and their success stories in newsletters and brochures (with their written permission) and give them importance, recognition, and appreciation. In return the patients, particularly the ones with strong social connections and a large circle of influence, will become human billboards for your practice. As with physicians, you want to you choose the right words and position the request as an opportunity for the patient and not a favor to your practice.

People don't like doing favors, they like returning them. Start by being at the giving end and you will soon find yourself at the receiving end of an endless flow of patients.

'PUSH' AND 'PULL' ADVERTISING

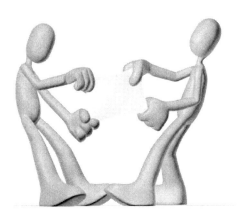

Successful advertising involves an understanding of the difference between pull advertising and push advertising.

A common error made by growing practices is push advertising. This means pushing down or rather forcing the information about your practice and its benefits down the throat of your audience.

This is the most traditional form of advertising and also the least likely to work. This is also called brand advertising. Large companies like Coca Cola, Wal-Mart and Sears can engage in this kind of advertising, where the messages primarily conveyed are:

✓ We are here and can serve your consumer needs
✓ We are nice people
✓ We are a brand
✓ Come in anytime and do business with us

These brands have the time, energy, and resources to 'play this game' over and over again until they build a loyal customer base. A small physical therapy private practice cannot afford to play Russian Roulette with advertising. Results have to be measured in hours, not weeks, or months.

THE DIFFERENCE BETWEEN PUSH AND PULL ADVERTISING

Rather than telling your customers and prospective patients about your practice (push), give your patients and other referral sources a reason to get in touch with you. Make them take an action that pre-qualifies them as prospects and encourages them to take an initiative (call your practice, bring in a coupon, ask for a special offer). Pull advertising generates high quality, compliant patients who are likely to refer friends and family also.

Pull advertising involves providing the prospects or referral generation sources with tools and incentives to communicate with you and seek you out as opposed to hunting them down to visit your clinic.

An example of push advertising would be to advertise in a local newspaper and tell patients or prospects about your clinic and its features, new equipment, and modalities. The truth is that this really does not matter to most patients. In this case you are expecting or hoping that prospects read about your clinic and come to you for physical therapy.

Pull advertising works differently. It encourages your prospects to take an action and places the decision of 'first contact' on them. This is the most effective form of advertising because it encourages the reader to take an initiative, such as scheduling an appointment with you.

An example of pull advertising would be providing the patient an invitation to attend a "Low Back Pain Seminar," a coupon for a free massage, a limited time offer for a complimentary evaluation, or a referral form encouraging your current patients to write down the contact information of their relatives who may be interested in your services in exchange for a free $20 Starbucks gift card. You essentially provide a product or service that has a high perceived value. Such a product can also be in the form of an informational product, like an audio CD or a DVD, which demonstrates a few exercises or tips. Such products are easy to produce and can be created for under $5.

Another advantage with pull advertising is that it gives you an opportunity to outline and recommend your services to your own potential market in an indirect, indiscreet, but fairly powerful fashion.

It is best for pull advertising to include patient testimonials which are crafted in such a way that they seem beneficial and not like 'sales messages' to your audience.

QUALITY OF PATIENTS

The big difference between push advertising and pull advertising is the quality of your prospects.

With pull advertising you are strategically spending most of your time, resources, and energy communicating with the prospects that have shown an interest in you and your physical therapy services.

With push advertising, you are hoping (against chance) that the prospect will respond to your offer and take you up on your services.

The secret to successful marketing is pre-qualifying target patients and weeding out patients who are unlikely to seek and benefit from your services. You want to avoid prospects that have a low probability or working with you or have a low interest in your services.

When you dedicate resources to interact with, build a relationship with, and sell to prospects that have shown an interest in your services. There is a high probability of acquiring patients who are going to be compliant and turn into strong referral sources.

6 STEPS TO BUILD YOUR REFERRAL SYNDICATE

When we treat a patient, it's best to think of the patient as an evolved consumer who does business with other establishments in your community.

The patient is therefore a 'client' at the local gym, enjoys the chicken salad at the Greek restaurant across the street from Joe's, has had the same dentist, Dr. Stanley for 15 years and uses Charlie Schmidt, the friendly neighborhood accountant.

It takes a great deal of time, money and effort for you as a practice owner to get a patient, treat them, and build trust with them. Other businesses do the same and have a list of clients that they have worked with. These businesses are known, liked, and trusted by those clients.

This little detail is very instructive from a referral generation point of view, since it underlines the importance of having your own 'syndicate' of referral sources. If you can build, control, and nurture your own syndicate (with you at the helm) you can derive all the benefits of referral generation without the associated hassles and costs.

The best way to do this is to offer to endorse other businesses to your patients and ask other businesses to do the same. This allows you to spread your wings by reaching more individuals in your community through endorsements instead of traditional advertising.

You should have at least 10 local businesses that are an active part of your syndicate. Also, it's best to create your own syndicate and hand pick the team members instead of joining existing syndicates like the local chamber of commerce and local business networks (which may or may not be active and motivated to help each other).

When forming your own syndicate, you want to identify and invite successful local business owners. They can potentially give you access to several thousand individuals, while the non-business owner will have a significantly smaller network.

Here is how you can go about it:

1. Compile a list of the top 30 professionals or businesses in your community. Be selective and choose only the most reputable businesses. A good place to start is owners of pharmacies, accountants, attorneys, gym owners, massage

therapists, health spas, and restaurants. Think about businesses your patients frequent and work at, then go backwards from there. You'll start off with the professionals you know personally and then you'll get them to help you in rounding out your list. This will be your core team of 30 business owners.

2. Create this list in an organized format. Create an Excel or Access database sheet with names, phone numbers, mailing addresses, and emails (if available) for easy reference. You have now built your own 'syndicate'.

3. Approach this list by phone call / letter to introduce yourself and the concept of building a 'referral network'. Tell them you would like to make them a part of your 'syndicate' and that the function of this group is to help each others businesses by encouraging referrals.

4. Inform the 'team' that you will make copies of this list and send them the updated version on a regular basis. By circulating this list you are not just helping grow your own practice, but you are also helping these business owners build their own businesses through referrals.

5. Each time you send an updated list, you will educate the 'syndicate' about your work and how you can help both them and the people in their network. Over time, they'll understand your practice more deeply and will know exactly when to refer people to see you. Because of the regular contact, you are going to be at the forefront of their minds and they'll want to refer to you because you are helping them.

6. Expand your role with the 'syndicate' by making special offers in your correspondence, by profiling other members and their offers to the group, and by helping them develop their own syndicate with you as their preferred physical therapist.

In this manner, you can transform a '*consumer*' of another business into a '*patient*' of your business and help other local businesses do the same.

LOCAL BUSINESS SYNDICATION TO GROW YOUR PRACTICE

You've heard of local business organizations like the chamber of commerce and probably noticed that many business organizations are fragmented entities that sound good on paper but never really bring in additional business for the entities involved?

The fact is that local businesses have the potential to help you grow your practice, especially in direct access states. In turn, you can promote those businesses by promoting them to your patients.

But if local business organizations don't cut it, what does?

The best way to fix the problem is by forming your own 'local business syndicate.' The word syndicate comes from the French word syndicat, which means trade union (syndic meaning administrator).

WHY ESTABLISH YOUR OWN SYNDICATE?

If you establish your own 'local syndicate', you immediately create a position of authority among members of the syndicate, since you initiated it. It's like forming your own local trade union, consisting of different professionals including one member from each of the following professions:

- ❖ Physical therapy
- ❖ Dental
- ❖ Medical
- ❖ Legal
- ❖ Accounting
- ❖ Food (restaurant owner)

Since each of these professionals has their own clients, they can cross promote each other's business. On top of that, remember that your patient is not just your patient; he/she is also a client / customer for some other businesses as well.

In other words, your patient is a buyer. They go to other establishments in your area. The goal of the syndicate is to provide a better, more affordable experience for the client with a 'collective service' power. Clients who do business with members of the syndicate can get special discounts, offers, services, and upgrades that they would NOT normally get elsewhere.

Your task, as the creator of the syndicate, is to align all your peers to constantly deliver value to the client and improve their health and lifestyle. Essentially, you want

Chapter 7   179

to protect the client from bad experiences and provide better service as a collective 'front'. The mission is to make sure the client is happy and satisfied. Once the client is 'wronged', everyone loses.

WHAT IS A LOCAL BUSINESS SYNDICATE?

It is a group of business owners that promote each other and grow each other's business. Keep in mind that you want 'players of a level playing field' in your syndicate. You want people who can add as much, if not more, value to existing members as opposed to 'value extractors'. For example, a large physician network is more important for your syndicate than a new physician who just opened his doors. The bigger the physician, the more important the cooperative relationship with them; the more referrals your practice will get as a result of their involvement in your syndicate.

HOW DO YOU CREATE A SYNDICATE?

Identify 10 people who are your biggest potential referral sources. Write down their specialty, the type of patient or client they work with. What is the NUMBER ONE OUTCOME their clients are looking for?

For example, how can you help that physician better manage their patients?

Give them something of significant value that they cannot ignore and help them manage their patients better. Keep in mind that not every business may show an interest in joining your 'syndicate' but the ones who don't respond are unlikely to be referral sources anyway. The physicians (and businesses) that really matter to your bottom line are going to be the ones that show an interest. The syndication offer therefore serves as a pre-qualifier to help you identify such businesses.

TRY TO SET UP A MEETING TO INVITE PEOPLE TO YOUR SYNDICATE.

Help each one of these physicians understand the opportunity by saying:

> *"I am having a little invite only, private industry meeting (5 people only) in XXX (city) and I'd like to share a breakthrough strategy I have been using to improve patient care with XXXXX"*

You will now position yourself as the "intelligent expert" and the "authority figure". Getting a team of physicians in a room, with you as the presenter is a significant achievement.

You can do this with multiple local businesses and offer to help them add more value to their clients and grow your network at the same time.

The bigger (and more influential) the players in your syndicate, the more likely you are to get referrals from multiple sources and grow your practice.

JOINT ENDORSEMENT REFERRALS:
CAN LOCAL BUSINESSES HELP GROW YOUR PRACTICE?

As private practice owners, we are conditioned to seek referrals from physicians and patients; but this is a very self-limiting, restrictive way to grow a practice.

Even if you are in a state with limited or no direct access, you should be able to 'consult' with a patient and then fax a referral request to the physician, converting a '*prospect*' to a '*patient*'.

Getting in front of these prospects can be done with traditional marketing like newspaper ads, postcards, radio ads, and Yellow Pages. The problem with these methods is that consumers are 'conditioned' to tune these messages out. Interruption marketing does not work.

Endorsement marketing, on the other hand, is more likely to get a consumers attention because the consumer now hears about your clinic from a trusted source when they get a letter or phone call from the other business (that they know, like, and trust) telling them about YOUR services.

The reason this works? Your patient is a CONSUMER and is likely doing business with OTHER businesses in your community. Your practice is NOT the only business that your patient (consumer) visits.

If your attorney, accountant or physician sent you a letter recommending a local dentist (who then offers a special discount or $25 teeth cleaning for you to respond by a certain date), are you likely to respond? (Endorsement marketing)

On the other hand, if you get the SAME offer from the SAME dentist in a postcard in your mailbox, chances are that it's going to end up in your trash. (Interruption marketing)

The best way to get joint endorsements from your own network of local businesses is to build such a network to begin with. It's best to form your own, private network. The goal of the network is for participants to promote each other and grow each other's business. Your network can include a prominent personal trainer, a pharmacy, several physicians (with different specialties), a massage therapist, a gym owner, a spa owner, a nail salon owner, and even a famous local restaurant. All these are businesses your patients may know or benefit from.

Local businesses (those located within a 5 mile radius or your clinic) are valuable allies and strategic partners for your practice. In particular, local businesses with large lists of clients are (strategically) better allies than new businesses that lack a presence (and goodwill) within your community. Make sure you identify and forge mutually

Chapter 7   181

beneficial referral relationships with providers you trust and have used in the past. Otherwise, negative experiences that your patients have with other businesses that you recommend will creep back to you and affect your reputation.

Each local business has its own set of clients and customer relationships, which can be leveraged in your favor with endorsements. Once you can identify local businesses that serve your ideal patient, you want to start building mutually beneficial referral relationships with them. You can do the same for other businesses. The big benefit with local endorsements is your ability to 'piggyback' on the reputation of other businesses, establish instant credibility with residents in your community, reach a new patient population, and minimize your new patient acquisition costs.

With a combination of a well-planned endorsement strategy (combined with an offer fueled by scarcity and urgency like the dentist example), you should be able to drive more patients and dramatically improve awareness about your practice and its services.

As private practices, we need to look beyond traditional referral sources like patients and physicians. Relationships with local businesses represent a new, untapped way to grow your private practice.

CHAPTER 8

The Road To The Celebrity Physical Therapist –

How To Win Over Everyone In Your Community

THE CELEBRITY PHYSICAL THERAPIST

A successful private practice owner is able to convince a patient / physician about his authority and expertise even before the treatment or referral occurs.

For most products and services, perception about value is subconsciously considered as reality.

This is called '*preframing*' and positioning.

Imagine you had to get an appointment for your next haircut. If you had to wait for your appointment like some other people, chances are that you would value the time of the service provider much more than if you could walk in to the hairdresser any time you wanted. The next time you eat at a fancy Italian restaurant with a reservation, as opposed to the 'never ending pasta' bowl at Olive Garden, ask yourself – why did you cheerfully pay four times as much for a meal that was almost the same?

How does this apply to your practice? Is it possible to convince your patients about your expertise and "*preframe*" them even before they step into your practice?

Is it possible to convince physicians that you are THE authority, even before you pick up the phone and call them?

Here's an example of '*preframing*' versus '*cold calling*' a physician's office.

COLD CALLING

> *"Hello, this is Jane Smith calling from ABC physical therapy, may I speak with Dr. Roberts please?"*
>
> *"Dr. Robertson is not available, may I help you?"*

The conversation continues… until you hear…

> *"Please leave your name and number and the physician will call you back"*

We all know how that plays out.

PREFRAMING

> *"Hello, this is Jane Smith calling from ABC physical therapy and recently featured in the _____ Times (a local newspaper), may I speak with Dr. Roberts please?*
>
> *"Oh, I know you. Hold on while I try to find the physician"*

Something significant just happened. You just made a BIG breakthrough and got past the gatekeeper, almost instantly. Since your position as an expert, an authority on physical therapy was already pre-established, it was much easier.

You were *"preframed."*

The good news is that anyone can do this. It just takes planning.

Imagine if you could apply this before anyone ever met you, how much would that help your practice?

A successful physical therapy marketing campaign, where you use different media to *"preframe"* your practice will hinge on three factors:

1. The cost effectiveness of the medium (internet, phone, mail, radio, TV)
2. The ability of the media to get your prospects in the right frame of mind even before they have called your clinic (preframing)
3. The ability of the media to identify potential referral sources, so that you invest time and resources creating relationships with those referral sources (pre-qualification)

HERE'S HOW THIS WORKS

Let's assume you write an article on injury prevention for a local magazine. You present valuable how-to information on pain relief, exercise 101, and injury prevention; resulting in positioning yourself as a likeable and insightful practitioner. The interview starts stirring discussions about you among patient and physician circuits. People get curious about your clinical skills and want to know more. This buzz turns out to be conducive to patient inflow and positions you as an expert.

You can leverage this media success to reach more media outlets and progressively build bigger media appearances. This free publicity "preframes" you in the eyes of patients and referral sources as an expert, even before you have had a chance to interact with them. You have discovered a way of making physical therapy marketing easier than ever.

Preframing is at work every single day and explains our predisposition for products ranging from personal care to supermarket food choices. When you walk down the supermarket aisle, the choices you make are largely dependent upon your perception of the product as opposed to its quality and cost effectiveness. The reason you might choose Kraft cheese and Coke over store-made cheese and Pepsi is a classic example of preframing.

Chapter 8   185

HOW DOES THIS RELATE TO YOUR PRACTICE?

A call from a patient seeking an appointment because you came recommended by their physician is a classical example of preframing.

The right kind of advertising not only informs the patient about the existence of your practice, but goes the extra mile to preframe them.

The phrase *"your reputation precedes you"* takes on new meaning.

RESOURCE

FREE WEBINAR:
How To Combine SMS, Voice Broadcasting and Email Marketing To
Automate Patient Communication and Transform Your Practice

In this live webinar, discover the emerging trends in mobile marketing and learn:

- ✓ Why is mobile marketing a trend you can't ignore?
- ✓ How you can take advantage of it
- ✓ How to get started

This training will help you if:

- ✓ You are looking for new ways to get and retain patients
- ✓ You have (or are collecting) patient's cellphone numbers and emails
- ✓ You want to save time and money by using mobile marketing and voice broadcasting to increase the effectiveness of email marketing campaigns

To reserve your seat, simply register for the webinar at the link below and click the "**Register Now**" button on that page. Hurry, because seats are limited!

www.mobilepatients.com

THE ENERGETIC PHYSICAL THERAPIST

A physical therapist that engages patients on a subliminal level, in addition to demonstrating effective skills as a professional, is an asset in any private practice. This therapist knows exactly how to speak with patients in a language that makes sense to them. He often uses words like '*pain relief*', '*move faster*' and '*do things better*' while avoiding technical terms. He has a way to relate with patients and always presents himself enthusiastically since he understands the needs and wants of his patients.

Such a therapist is successfully able to transform a great majority of his patients into raving fans of physical therapy (his practice) and is able to create human billboards out of a majority of patients.

THE FIRST 30 SECONDS

Within the first 30 seconds of interacting with you, the patient will form an opinion of you as a practitioner and of physical therapy as a service. They may think of you as a torturer, one who is going to cause them pain in an effort to relieve their pain. They may think of you as a warm and energetic individual, dedicated to their health and wellbeing.

The initial opinion that a patient forms of a physical therapist is important, not just to the success of the therapy process but to the long term financial value and the referral generation potential of that particular patient. The first impression is truly the last impression. The first 30 seconds that a patient interacts with you will set the stage for a long-term relationship with the therapist and in turn with the private practice. When you are meeting the patient for the first time there are many things that you can do in order to make the patient more comfortable with you.

TIPS TO INCREASE PATIENT COMFORT LEVEL

First, start with a warm greeting in an empathetic manner. Show them that you really care. Don't give them the impression that they are simply numbers, information on a form, or they are simply an insurance record. Try to be punctual and respect the patients' time as much as possible.

Maintaining eye contact with the patient when you first see them is extremely important. Don't allow yourself to be distracted with other patients or with other things going on in the clinic.

A firm handshake is not mandatory, but indicates a level of trust and professionalism from the word go. You want to introduce yourself properly by saying, *"Hi! My name is Joe Johnson I will be your physical therapist today."*

All of these factors are a combination of maintaining eye contact, shaking hands firmly, and greeting them by their first name can be reinforced and made even more powerful by maintaining an open friendly posture and doing something as simple as smiling.

ENERGY

The energetic physical therapist is the glue that holds a physical therapy private practice together. It is important to convey a high level of energy and enthusiasm, since this rubs off on all of your patients. There is a social benefit and a strategic motive here. It makes patients more accountable to the therapist and themselves because they now recognize the energy and the effort that the therapist is putting into them with each and every appointment.

Your goal is to provide a high level of enthusiasm, energy and excitement and to get the patient as interested, as excited, as hyped up about physical therapy and its benefits as you are.

The principle of enthusiasm is actually grounded in the principle of reciprocity. We as human beings tend to reciprocate what we get. Nobody wants to feel a sense of obligation towards another person. We want to 'give back' what we receive.

Let's say you walk into a mall and someone walking ahead of you decides to be polite and hold the door open for you. You instinctively say *"Thank you"* to the person and maybe even smile.

Let's say you came across the exact same person in a crowded restaurant and passed by him. Chances are, you would not have given this person a second glance.

Do you know why?

You returned the gesture of politeness in the mall since you did not want to feel obligated to this person.

In a physical therapy appointment, there is an underlying sense of obligation that a patient feels towards the physical therapist for the treatment they are getting. As a therapist, you can 'consolidate' this obligation and reinforce it by using some of the strategies mentioned. You want to smile, you want to have open body language, you want to be able to address them by their first name, you want to maintain eye contact with them and have a firm hand shake.

All of these things go a long way in actually establishing a positive vibe that is the hallmark of a successful physical therapy private practice.

POWER OF THE PATIENT APPRECIATION DAY

One of the best ways to promote a physical therapy private practice is to consistently market your clinic. Marketing strategies can be both offline and online. The best offline marketing strategies allow you to leverage your time by allowing you to reach out to several people at one time. The best online marketing strategies create a new wave of patients that find you on the Internet and reach out to you for their physical therapy needs.

Here is a secret that many professions have been using for a long time. Offline and online strategies should ideally culminate in an event that generates an incredible amount of hype for your clinic.

So how do you get the patient's attention in a world that is getting busier by the day? The best way to create tidal wave marketing for your clinic is to announce a 'Patient Appreciation Day.'

So what is a patient appreciation day? Essentially, it's a big party that you throw for your patients. The patient, his or her family, their pet poodle, and everyone else they want to bring are invited. You provide lunch or dinner, some light entertainment, and a fun relaxed atmosphere in which you can interact with all of your patients in an informal environment outside of physical therapy.

Fundamentally, it is a day in which you appreciate all your patients for their excellent recovery and give prizes to patients who have shown the most recovery and referred their friends to your clinic. Some great ways to make this event successful are:

❖ Announce a whole range of prizes, most which can be sponsored by local businesses, to the most outstanding patients, graded by compliance and extent of recovery, as judged by you.

❖ Have the whole event captured on video. Acquire the patients' permission to gather pictures, video, and audio testimonials that can be used on your web site and marketing brochures.

❖ Invite key people from local businesses like massage therapists, accountants, attorneys, and community leaders to learn more about your practice and the initiatives you take for your patients.

❖ If you have some connections in your town and have treated a restaurant owner, a local celebrity, the mayor or some key decision maker in your town, ask them to come along and bring all of their friends.

❖ Make the event as entertaining as possible by including events like lotto, a movie screening, or a stand-up comedy routine. Remember, everyone is there to have fun and toast to you and the success of your practice.

The secret benefit to an event like this is the referral incentive you can subconsciously instill in all of the attendees. Besides the implicit appreciation of your practice, you can get on the stage and hand out prizes to patients who have referred other patients. Presenting your appreciation in a warm, open, appreciative, and fun manner will be perceived as a powerful practice building tool; as opposed to being perceived as an unethical practice. The success of an event like this is all in the presentation.

The words and phrases that you use to describe the event and the quality of your product or service will transform this promotional event into an annual phenomenon.

Persuasive statements such as "I would not be standing here today if it were not for all of you", "I am glad the pillars of the community are here to celebrate our success together", "Your satisfaction is our business", "Physical therapy is an investment in your future" and "This event is dedicated to all those special people in my life" can help bridge the gap between a tacky promotional event and an energetic crowd puller.

The very act of promoting the patient day, in and of itself, is a referral generation exercise for your practice. Use a combination of print, word-of-mouth, and online advertising mechanisms to make this an event the town will remember. With the right approach this can become an annual event that results in a massive surge in your practice.

Running ads in local newspapers is effective, but it is the old school way of doing things. Engaging in online promotion mechanisms like optimizing your web site and having your own physical therapy block is an important component for new age physical therapy marketing. Connection between you and your patients by using the benefits of audio and video marketing cannot be understated. Use a digital video camera to capture short video clips lasting 30 seconds to one minute; put them up on video sharing websites and host them on your web site or blog. Give patients the opportunity to get to know you better and attach a face and a voice to a name. The internet allows us the opportunity to leverage time and reach out to scores of people with a single, concentrated, and planned effort.

In today's world however, we cannot undermine the importance of one-on-one personal, relevant communication. Speaking of old school, there's one strategy most therapists have forgotten. It works like a charm, especially when promoting an event like the Patient Appreciation Day. We all know that the best way to get a surge in your physical therapy private practice is to reach out to former patients. Most private practices have hundreds of former patients in their database. The single best thing you can do to grow your practice is to pick up the phone, speak with these patients, and educate them about the benefits and the value of your brand of physical therapy. Just collect the phone numbers of 5 to 10 patients you've had a good relationship with and call them to invite them to your Patient Appreciation Day. For best results use a call script, which provides a step-by-step outline of what you can say during the phone conversation. If you can repeat this process five days a week you will be reaching out to 15 to 20 former patients every week. You see the results within two to three weeks with new patient referrals, RSVPs for the patient appreciation day, and enhanced credibility for your practice.

OUTREACH: HOW TO BE A COMMUNITY LEADER IN PHYSICAL THERAPY

The backbone of any physical therapy practice is the development of referral relationships. Cultivating such relationships with patients is the key to establishing yourself as an opinion leader in your community.

There is a consensus among physical therapists that personal contact with patient referral sources, the patient community, and insurance companies is the most powerful way to boost your credibility as a provider and cement your position as the provider of choice in your community.

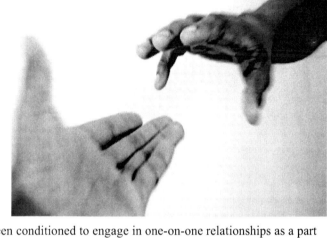

The problem with personal contact is that we, as physical therapists, have not been conditioned to engage in one-on-one relationships as a part of our education. Physical therapy school teaches us to be excellent clinicians with a strong ability to evaluate and treat patients. However, marketing is an entirely different ball game and it's not something we are taught in school.

Marketing physical therapy requires a high level of personal contact with patients, physicians, and the local media. It seems much harder than it actually is, for most therapists. Feelings of self-doubt emerge, "*I feel like a salesman*," "*I don't want to be treated like a pharmaceutical representative*," or "*I don't want to be disrespected*." I believe that perception is reality and you must present yourself as an expert if you want to be recognized as one. Personal contact is an art form and a formula that works over and over again when skillfully mastered.

THE IMPORTANCE OF PERSONAL CONTACT

Remember, the best way to promote yourself as a physical therapist is to go out into the real world and meet people with the intention of letting them know about you. A simple strategy that has worked for us in our clinic is a "Thank You" card. Remember, a "Thank You" card to a physician is much more effective when it comes from the patient and not from the provider. For example, if you, as a provider, send a "thank you" card to the physician as a way of expressing gratitude for the referral, the card may not be read at all. Try another strategy, which is far more successful. This card should come from the patient. When you treat a patient, ask the patient during one of their visits to stop for a moment and fill out a quick thank you card they receive from the receptionist. Your friendly receptionist or staff can offer to mail the card to the physician on behalf of the patient. This little "Thank You" card from the patient, addressed to the physician, is a powerful way to enhance quality patient referrals from the same physician. Physicians and their staff are more likely to read notes and "Thank You" cards that come from patients than those coming from providers.

Another great approach is to contact physician groups and hospitals in your area and to ask to speak with the education director. Many physical therapists don't even know about the existence of an education director in such organizations, so this is where you can get ahead of the competition. When you speak with the education director, be polite, friendly and professional. Introduce yourself as a physical therapist with a specialty in your particular field and express your desire to speak to a patient population as an expert, in the form of a seminar, at no charge. Be prompt in sending your resume, a well-designed press release, and a seminar outline to the education director. The next step is to follow up with this individual in three to four business days and request an update on the possibility of conducting a seminar or lecture for local residents.

When you follow the system, it is guaranteed to work, and you will end up with several public workshops and seminars. This is an extremely effective way to reach out to the local community and introduce your services as a physical therapist and healthcare professional.

When patients come in to your clinic to see you as a physical therapist, they will be ready to pay cash for your services as long as they have faith in you and your services. The key is to describe all the benefits of your program and describe it in such a way that the patient feels they cannot get those services elsewhere. In fact, you have to be so adept at selling the program over the phone or in person that you should get the patient wondering if this program is covered by insurance at all! Patients are more likely to pay cash if they know you, like you and trust you. In order to cultivate this sort of relationship with your patients, you need to be friendly, approachable and professional at the same time. This is the essence of marketing physical therapy services.

Another great way to boost referrals is to generate educational handouts for referral sources. Imagine providing an orthopedic surgeon a handout on "postoperative tips for recovery from knee or back surgery." When the surgeon hands out these pamphlets to his patients, take a guess as to which physical therapy provider these patients are more likely to choose. It's important to remember that these brochures and pamphlets should provide patients with valuable information that can be used in day-to-day life. It can include your clinic name, address and contact information, but it should not be promotional in nature. The idea behind any informational handout is that it should save the physician time in explaining common ailments. You can also go one step further and provide high-quality information with a blurb at the end that suggests that patients call you if they need more information.

At the end of the day, referrals and personal contact are the most reliable way to consistently gain patient referrals and boost patient loyalty. In our experience, we have found that callback programs to patients have been extremely successful. Imagine that you are a patient who has just been discharged from physical therapy. Wouldn't you love to hear from your therapist? It is amazing how a simple phone call can do wonders for the patient's perception of physical therapy, in addition to increasing their likelihood of referring new patients. In my experience, many patients have been very happy to hear from their physical therapist. They often develop a personal connection with their physical therapist, to the point that they take the initiative to inform their physician about their satisfaction with physical therapy. As a physical therapist, all you have to do is pick up the phone and ask the patient, "How are you doing? What was your experience with physical therapy?"

The patient is likely to be impressed with the phone call and express any concern or difficulty, if any. This is a wonderful way for the patients to express themselves and offer feedback to the physical therapist about their treatment process and future goals. In the event the patient requires further assistance, the physical therapist can ask the patient to come in for a re-evaluation or a brand-new evaluation, presuming the condition is different. At the end of the day, the physical therapist and the patient are able to communicate better, resulting in better standards of care. The receptionist and your staff can take this one step further and call the patient on birthdays and anniversaries. Your office can also offer a courtesy screening for a friend or family member.

Chapter 8   195

SHOW YOUR PERSONALITY
IN YOUR PRACTICE

Imagine your patient at lunch with a friend, 3 months after being discharged from your clinic.

Your name comes up during a conversation, since the patient's friend is looking for a physical therapist. The patient searches for words to describe you, and uses one of 3 descriptions to paint a picture:

a) That therapist... I can't remember his name, but I got some massage, exercise, and electrical therapy.

b) John was an excellent therapist, helped reduce my pain and I like his sense of humor!

c) That therapist was a punisher, I dreaded the appointments.

The second choice reflects camaraderie; a strong, positive rapport between patient and therapist.

The more patients you have and the more they get along with you as a therapist, the more successful your practice. With the right planning, you can use your personality to get more patients and improve relationships with existing patients. This is personality driven physical therapy.

In order to get more patients, you need:

a) Contact information of previous patients who know you, like you and trust you as a therapy provider. As a therapist, you maintain relevant, professional contact with them to remain 'top of mind' for future physical therapy needs.

b) The ability to reach a new set of patients through physician referrals, local media, public speaking engagements, websites, and blogs.

c) A patient base with the need for your services, the commitment to make and keep physical therapy appointments, and a strong desire to improve functionally.

Most private practices ignore (a), work hard at (b) and have (c). For a successful practice, all 3 components should be in place.

The link between (a) and (b) is quite simply you, the practitioner. Physical therapy is the tool / service while the craftsman or technician is you, the therapist. One of the best ways to achieve (a) and (b) and defining yourself as a therapist is by setting up your own physical therapy blog and posting video updates, not just text updates, to your blog.

It's free to set up a blog and can be done within minutes. Just search for 'free blogs' online, choose your own blog name, and you will be up and running. Blogs are generally favored by search engines, as opposed to static websites, since search engines prefer dynamic content; information that is constantly being updated.

A blog is an online diary of your life and can be maintained with 5-8 minutes a day of short entries entered in-between working with patients. It allows patients and visitors to catch a glimpse of your life and allows them to associate the professional therapist with a likeable human being.

Authenticity matters. It's important to be consistent, transparent, and provide valuable information. Each one of us is a unique individual and has a story to tell. You must be interesting and present your personality with your blog posts.

It's not important to write a long blog post every day. Short posts, 100-150 words once a week are sufficient as long as the information you provide is valuable and relevant to the patients. Avoid technical language and use the blog as a medium to unwind and communicate with patients. The first 3-4 weeks of posting may seem arduous, but once you get into the groove of writing blog posts it will become a tough habit to break.

Using video and audio is the best way to add an extra dimension of personality to your blog. A digital camera or a handheld camcorder is sufficient. Once a week, have someone point the camera at you and follow these suggestions to capture your personality on video:

a) The camera should capture your head, neck, and shoulder. Close-ups are preferable, since they allow the viewer to better identify with you.

b) Keep your head and neck steady, with a relaxed smile on your face while you look straight at the camera.

c) Introduce yourself and the name of your clinic. Speak for 30-45 seconds (research shows longer clips result in a significant reduction in visitor interest). Tell the viewer about your day in 2-3 sentences and then spend 20-30 seconds providing the viewer with useful, patient friendly information.

A SAMPLE SCRIPT IS:

"Hello, my name is John Doe from ABC physical therapy. I just finished treating patients for today. I had a wonderful day and hope you did too. This is a reminder about the importance of physical activity. Remain physically active, within the limits of pain and heed any restrictions established by your physician or physical therapist. Listen to your body and communicate any signs and symptoms of discomfort to health professionals. Physical therapy is intended to relieve pain and improve function. We are always here to assist you. That's it for today. Thank you and enjoy the rest of your day".

Vary this script to suit your style and message. Change the message often and convey information about your practice, services, and features. This video can be uploaded to the internet on various video sharing sites like YouTube and easily made available on your blog or website.

Use a blog and video updates to reflect your personality and define your practice. The next time your name comes up in a conversation, patients will seem like raving fans.

THE VIP PATIENT EXPERIENCE

You get just one chance to make an impression with patients, especially in the current times. Patients are constantly evaluating the need for and the benefits of various services (including physical therapy) and it's critical for therapists to recognize this subtle perception and mold it in their favor.

FIND YOUR RAVING FANS

Start by determining who your 'raving fans' are and how you can nurture them. There is a big difference between a patient and a raving fan. A patient is some who has received treatment in your facility, either in the past or present. Develop a relationship with them. Make their experience memorable and they'll become repeat clients or refer other friends and family to you. Get your patients talking about you by over-delivering, and they won't be able to stop talking about you.

A raving fan is a rare breed of patient. These are patients who believe in your treatment and swear by its efficacy. They are happy to tell their family and friends about you and often result in repeat referrals. Meet and exceed their expectations and you will see an abundance of referrals.

GOOD SERVICE IS CRITICAL

Good service is paramount. You **get** successful in a private practice by satisfying the patient's needs and wants. Remember, it costs a lot more to get a new patient in the door than to keep the old ones coming (and being loyal to you for future treatments). That's how you increase revenue; with repeat business.
Try writing up a contract for a *"Patient Bill of Rights"* and hang it up on your wall. To those who might have a complaint, but won't complain to you, this will encourage them to voice their opinions BEFORE taking their business elsewhere.

DEALING WITH ANGRY PATIENTS

Dealing with angry or upset patients and minimizing negative comments is important. The most damaging word-of-mouth comes from an angry patient. Below are 3 quick tips to help resolve an issue with an angry patient.
Do not undermine the patient's frustration; recognize it and acknowledge it immediately.

Chapter 8   199

✓ **Acknowledge that the person is upset.** In a calm, gentle tone, you want to say" *I can see that you are upset"*. Demonstrate empathy and immediately attempt to resolve the problem by going out of your way. A good statement is: *"I'm sorry that you had a problem and I'm glad you are bringing it to my attention"*. Make positive comments like *"I will resolve this for you, this is what I am going to do..."*

✓ **Involve the patient... just enough to show them respect.** The next step is to ask: *"Here is what I am going to do... I trust this will make you happy?"* This comment changes the frame of reference for the patient from upset and agitated to involved and reasonable. Be careful not to 'hand over the reins' to the patient since you want to demonstrate your authority. Retain control of the situation while seemingly 'giving in' to the patient.

✓ **Go above and beyond... SURPRISE the patient.** This is where you really turn the tables in your favor by showing even more respect towards the patient and surprising them with kindness and goodwill. You do this all while defusing the situation completely. Here is the script to use:

"I sincerely apologize. Your feedback is greatly appreciated and will assist us in improving our standards of service. In return for your kind feedback, allow me to _____ .I want you to know you are a valued client and we are committed towards your goals at all times."

Always avoid confrontations or harsh words. Do not react with your own emotions. Never take things personally.

Give patients the right first impression. Remove all negative connotations and signs, in your practice.

Everything in your practice SPEAKS to the prospect or patient walking in the door. For example: how clean is the waiting room or treatment area? How much time do they have to wait to be treated? Are the magazines in the waiting room outdated? Are their insurance benefits explained to them in a manner they understand? Do they get a clear explanation of their problem/diagnosis? Does the staff genuinely care?

The patient is subconsciously thinking about and forming an opinion about all these things during their visit. Everything about your practice – the image, the appearance – speaks to every patient who walks in your door. The little things matter.

REMOVE THE NEGATIVE SIGNS

Take a look around your practice. Remove any signs that say or imply "No".
- No credit cards accepted ("We prefer cash")
- Closed on weekends ("We take a break on weekends so our employees can enjoy their families… we hope you enjoy your weekend too!")
- Cash and checks accepted only ("Cash and checks preferred")

Change the atmosphere in your practice by saying positive things and your patients will take notice.

THE STARBUCKS™ OF PRIVATE PRACTICE

It's hard to forget my positive customer service experience with Betty at the local Starbucks™ last week. It's the local Starbucks™ where I usually pick up my $4 soy decaf blueberry latte every day at 7.30 am.

> *"Hi Nitin, great to see you! I see you are running a couple of minutes behind today. I don't want you to be late for work, so is it going to be the same? I suggest a dash of hazelnut – it just came in today and I think you'll really like it!"*

One thing was clear. Each time I visited Starbucks™, I got more than a cup of coffee; I got an experience. I was made to feel special.

The Starbucks™ business model has changed the coffee industry as we know it. Customers are able to customize their beverage with the hand-crafted assistance of a 'barista' (the Italian equivalent of a bartender). This customization adds a heightened level of satisfaction for each consumer with simple, yet delightful additions like soy milk and various 'pumps' of flavor and sweetener. Compare this with a system-based, automated approach like your order at McDonalds™ and you'll see why people (myself included) seldom hesitate paying $4 for a cup of coffee that would often be 50% cheaper at McDonalds™.

When your patients and referral sources think of you, are you the McDonalds™ or the Starbucks™ of physical therapy private practices in your community?

The truth is that what a consumer pays for is not always what the customer wants. A customer who pays $4 or more for a latte is paying for the experience, the 'feel good' factor, the human connection, and not just the drink. In fact, the customer subconsciously knows he/she is overpaying, but still continues to pay top dollar for a premium service. Consumers in a new economy, a sophisticated, fast-paced world will pay for a genuine, 'warm fuzzy feeling' human connection.

This 'human touch' is one of the factors that add to the perception of quality. In a service related profession like physical therapy, success has a lot to do with perception since perception is perceived as reality.

Starbucks™, like every other conglomerate, started with one store. Founder Howard Schultz said,

Chapter 8   201

> *"The success of Starbucks™ demonstrates that we have built an emotional connection with our customers… We have a competitive advantage over classic brands in that every day we touch and interact with our customers directly."*
>
> *"Our product is not sitting on a supermarket shelf like a can of soda. Our people have done a wonderful job of knowing your drink, your name, and your kids' names."*

Similarly, in private practice the patient interacts with the therapist several times during the course of the treatment. This presents the clinician with several opportunities to provide a 'blue chip' patient experience. The patient could easily go to a Walgreens and pick up some OTC medication or visit other professionals, including personal trainers and chiropractors. The fact that we get the patient's undivided attention during the course of the treatment several times before discharge is a significant opportunity.

Leadership at Starbucks™ spends a great deal of time, effort, and energy educating the partners (staff members) about customer satisfaction and in doing so, they build a brand. This is a commitment to the shared good of all employees and customers. Starbucks™ consistently spends more on training than it does on advertising. They go beyond stock options and health insurance. Staff members who work more than 20 hours a week are called '*partners*'. Partners get extensive training in product knowledge, success principles, self development, and human interaction skills to improve customer experiences. This helps significantly with staff and customer retention, along with new client acquisition.

That's why you have a better experience with Betty, who accepts your order at Starbucks™ than Joe, who's looking at the line behind you while taking your order at McDonalds™.

Dave Olsen, senior vice president of culture and leadership development at Starbucks™ states that:

> *"It doesn't matter how many millions or billions of cups of coffee Starbucks™ has served, if the one you get does not suit you. We will deliver a drink that suits you every time and create an experience in the process. The experience must fit the customer."*

Starbucks™ strives to maintain a high level of consistency and quality for that particular customer and that is their promise.

Starbucks™ encourages employee individuality and avoids scripted customer service approaches. Staff members are provided a structure to engage with clients in productive, meaningful ways. Management at Starbucks™ calls this the "5 Ways Of Being"

    1. Be Welcoming

2. Be Genuine
3. Be Considerate
4. Be Knowledgeable
5. Be Involved

Starbucks™ has successfully mastered the application of the most basic principle of giving the customer an experience to remember. This has helped the company build its brand and keep their customers coming back.

How can the "5 Ways Of Being" work in your practice? Ask yourself:

✓ Is your practice giving your patients those memorable experiences?
✓ Are you or your staff connecting with your patients on a human level?
✓ Is there a sense of community within your staff?
✓ Do you share your knowledge with others (including staff) to generate passion and awareness for your practice?
✓ Is the staff engaged and willing to contribute ideas or suggestions to boost your reputation and efficiency?

In a private practice, the way your team interacts with a 62 year old patient recovering from a fall injury must be different from a 17 year old high school athlete with a torn meniscus. This goes a step beyond clinical intervention; it's the human interaction that leaves a lasting impression with the patient (customer) long after discharge. Patients want more experiences with individuals like Betty in your clinic. It is the experience that will be what they remember most and that's what will keep them (and their friends) coming back.

THE LAWS OF PREFRAMING AND PREQUALIFICATION

THE LAW OF PREFRAMING

Let's assume you write an article on injury prevention for a local magazine. You present valuable how-to information on pain relief, exercise 101, and injury prevention and position yourself as a likeable and insightful practitioner. The interview starts stirring discussions about you among patient and physician circuits. People get curious about your clinical skills and want to know more. This buzz turns out to be conducive to patient inflow and positions you as an expert.

You can leverage these two media successes to reach more media outlets and build progressively bigger media appearances. This free publicity 'preframes' you in the eyes of patients (and referral sources) as an expert even before you have had a chance to interact with them.

Preframing is at work every single day and explains our predisposition for products ranging from personal care to supermarket food choices.

A call from a patient seeking an appointment because you came recommended by their physician is a classical example of preframing.

The right kind of advertising not only informs the patient about the existence of your practice, but goes the extra mile to preframe them. The phrase "*your reputation precedes you*" takes on new meaning.

Interestingly, the cost of a medium is not related to its ability to preframe. A free press release or an editorial article about your practice in a local paper will do a lot more to preframe patients and physicians about you than a paid advertisement in the same publication.

To preframe your audience, try the following strategies
   a)   Select media that are accessed by your target audience. Survey patients to determine which magazines they read, websites they visit, and radio stations they listen to
   b)   Approach the editorial departments as a qualified contributor, not an advertiser or submit a free press release
   c)   Make references to successful treatments, use positive feedback from past patients, and clearly explain benefits and anticipated outcomes to give patients a strong reason to contact you with your contributions
   d)   Leverage small successes to open doors for bigger media

e) Strategically use media appearances – big or small – to forge new relationships with potential referral sources. Have your trained receptionist or support staff contact potential referral sources with strong scripts that imply stature, specialization, scarcity, exclusivity, and a clear directive. A rule of thumb is; the more accessible you are, the lower the appearance of exclusivity.

Here is a sample script for your receptionist to use when calling a physician's office:

> *"Hello, this is Amy calling from ABC Physical Therapy. I am calling on behalf of John Doe, our lead therapist. John was unable to make the call himself since his schedule has become even more hectic with his media appearances surrounding his new techniques on "Instant Pain Protocol Prevention", but he would like to personally offer Dr. James an exciting joint venture opportunity to drive more patients to your practice. His schedule is extremely limited, but I can see that next Thursday at noon is available for him to speak with Dr. James. Does that work?"*

Observe the elements of stature (media success), specialization (name of the program – instant pain protocol prevention), scarcity (limited schedule), and direction (asking for a confirmation on Thursday at noon).

In some cases, you might want to make a call like this on your own; but for the most part, minor customizations of this script and execution from support staff will work well to secure appointments with referral sources.

THE LAW OF PRE-QUALIFICATION

When you speak with physicians and local businesses, bring something to the table for them. Tell them that you will promote their services to your patients and would like them to refer patients back to you.

Create a simple outline of what you want them to do and what you can do for them (direction). Use a combination of emails, regular mail, phone calls, and faxes to convince them that a partnership with you is in their best business interests. The referral sources who respond positively automatically point themselves out as key referral sources (pre-qualification).

Preframing substantially increases the success rate of pre-qualification, since prospective business partners (referral sources) are more likely to want to do business with you.

The success of future marketing campaigns will no longer depend on the size of the budget, but the type of media and its ability to preframe and pre-qualify the patient and referral source.

PRICELESS PATIENT GIFTS

When was the last time someone you worked with gave you a surprise gift?

Did it feel good?

Chances are, you were impressed and told some friends about it.

What if you impressed patients with gifts and they started talking to their friends about you?

Patients love getting souvenirs from clinics, particularly if the souvenir has a high perceived value. The key is to keep your budget to a minimum, but over-deliver to your patients by providing a perception of value. A few dollars spent on gifts can become a great way to brand your clinic and stimulate patient to patient referrals.

1. **INTERVIEW SOME OF THE TOP PHYSICIANS IN YOUR AREA, IN AN EFFORT TO PROVIDE PATIENTS WITH AN INFORMATIONAL AUDIO CD**

If you don't have a monthly patient newsletter or an audio CD that you provide patients, now is the time! You probably have a network of physicians and healthcare professionals who refer to you. You can use this as leverage to improve your relationship with them and provide additional services to your patients at no additional cost.

Consider interviewing these practitioners and providing your patients with an informational interview format audio CD. This is pretty simple to do. Communicate with a referral physician you wish to interview and tell them that you're setting up an interview program and you'd like to have 20-30 minutes of their time. **Inform them that you plan on recording the interview and making it available to your patients as a free informational audio CD**. You will rarely get an objection. All the physician has to do is to send you a bio of themselves, answer the phone at a particular time, and talk to you. All you do is talk to the practitioner about the subject that they specialize in. You can interview an orthopedic surgeon specializing in knee injuries, a bariatric surgeon specializing in liposuction, or a general physician. Ask several questions that are relevant to patients and empower the patients with valuable information. Then, at the end thank your practitioner profusely for their time and mention their clinic location. **Do this once a month with a different practitioner and your patients will really benefit and perceive you as the expert, even though you're just asking the questions!**

So how do you conduct a phone interview and record it at the same time without investing in expensive equipment? Its simple, you can download free programs on the internet that record your voice, when you make an outbound call from your computer to the physician's office. You will need a headset and a microphone that connects to your computer. The software automatically allows you to record the conversations directly to your computer as an MP3 file. At the end of the phone call, just copy your conversations to a regular CD and provide it your patients! Your patients can now listen to the interview on their computer or on their CD players!

2. HEALTH AND WELLNESS MAGAZINE SUBSCRIPTIONS

Some of your patients like to read magazines on health, fitness, and physical therapy. As long as the magazine is health-related, consider getting a magazine subscription as a gift for some of your patients. This is an unusual strategy that has worked wonders for my clinic. Some patients want to eat healthier and want great recipes, get them a healthy recipe magazine, or Gourmet. The unique thing about a magazine subscription is that it allows you to remain in the patient's mind. **Add a magazine subscription to a personalized bi-monthly e-mail newsletter and you have a winning combination.** Patients are hungry for information, specifically the right information. Over a period of time, they will consider you to be the primary source for physical therapy in their community.

The key to building patient value over a period of time is to be in constant contact with patients, without being physically present in front of them. This is the challenge we struggle with as therapists on a day-to-day basis. Fortunately, the solutions are available and easily applicable. Most magazine subscriptions are inexpensive.

3. NEW EXERCISE TOOLS AND THERAPEUTIC EXERCISE HANDOUTS.

Every three to four visits attempt to introduce a little variation in the exercise routine of the patient. I can introduce an exercise ball, some dumbbells, a medicine ball, balance disk, etc.; anything that will enable them to get results faster and promote functional independence. The key is to teach the patient how to use this new tool and use it independently at home. **Most patients enjoy learning new exercises with new tools. In such cases, I surprise some patients by allowing them to take the new tool home!** Most of these tools cost less than $10.

4. FIELD TRIPS, PICNICS AND BARBECUE PARTIES. ($5)

Everyone loves a get-together, especially if it's organized by someone they like and respect. Most patients enjoy social events like field trips. **Such events foster relationships with patients, plus they are fun!** There are several types of field trips. This can be a picnic or an outing at a park, a trip to a baseball game for your baseball clients, a local hockey game for your hockey kids, etc. Try to get a group rate for tickets and offer your patients a discount, so your cost is less than five dollars per patient. Your patients can meet you at the venue and you don't have to be concerned with the logistics and transportation. What matters is the thought and the social component behind the event.

5. BIRTHDAYS. (FREE, UNDER $15)

Two pieces of information that every physical therapist should start to gather from patients are e-mails and birthdays. As I mentioned before, the e-mail is a critical component of e-mail marketing. Birthdays are self-explanatory and almost always ignored by physical therapists. Everyone loves getting presents, particularly your patients!

During the treatment process, try to determine what would be a good gift for the patient and make a note of it in your diary or day book. As a general rule, spend less than $15 on the gift. Even if you or a member of your staff doesn't have the time to buy a gift, a simple phone call works wonders. **On the big day, call them and wish them a happy birthday. This is an absolute winner. Most of their family members might forget, but not you!**

RESOURCE

REFERRAL IGNITION: The Only Real 'Done-For-You' Marketing System Guaranteed To:

✓ Help you be on pace for a full patient schedule
✓ Flood your practice with new patients
✓ Provide a blueprint to open multiple clinics run by *other* therapists
✓ Skyrocket your profits with the 'group physical therapy' and the 'post rehab' business model
✓ Deliver several plug-and-play systems that attracts patients magnetically
✓ Allow you to have more free time, money and freedom to do what you really want

While most private practitioners are frustrated with **vested financial interests from physician-owned private practices, competition from hospital owned clinics, the inability to get a physicians attention, the lack of time, money and effective strategies to market effectively**

... there is a select group of private practice owners who have mastered the "Referral Ignition" marketing strategies to effortlessly ignite referrals, bring home the bacon and grow their private practice in a clinical, automated fashion without spending tons of money on marketing.

Which side are you on?

The truth is, for the first time ever, I'm in a position to show you how they do it.

Here are the patient referral problems that plague most private practice owners.

❖ You can't find those 'hooks' that make people sit up and take notice of YOUR practice over others.
❖ You just **can't get past the gatekeepers when you call physicians' offices**
❖ You just don't have the time and money to market your practice.
❖ You can't seem to get enough physicians and hospitals to try you out
❖ **Not enough patients and physicians know about your services**

The problem you are facing is common. **How do I get physicians to sit up and take notice of my practice in these tough times**? As an expert on this subject, I can tell you that:

...this is entirely possible

...there are several ways to achieve this.

This is exactly where I come in, to stand by your side and cut through all the hype to finally help you achieve the practice success you have always wanted with Referral Ignition.

WHAT WILL YOU GET?

- ✓ The 'Ignition Box' consisting of 7 Audio CDs, 10 DVDs, 4 Manuals and a Handbook
- ✓ Access to the exclusive 'Referral Ignition' member's area with a username and password
- ✓ Done-for-you marketing campaigns (postcards, letters, emails, PowerPoints, website templates, reactivation sequences, patient stimulator books)
- ✓ 4 weekly modules with audio / video content updated every week in the member website
- ✓ Weekly group coaching calls to ensure implementation
- ✓ LIFETIME access to call recordings and all study material in the member's area
- ✓ A SPECIAL BONUS - LIVE 2 day workshop every year for Referral Ignition members
- ✓ Unedited video recording of the ENTIRE workshop if you miss it

For years I have coached and mentored groups of success-minded private practice owners on ways to increase referrals, build lifelong relationships with patients, and leverage some of the most powerful methods to take their private practice to new heights.

Gone are the days of marketing to physicians with fruit baskets and lunches. Certainly, physicians are an important part of the referral equation, but there is a whole new world of patients waiting to work with you. **We start by identifying prospects even before they become patients**. That's what **Prospect Ignition** is all about.

www.referralignition.com

MODULE 1: PROSPECT IGNITION: **How To Identify Prospects Even Before They Become Patients**

- ✓ How to get LISTS of prospects (individuals with low back pain, knee pain in your area)
- ✓ Determine how you can help them IMMEDIATELY even before they have met you
- ✓ Build a list of such individuals using patient stimulators and joint ventures
- ✓ How to get your postcards and print ads to jump out at prospects, immediately facilitating a call to your clinic
- ✓ **Done-for-you scripts to reactivate former patients and convert them into referral sources**
- ✓ Plug and play templates and print ads to jump out at prospects, immediately facilitating a call to your clinic
- ✓ 10 minute Facebook marketing to find new prospects in your community
- ✓ Use our done-for-you blog to create a new web presence and visibility with prospects and local businesses

MODULE 2: PATIENT IGNITION: **How To Condition Patients To Refer and Transform Them Into 'Human Billboards'**

- ✓ Condition patients for referrals with ready-to-use scripts and 'emotional triggers'
- ✓ How to judge the frequency (and relevancy) of contact with your patient list
- ✓ The 'Ascension Ladder' principle
- ✓ Get (and leverage) testimonials from patients
- ✓ Recognize and motivate patients to appreciate you and make referrals
- ✓ Setting up a "Patient Appreciation Day"
- ✓ Stimulate word of mouth referrals
- ✓ Get patients to know you, like you, and trust you

www.referralignition.com

MODULE 3: PHYSICIAN IGNITION: **How To Get Physicians To Finally See You As An Authority**

- ✓ Identify the 20% of physicians that will provide 80% of your referrals
- ✓ **Physician database (a list of physicians in your zip code; $1,999 value)**
- ✓ How to get them to refer to you instead of your competitors
- ✓ **The 3 Step Fax Campaign to trigger referrals from unknown physicians**
- ✓ The Giving Hand principle
- ✓ The Press Kit principle (give them a done-for-you press kit)
- ✓ The Press Release principle
- ✓ **The Physician Interview script (how to ask for an interview, what to ask during the interview)**
- ✓ The Workshop Approach (with done-for-you PowerPoints)
- ✓ The Newsletter Joint Endorsement script

MODULE 4: COMMUNITY IGNITION: **How To Become An Overnight Celebrity In Your Community**

- ✓ Gain recognition and visibility in your community on a shoestring budget
- ✓ Media database (a list of health and wellness journalists in your area; Radio, TV, columnists; $1,999 value)
- ✓ **Get noticed by the press with plug-and-play press releases**
- ✓ Joint Endorsement strategies with local businesses
- ✓ The community events you should (and should not) focus on
- ✓ Done-for-you PowerPoints for community speaking engagements

WE WILL CREATE A PLAN FOR YOUR PRACTICE IN THREE PRIVATE ONE-ON-ONE COACHING CALLS

- In addition to everything above, you get **THREE** coaching calls with me to help you implement the entire program.
- Each coaching call can last up to 30 minutes.
- You will be told EXACTLY what to do to grow your practice.
- **Just implement what I say and see your patient referrals soar**

SECTION III

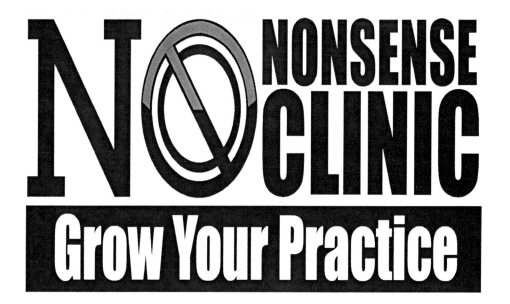

CHAPTER 9

How To Use Newsletter Marketing To Get Patients To Know, Like, And Trust You

HOW TO GROW YOUR CLINIC EXPONENTIALLY WITH NEWSLETTERS

I f you are reading this book, chances are you already know what a newsletter can do for your practice. It's a great way to stay in touch with patients in a consistent and relevant manner.

This chapter is going to be valuable whether you have a newsletter or not.

If you're not using newsletters in your practice, by the end of this chapter you will be saying to yourself, "*I should be using newsletters*" and you'll implement them in your practice.

Now if you <u>are</u> using newsletters in your practice, by the end of this chapter you'll be saying to yourself, "*I learned a lot of tricks here that I could be adding to my existing newsletters in order to substantially increase their effectiveness.*"

CONTENT CAN MAKE THE DIFFERENCE – YOU WANT THEM TO READ IT

One of the things that I always talk about is that it doesn't matter how good your newsletter is if it doesn't get opened and read.

When you are talking e-mail marketing, the best way to get the newsletter opened is by using a strong subject line. When you are talking direct mail, the best way to get the newsletter read is by using a combination of **clinical, bonding, and authority content**, which we will cover in this book.

If you are using newsletters and you're not seeing the kinds of results that you expect, there are two reasons:

1. The content is boring – you want people to read it from cover to cover
2. The delivery method is incorrect or insufficient – reliance on only e-mail as a form of delivery

I've been creating and sending newsletters for many years now as a private practice owner. I have reviewed over 1,547 newsletters from different clients and I am about to share all of the lessons from those newsletters in this one book. That's a pretty amazing amount of

information! However, before we begin, let me ask you – "*Why are newsletters the best overall media that there is?*"

First of all, they're a forum to change people from customers to belonging to a community.

REDEFINE YOUR CUSTOMERS

In your private practice, you want to redefine the way you look at customers. You don't want to call them patients. You don't call them clients. You don't call them prospects. So, what should you call them?

You should call them *insiders* or *members*. The phrase indicates that these individuals have a feeling of belonging in your clinic and a newsletter is a great forum to help somebody feel as though they belong to a community.

Your newsletter should be perceived as an exclusive, insider report; a legitimate publication, not as advertising.

This is the ONLY way for you to get past the massive clutter of email and piles of junk mail that your clients get every single day. When you check your mail, the first thing you try to do is eliminate the mail from the advertising category; your "junk mail."

Newsletters are not perceived as advertising, they're perceived as publishing. They build trust with people and they also build relationships. When you put those things together, it substantially increases how people perceive a newsletter.

In a world that is dominated by media and advertising, the patient is looking for a provider they know, like, and trust. This is what separates you from the large nameless, faceless corporate clinics. People like to read information and find out more about what's happening with people they know, like, and trust.

NEWSLETTERS PROVIDE VALUE AND CONTENT

Since newsletters provide content, they have more credibility than an advertisement. A newsletter is a huge credibility booster. Newsletters are perceived as a publication, making you an expert in your industry. So now if you write a publication, you must be an expert. It's the same thing as if you are the author of a book; you have to be an expert. So whether it's a book or it's a newsletter, it immediately makes you an expert and patients are more likely to want to work with an expert then a salesperson. In addition to that, I will pay an expert more than I will pay a salesperson.

A newsletter is an ideal forum for the demonstration of testimonials. You could highlight customer successes. You can show referrals and you increase patient referrals. It's easier to convince current clients who read your newsletter about how wonderful you are compared to the effort involved in trying to get new patients. Newsletters

have a tremendous amount of "pass-along" value with current patients also.

So when you send somebody an advertisement, they get the ad and they read it. If they get a newsletter that is positioned as educational, positioned as being informative, they're going to save it. They're going to pass it along to somebody else. When things are positioned as educational, people want to show them to other people. When was the last time someone said to you, *"Hey take a look at this ad in this magazine?"* On the other hand, when was the last time someone passed on an article to you?

How do you know if your newsletter is generating that pass along value? You will start to get requests from members asking if it's okay for them to reprint some of your articles to show employees or friends.

Newsletters have a longer shelf life than most other mediums have. How often have you been in a waiting room somewhere and in the waiting room there are newsletters sitting in the waiting room? In fact, in most of the clinics of my mastermind clients, patients have actually said to them year after year that they want a place to save all of their old newsletters. The patients like to go back and refer to them over and over again. So the newsletters have a longer shelf-life and they last longer.

YOU'RE TOO BUSY TO CREATE A NEWSLETTER REGULARLY

If you're saying to yourself, *"I can't do newsletters in my practice"* or *"I already have one and I'm happy with it"* then I want you to pay close attention to what I am about to reveal. You're saying to yourself, *"I already write a newsletter and I don't want to change it in any way, I already got it sort of figured out, I know how I'm doing it, I want to keep doing it the same way."* It's also likely that some of you are saying to yourself, *"I've tried it and it doesn't work."*

What I'm asking you is this; follow what I'm about to teach you step by step in this and try it for just twelve months. That's the only way for you to see the kind of extraordinary results that a <u>real</u> newsletter is going to bring you.

If you send out a newsletter using e-mail alone for one to two months, you will see a trickle of responses.

If you start using multiple modes of distribution (email, print, regular mail, fax) followed by phone call follow-ups for twelve months, you will see a snowball effect. You will get exponential results as you continue to do it the right way.

How do you know when newsletters are really working?

There's a simple test for this. Just take one month and don't send it out. If your patients call you up and say *"Hey, I didn't get my newsletter last month"* then you know they're really working because now people are looking forward to getting them.

Print vs. E-Mail Newsletters

So first things first, let's address the big question which is <u>print</u> versus <u>e-mail</u> newsletters.

The question that I get all the time is, *"Can I send out an online newsletter or should I use a print newsletter? Isn't a print newsletter much more expensive?"*

Let's talk about the e-newsletter first. First of all, they're relatively low cost to produce, which is the reason they're very attractive to most people. Secondly, you can deliver as often as you like with simple, short topics. Now there's good and there's bad to that.

The "good" is that you can deliver them often. The "bad" to it is that they're very difficult to get people to consume large quantities of information on e-zines because people, by nature, want small quantities of information when they are getting information online. So if you're going to do large quantities of information, the e-zine pretty much will not work for you because you'll rarely get anybody to completely read it all.

You can still develop relationships with an e-newsletter, but not like a printed newsletter can. Yes you can, without a doubt, create relationships with newsletters. Patients tend to change their e-mail address much more often than snail mail addresses.

As I said, e-mails actually change quite often. As a matter of fact, 20% of all e-mail addresses change every year. So the problem is that when you're e-mailing out your newsletter, since 20% of them are changing every year, it's very difficult to know whose e-mail address has changed. In most cases it requires somebody to take action on the bottom of your e-zine to actually update their information and very few people ever do that.

The other problem with e-mail newsletters is that often times they're not being read by all the recipients. You need to utilize the subject line to its fullest to get them to open it. This is very important with e-newsletters. The subject line <u>must</u> create enough curiosity to get the email to be opened.

Here's a startling observation about email open rates:

On average, only 20-30% of all e-mails get opened and read; even from people who know you already and trust you. That means that 70-80% of all e-mails never even get opened, even if they already know you.

The bottom line is that you've got to really strategically think about your subject lines on your e-mails in order to even get them opened up. Here's another issue with e-newsletters; you are restricted by how many characters you can use on your subject lines. It's not like a print newsletter where you really have your whole palette that you can deliver your information on.

In essence, an emailed newsletter should be an adjunct to your newsletter marketing strategy. Remember, email is just ONE mode of delivery. Rely on this mode of delivery alone and it's like having your entire 401k invested in one stock.

Print newsletters are, by far, the preferable way to consume large amounts of information. So this is the opposite of the e-newsletter. It's also a much better media to develop relationships. Let me prove it to you.

Let's say it's your birthday and your mother is going to send you a birthday card. How would you feel if you were to get a birthday e-card delivered online from your mother versus a birthday card in your mailbox? Obviously you're going to feel like mother should have bought a birthday card and put a stamp on it.

When a newsletter is delivered to you via snail mail, in your mailbox, it has a much, much higher perceived value that's coming to you and it's much stronger to build the relationships with.

My recommendation on newsletters is that I strongly suggest you use an e-newsletter to supplement your printed newsletter. Another question I get all the time is, *"Can I do one or the other?"* If you're going to do just one, my recommendation is do the printed newsletter.

One of the smart ways to actually do both versions is to take the printed newsletter and divide it into smaller sections and deliver the e-newsletters more frequently over time. But again, it just supports the printed newsletter that you send out. So again, the formula here is that you've got to use a printed newsletter. This can't just be an e-newsletter.

MOST COMMON FORMATS

First of all, one of the most common formats is the one page front and back newsletter. This is approximately 46 cents to a dollar out the door to mail.

MY OVERALL RECOMMENDATION ABOUT ENVELOPES VERSUS NON-ENVELOPES OR "SELF-MAILERS":

My recommendation is that it's a lot better to do one or the other as opposed to doing nothing at all. However, my overall recommendation is to always use an envelope when you can.

The envelope – the increased price for the envelope is almost negligible because the biggest expense of a newsletter is what?

Postage. Postage is the biggest expense. So when you realize you're adding a couple of pennies by adding an envelope to it, it doesn't really cost that much more because the postage is the biggest expense.

THE IMPORTANT EELEMENTS OF YOUR NEWSLETTER

Ask yourself, *"What do I want to accomplish with my newsletter?"*
Do you want new patients? Do you want more referrals from existing patients? Do you want to stay in touch with patients and referral sources?

THE IMPORTANCE OF THE NEWSLETTER BANNER

I highly recommend that every clinic have a customized banner at the top of their newsletter to give you an identity of your own.

This banner should include your clinic name, a *'hook'* about your clinic, a call to action, and your phone number and address. You want a uniform identity on the top of your newsletter to make it feel like every time a patients gets this every month, it's part of continually growing the brand of your clinic and the familiarity with your newsletter every month.

OPENING ARTICLE

The next thing is that you want an opening article. The opening article is really, really, really important in your newsletter. The opening article, in most cases, should not really be about your practice. The opening article should really be about people living their life with you. It should include elements of your life that they can possibly identify with. It is their "connection" with you.

Let me share an example of an opening article:

Dear Friends,

I just came back from celebrating with my in-laws, Pat and Justin, their sixtieth anniversary – no surprises why they made it to 60 years. Their marriage is evergreen. After 60 years of living together, they still treasure each and every day together. (Photo of in-laws holding hands together) It just makes my heart sing. I'm so thankful to have been a part of it and that we met them - Theresa, my wife, and our two girls got to spend time with their grandparents. We all boarded a Carnival Cruise for five days. What a great time. No drama. Everyone brought their best attitude and behavior. The family knows how to laugh, spend time together, play games, connect, share, and enjoy life together to make time and family count. Mom and Dad may not know it, but they're showing me and the rest of the kids what a great relationship is and what it takes.

> I'm paying very close attention because their grandchildren, our children, are watching us very closely. What we are showing them – that's how they learn and behave. This is what makes your heart sing.

Now you may be asking, *"What does this have to do with your private practice?"* My answer is simple… absolutely nothing.

What did it have to do with connecting the reader with the writer? Everything.

What did you feel about the writer after reading it? He's got great family value. He showed a photo of his in-laws holding hands together. This is about connection. Every month, when patients get this newsletter, they want to find out what's going on with the private practice owner. It has nothing to do with his practice or his expertise.

THE TYPE OF CONTENT IN YOUR NEWSLETTER

First off your newsletter should have headlines and sub headlines. Your reader should be able to scan things in order to figure out where they want to go with each newsletter.

Next, you want <u>three</u> types of information in your newsletter.
1. You want **clinical information** that helps the reader in their day to day lives.
2. You want **authority content**, which demonstrates your expertise and success as a private practice owner.
3. You also want **bonding content**, which helps the reader identify with you and get to know you better.

The biggest mistake most private practice owners make with their print newsletter is the presence of MOSTLY clinical content.

The whole newsletter is about clinical information. The whole newsletter is filled with articles about *"How to decrease pain in your lower back"*, *"How to reduce headaches"* or *"How to take care of your teeth,"* etc.

In your own practice, think of what you do when you're sending out a newsletter and avoid the temptation to make the entire newsletter clinical in nature.

Every newsletter must provide the reader some information about a particular condition and lead them back to you with a call to action for them to pick up the phone and call your clinic. Don't do anything else in the newsletter and don't try to do too much, since this will dilute the effectiveness of the newsletter. Be very selective about what you offer. Remember, the main purpose of the newsletter is to build a relationship with your patients and retain them for life. With relationship comes retention.

For best results, if you are offering something to the patient (promoting something) you should use an insert in the newsletter. Try to keep the newsletter sacred with really good information and also connecting with people. The insert can do the job of actually selling something. The newsletter in fact, sets up the insert.

Here is how this works.

With the newsletter, since it is coming as from an expert and because of the fact that it is good relevant information that helps you to connect with the person; you have now established enough credibility to make a recommendation to the reader.

Most people try to promote themselves before they have set the stage with the newsletter. If you're starting a newsletter from scratch and you haven't sent it out to people yet, I would highly recommend that you not try to market anything to them for at least four to six months. First build the relationship with a combination of email, print, faxed, and mailed newsletters. Once you build a relationship and you get them to be looking forward to getting it every month, then you can start putting inserts into your newsletter.

CONSUMPTION IS CRITICAL

There is nothing more critical than consumption of your newsletters. If they don't read it, then nothing's going to happen. What is the single biggest problem with most private practice newsletters, the single factor that DOOMS consumption?

The newsletter is boring.

Here's the secret to maximize consumption of your newsletter.

Clinical content should be no more than 40% of your newsletter. Everybody

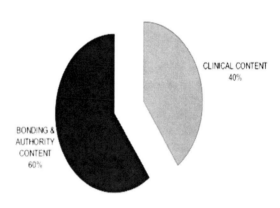

TOTAL CONTENT OF NEWSLETTER

CLINICAL CONTENT
40%

BONDING &
AUTHORITY
CONTENT
60%

wants 100% of their newsletter to be clinical content; but, it should be no more than 40% of your newsletter. This means that 60% of your content should be bonding and authority content.

AUTHORITY CONTENT

Here are some examples of authority content:
- ❖ **Always welcome new patients.** So what does that show? That shows that you're getting more patients. List the first names and initials of last names of patients who came to your clinic – this allows you to demonstrate social proof without violating any patient privacy or HIPAA laws (you are not giving out any medical information). That's a powerful demonstration of all the new patients that come to your clinic each month.

  It's also a demonstration to all the existing patients that they are in the right place because if all these other people keep coming to your clinic every month, they should be continuing to stay active every month.

❖ **Highlight a patient of the month.** Consider using the entire opening article of your newsletter to spotlight one of your patients.
  You are publicly praising a patient for his success, elevating your status as an expert clinician, and getting other people to talk about your success at the same time.

❖ **Next you want to do employee spotlights.** Write fun stuff about people that work in your office, which gives you a better connection with the staff.

❖ **The next one is Q&A.** Q&A is a very smart thing to be putting in your newsletter. It immediately establishes your authority. Make a list of commonly asked questions from your patients and then you answer them.

❖ **Next you want to share testimonials.** Testimonials are a very, very smart thing to be putting in your newsletters each month.

❖ **Show people holding up your newsletter** since this indicates consumption and authority.

❖ **Feature local physicians**. You can also feature local physicians in your newsletter. This is what I call the *'physician profiling'* principle.

CREATE AS MUCH RECIPROCITY AS POSSIBLE WITH YOUR NEWSLETTER

The simplest way to trigger reciprocity in a referral relationship with the physician is to feature the physician as a provider of choice in front of your own patients.

You can do this easily with a newsletter.

If you publish a newsletter, send e-mails, circulars, or communicate with patients on a regular basis (an important strategy), you can approach a local physician and 'offer' to feature him as a provider of choice in your next newsletter. This is called the *'physician interview'* principle. Even though some physicians will not take you up on this offer, the ones who do are likely to be important referral sources for you in the future.

When you explain the proposal in this manner, the physician perceives importance, opportunity, and urgency. The good news is that these three emotions can trigger the most wanted response for you, the need for reciprocity.

Use this principle with multiple physicians in your area (as long as they are not right next door to each other).

As we discussed earlier, you can use the same principle of reciprocity with patients. Feature patients and their success stories in newsletters and brochures (with their written permission) giving them a feeling of importance, recognition, and appreciation. In return the patient's, particularly the ones with strong social connections and a large circle of influence, will become human billboards for your practice. As with physicians, you want to you choose the right words and position the request as an opportunity for the patient and not a favor to your practice. People don't like doing favors, they like returning them. Start by being at the giving end and you will soon find yourself at the receiving end of an endless flow of patients.

HIGHLIGHTS OF LAST MONTH'S NEWSLETTER

Let patients know what they missed in last month's newsletter.

Again, this is all about getting more consumption for people to be reading it because now if they missed it last month, they don't want to keep missing it every month. So now they are going to be reading it more carefully every month.

Keep extra copies of the newsletter in your clinic.

Print up extra copies of your newsletters and leave them in your clinic for people to take with them or read while they're there. Keep copies of last month's newsletter in your office for patients to look at while waiting in your waiting room area.

DEMONSTRATION OF REFERRALS

This is my top recommendation for every newsletter. Acknowledge people who have referred to you. Thank your patients for referring and if you send your newsletter to other physicians, thank them for referring also.

The showing of referrals is a really important thing to do because it tells people that the right activity, the right behavior for them, is to refer to your practice. You are demonstrating that the right behavior is to refer others to your practice, because you appreciate them for doing so and acknowledge that each month in your newsletter.

PROVIDE INFORMATION ABOUT OTHER SERVICES YOU OFFER AND EVENTS YOU ARE CONDUCTING

Most of the people that get your newsletter may be interested in one or two more services from you. Don't make the assumption that *'they read the sign and will know about it'* when they were visiting your practice.

Put a little box on your newsletter that talks about other services you offer. It's a very smart thing to do.

BONDING CONTENT

Now we move to **bonding content**. The first way to utilize bonding content is to use trivia, jokes, crossword puzzles, fun stuff, cartoons, quotes, etc.; that's bonding content. Believe it or not that's probably the thing that gets you more consumption than anything else.

As counterintuitive as this may seem, it's the kind of thing that people really enjoy when they get their newsletter and this increases their involvement with it. It has nothing to do at all with your practice and what you can do for the patient but it helps increase consumption of your newsletter!

❖ **Crossword puzzles** are extremely appreciated, by the way. It's amazing to me how many people really get excited about crossword puzzles. So they're very easy to get and you could be putting a different one in every newsletter each particular month.

❖ **Talking about holidays** and what you are doing during the holidays is another great way to bond with patients.

Meaningful occasions for you like your birthday, your wedding anniversary, or even the anniversary of your clinic are additional ways to bond with your audience.

❖ **Photos in your newsletter** are an excellent way to bond with clients. Use as many photos in your newsletter as you can. They are a great way to actually fill up space in your newsletter if you are running short of content.

Photos with celebrities will allow you to show '*fame by association*'. Find someone local who is well known and get a picture taken with them, which makes you a celebrity.

❖ **Charity tie-ins** are a very smart thing to be talking about in your newsletters because people will feel better about you if you are actually doing good things in your local community. So if you're doing good things in your local community, use it in your newsletter each and every month.

❖ **Contests** are a fun addition for the patients. Conduct contests where you give away cool prizes. In the following month, show the people who won the contests in your newsletter.

Month number one, you announce a contest and month number two you show the people that actually won the contest.

❖ **Seasonal themes**, depending upon the time of year, are a good way to add flavor to your newsletter.

So again, authority and bonding content should be about 60% of the entire newsletter. I repeat, about 60% of the entire newsletter. Most private practice owners are very guilty of putting in too much clinical content and boring the audience.

❖ **Personalization**

You can make people read your newsletters even more if you take advantage of personalization. **Personalization** will increase response whether you use it in e-mail or regular mail. Most email sending programs will allow you to personalize the name of the recipient and if you know how to use the mail merge feature in Microsoft, you should be able to personalize your print newsletters as well.

HEADLINES AND SUB HEADLINES

Always have lots of **headlines and sub headlines** in your newsletter, so it becomes readable for people who 'skim' through it.

Nobody's going to start your newsletter from beginning to end unless you can get their interest with eye catching headlines and sub headlines. Once you get their interest, then they might very well read it beginning to end or they could make a decision even before they finish it. Most of your readers will scan your newsletter real fast, so if they want to read it they can pick out areas that they are interested in. Rarely do people read the entire newsletter.

COLOR MAKES A DIFFERENCE

Always use color, since it is more visually appealing than black and white. Keep mixing up the colors in the newsletter each month.

FEATURING PATIENTS

If you feature a patient in your newsletter, print up a copy and frame it for people you feature to hang up in their office.

Let's assume you feature a different patient each month. The front cover of the newsletter is all about a patient profile. What you should do, each month, is to take that front cover, put it in a frame, take it over to the patient's place of business, present it to them, and help them hang it up on the wall.

Underneath it, on the bottom of the frame, make sure the name of your office and also office information is listed so that people can contact you. Now you get zero cost promotion in the patient's place of business and the patient is happy that you recognized his success. You should have these frames all over your town, of people throughout the years that have been featured in your newsletter.

HIGHLIGHTING YOURSELF/BE INTERESTING

At the end of the day, one of the big priorities of your newsletter is that it should make you appear as a very interesting person.

By the way, if you don't want yourself to be the interesting person, I have two things to say to you. Number one is re-think it and decide hey, I really am willing to do that. Now there is a price to pay on that because you have to reveal things about yourself that you probably would not want to do, but it really makes a big difference. If you still won't get past that, where you just absolutely refuse to make yourself into an interesting person, then create sort of an interesting person profile that you feature in your newsletter. In some cases, we've actually seen that it's an animal. It could be your dog that you turn into the interesting person.

❖ **Stimulate patient referrals with the built in 'refer a friend' technology for patients and 'one click' unlimited faxing to physicians!**

Every content rich newsletter is specifically engineered to promote internal referrals. The built-in 'refer a friend' feature in each newsletter dramatically stimulates exponential, viral growth of your brand. Transmit the newsletter to hundreds of physicians with the push of a button using the integrated fax capability, allowing you to flood your community with your message and content.

❖ **Print and hand out your newsletter to patients, physicians and local businesses**

If you thought this was an email only program, think again! Your newsletter is available as a beautiful, completely customizable word document twice a month, giving you the ability to **instantly customize and print high quality color or black and white newsletters** that can be distributed to patients, physicians and local businesses, further enhancing your reputation as an expert.

The best way to distribute the newsletter is to follow the 'distribution trifecta'. We provide you with an automated emailed version, a printer friendly version (which you can easily print in your office) and a ready-to-fax PDF version that can be faxed to hundreds of physicians with the click of a button.

It's never been easier to market your practice.

Therapy Newsletter keeps your message 'top of mind', resulting in more referrals from patients, a boost in recognition from physicians and instant celebrity status in your community.

❖ **Quickly collect email addresses from patients who visit your website by providing them with instantly downloadable eBooks (which they can access after they enter their name and email address on your website).**

When it comes to marketing your private practice, the best way to communicate with your patients is with the use of email. If you don't have a list of emails, don't worry because we teach you TWO methods to build your email list. In fact, patients will **happily** give you their emails when you implement any of our proprietary techniques.

We make it fast and simple for you to build your email list. You get several, done-for-you "patient stimulator" eBooks (which you can customize and re-use in any way you like including print and online distribution) on several topics ranging from low back pain to shoulder pain and weight loss.

You collect patient's emails in one of two ways. On one hand, your patient comes to your website and enters their name and email address in a form on your site. Once they enter that information, the data is automatically stored in your Therapy Newsletter account and they start getting your newsletters twice a month (every patient has the option to unsubscribe from your newsletter at any time).

Once the patient enters their name and email on the form on your website, they can automatically access the FREE eBooks on various subjects like low back pain, secrets to good posture, how to beat arthritis, shoulder pain, weight loss and much more. In this manner, Therapy Newsletter gives you ready-to-use lead generation 'hooks' that are completely customizable and serve as 'lead generators' for your clinic. This allows you to build your email list.

You can also send them email sequences (new patients get a welcome sequence, discharged patients get a 'thank you' sequence, patients who miss appointments get reminder sequences and so on). You can also build trust and recognition with your patients by sending them **automated birthday greetings!**

Another way for you to collect your email list is to simply call patients and use our proprietary script.

> *"We have great news for you. We are giving away FREE eBooks on...* *(choose from a variety of eBooks we provide you once you become a member and make those available to your patients) and these books are delivered digitally since we want to save on the cost of printing and shipping. What is your email so we know where to send the books?"*

That's it. This script works like a charm every time you use it. When you use this script by phone, in person or with a letter, over 90% of your patients will **gladly** give you their email address. Once you add this email address to Therapy Newsletter, the technology does the rest.

Get started: **www.therapynewsletter.com**

Tip: It's a good idea to ask patient's to provide their email address on the patient intake form. Don't make it optional. In case they ask, just let them know they will be getting FREE eBooks and a FREE subscription to your emailed newsletter. The technology allows them to opt out at any time.

❖ Completely automatic, no technical knowledge, no website, no email list of patients required

Even if you don't have a website or a 'list' of emails, Therapy Newsletter can work as your one-stop communication system to stay in touch with patients, build trust and loyalty, condition patients to become more compliant and transform them into 'human billboards' for your clinic. In 20 minutes or less, we can have you up and running and completely automate your referral generation efforts.

Please go to Therapy Newsletter website to register for the Newsletter Code Webinar. You'll learn how an inexpensive, automated, done-for-you newsletter system can quickly flood your practice with new patients, slash marketing costs and FINALLY help you achieve freedom and independence in your practice.

❖ Content Repurposing - Current members can re-use the content on websites / newspaper columns / patient handouts since they own the copyright to the content

If you were to hire someone to write, edit, deliver the newsletter in multiple formats (email, video, print, fax), the cost could run into **HUNDREDS of dollars** each month, not to mention the lack of consistency and quality in the writing, formatting and distribution.

Fortunately, you don't have to bother with any of this, because we take care of this for you. Each month, professional writers create and deliver the content to you not once, but twice.. Just login to your account, access the content and make as many changes as you like. You can edit every single component of the newsletter (logo, template, contact information and content). It's like having your own, in-house team to write, edit, format and distribute your newsletter **twice a month. How much would you pay for a service like this that can literally save you hundreds of dollars each month?** Here's the best part - as long as you remain a member, you have unrestricted use of all eBooks, all newsletters in any manner you like. You can use the content on your website / in a local newspaper column and patient handouts since you own the copyright to the material. Please keep in mind that if and when your account is cancelled, you are not permitted to repurpose any of the content.

❖ Area Exclusive License to edit any picture, logo and
every single word on your newsletter, with 7 different
templates and unlimited color selections to choose from

Take advantage of our click-and-edit technology and enjoy complete creative control. Give your newsletter your personal look and feel with custom headers, footers, colors, and even format with our advanced editor. Easily add content, edit content, or remove any part of the newsletter to reflect **your specific treatment philosophy**. It gets much better. You enjoy an **area exclusive license to the Therapy Newsletter,** which means your competitor will not be allowed to use the same technology to market to physicians and patients in your area. A patient who is already on your email list will **never** get another email from another Therapy Newsletter client. Period.

Get started: **www.therapynewsletter.com**

Discover How Therapy Newsletter Helps You Stay Connected With Patients and Physicians, Positions You As The Primary Provider In Your Area and Stimulates Referrals On Autopilot...

✓ Reactivation of past patients with automated marketing
✓ Boost internal referrals from patients with word-of-mouth promotions
✓ Done-for-you service with full control over frequency, content and delivery
✓ Valid reason to communicate with physicians and 'stand out'
✓ Convert website visitors to patient visits
✓ Capture emails and other contact information with plug-and-play books
✓ Automatically deliver valuable content with inbuilt 'call to action' for patients
✓ Condition patients and physicians to recognize you as THE private practice expert

Therapy Newsletter Can Do So Much For Your Private Practice ...Take a Look!

Newsletter Success Formula	THERAPY Newsletter	In House Solution	Website Providers	Generic Content	Custom Created
Original Content	✓	Maybe	Possibly	No	Possibly
Prospect Stimulator Books	✓	No	No	No	No
Integrates With Website, Facebook	✓	No	No	No	No
Patient Friendly Content	✓	Maybe	No	No	Possibly
Call To Action For Patients	✓	No	No	No	No
Builds Trust, Loyalty	✓	Maybe	No	No	Occasionally
Written By PTs	✓	Maybe	Possibly	Maybe	Possibly
Automatic Email Distribution	✓	No	No	No	No
Separate Word Doc Version	✓	No	No	No	No
Fax To Physicians	✓	No	No	No	No
Web, Print Version Customizable	✓	Maybe	No	No	Maybe
Video Newsletters	✓	No	No	No	No
Affordable	✓	No	Maybe	Maybe	No
Money Back Guarantee	✓	No	No	Possibly	No
Area Exclusive License	✓	No	No	No	No

Chapter 9   233

❖ **Completely Automated, Done-For-You System**
It cannot get any easier than this. We write the content every 2 weeks. **You customize it just once.** Every 2 weeks, the content portion of the newsletter is updated (and your contact information, company logos stays the same unless you change it). This new newsletter is automatically delivered by email to your list every 2 weeks. The process is then repeated.

❖ **On-Demand Email Blast To Your Patients**
You get a lot more than just a done-for-you newsletter service with Therapy Newsletter. You get the ability to send your patients an email blast at any time, as many times as you want.

If you have something to announce or promote to your patients, take advantage of our sophisticated email broadcast system. No fancy website skills are needed, if you know how to use Microsoft word, you will know how to use this feature. Just type in your message and click 'send'.

NEW! Personalization fields are also included, so Amanda can get an email saying "Hi Amanda", John gets an email saying "Hi John" and so on, allowing you to **personalize your email contact with patients and other referral sources.**

❖ **Add Your Own Content, Pictures and Logos**
Give your newsletter your personal look and feel with custom headers, footers, colors and additional aesthetic options with our advanced online editor. With our unique technology, Therapy Newsletter allows you to match your newsletter with your unique corporate image.

❖ **You Control EVERY Little Thing On Your Newsletter**
We invest heavily in the content and message of your newsletter every single time. Every newsletter article and every line of content is meticulously researched and engineered in-house by our team of talented and licensed physical therapists.

But it doesn't stop there. YOU get total creative control. Easily add content, edit content and exercise complete control to reflect your own company brand, image and treatment philosophy.

Get started: **www.therapynewsletter.com**

❖ **Quality Content Written By a Team of Licensed Physical Therapists**
Every issue is content rich and crammed with valuable, practical information that your patients will LOVE. It's not old school, boring, dry stuff that people will ignore, it's cutting edge, timely, well researched, informative content that is fun to read.

That's not all; every newsletter comes with a set of 'action steps' for patients to take and inspirational ideas. That's why your patients and prospects will be eager to forward a copy of your newsletter to their circle of influence.

❖ **Done-for-you "Prospect Stimulator eBooks" and Website Banners Designed To Attract More Subscribers For Your Newsletter..**
You get done-for-you prospect stimulator eBooks, which act as 'hooks' for patients to part with their name and email address, allowing you to build your newsletter list (and everyone on your list automatically gets the newsletter twice a month).

The best way to transform passive website visitors into active newsletter subscribers (and finally patients) is to capture their contact information to begin with.

Therapy Newsletter completely automates this **critical process** since we give you plug-and-play forms that you use on your website to instantly transform website visitors into loyal newsletter subscribers.

❖ **Quickly Grow Your Patient List With Internal Referrals**
A happy patient, who is also on your newsletter list, is highly likely to reward you a referral. That's why we created the "Refer a Friend" feature, which is unique to your account.

Through a sophisticated feature programmed into the newsletter, your patients are encouraged to refer their friends, family, and coworkers who they feel would enjoy receiving your newsletter. This is viral marketing at its best and it's one of the fastest and easiest ways to grow your patient and prospect list.

When a patient refers a friend, you'll automatically receive an email with the information you need to contact your new prospect and schedule a possible consultation. These 'referrals' are also automatically subscribed to your newsletter and will start getting your newsletter every 2 weeks.

❖ **NEW! Newsletter Archive Feature - Access Library, Edit and Send Past Newsletters**
Get the most out of this system. You can showcase your newsletter archive on your website.

Give your website visitors a library of content and access to past issues. This is a great way to showcase your expertise and build your brand.

❖ **Email List Management**
If you have an existing list of patients and their emails, it's simple to import it and make it bigger with Therapy Newsletter. We give you plug-and-play forms for your website (we call these "email stimulator" boxes) which allows you to capture your visitor's contact information.

You can also View, edit, export, and manage your subscriber list with a simple click.

❖ **Track and Analyze Mailing Results**
Easily track open percentage, broadcast dates, and always maintain a clean list with our exclusive hard bounce email removal system that automatically removes bad, invalid and mistyped email address resulting in high delivery rates for your newsletter.

❖ **Email Exclusivity**
We don't allow your subscribers to receive newsletter from our system, which gives you the ability to exclusively market to your patients. This unique feature is called 'Email Exclusivity.' When a lead or prospects opts into your newsletter system they can't be added to another Therapy Newsletter account with the same email address.

❖ **Print Your Newsletter In Word - Create Beautiful, Content Rich Handouts**
Want to get maximum exposure? It's easy with Therapy Newsletter. Use the print feature to print out copies of your newsletter and pass them around to patients, physicians and local businesses.

Use our proprietary "Physician Profiling Principle" (outlined in the member's area) to get physicians to feature **your newsletter in their clinics.**

Get started: **www.therapynewsletter.com**

CHAPTER 10

NO NONSENSE CLINIC

Leveraging Mobile Marketing To Engage

Existing Patients And Get new Patients

Grow Your Practice

MOBILE MARKETING 101 FOR PRIVATE PRACTICE OWNERS

Most private practice owners have a list of patients and their cell phone numbers.

A cell phone number is a valuable piece of data; much more important than the patient's email or home address, from a marketing point of view. After all, there are only THREE things that everyone carries with them when they walk out of their home; their keys, their wallet/purse, and their cell phone.

What consumers take with them

More than 95% of the US population owns a cell phone. Text messaging plans are very affordable these days and 95% of individuals check their text messages within 5 minutes of receiving them.

Every private practice owner knows it's important to stay in touch with patients, but there are a few problems associated with the 'common' modes of communication.

All Other Local Ad Solutions are DEAD

Traditional advertising mediums are loosing their effectiveness

Phone Directory	Where is yours?
Newspapers	Declining Rapidly
TV	DVR/TiVo
Telemarketing	Do Not Call List
Direct Mail	1%-2% Yield
Print Ads	Rising Costs
E-Mail	Spam Software

- Email – not always opened, spam filters are making it increasingly more difficult to get emails read
- Regular mail and print ads – rising costs, difficult to measure response
- Newspapers – readership declining rapidly, since more people go online for information
- Phone directory – do you even know where yours is?

The number of individuals with Smartphones and mobile web users has increased dramatically in the past few months and jumped 34% from July 2008 to July 2009 alone, according to Nielsen Co.

Bango (*a mobile analytics specialist*) reported a 600% increase in traffic to mobile websites in the past 12 months. This means that not only do patients have cell phones capable of receiving text messages, but also more and more patients have 'Smartphones' like the iPhone, Droid, and Internet capable phones that enable them to browse websites using their cell phone. So what does this mean for your practice and where does it come into play with marketing?

HERE IS HOW THIS APPLIES TO YOUR PRACTICE:

✓ If you have cell phone numbers of your patients you should be communicating with them using text messages. The fact that they gave you the information during patient intake gives you the right to communicate with them (and they can always text STOP if they don't want to hear from you).
✓ Since you are communicating with patients directly, it's important for your message to be short, precise, captivating, and beneficial.
✓ Your website should be 'mobile optimized' since patients will quite possibly browse your website from their mobile phones
✓ You should be engaging your patients with mobile votes, surveys, and polls. You should be using automatic appointment reminders to boost compliance and minimize cancellations.

Speaking of appointment reminders, here is a simple way in which text messaging can boost patient compliance and minimize cancellations.

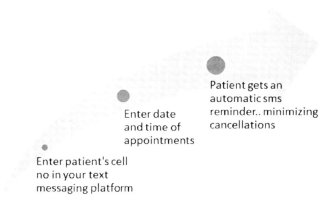

Patient gets an automatic sms reminder.. minimizing cancellations

Enter date and time of appointments

Enter patient's cell no in your text messaging platform

To understand how mobile marketing works, it's important to understand a few key terms. Let's say your practice name is "Healthfit Physical Therapy".

Now, if you ask a patient to text the word HEALTHFIT to 77453, then the word HEALTHFIT (doesn't matter if they text it in uppercase or lowercase) is called the 'mobile keyword'. The number 77453 is called the 'shortcode', which is provided to you by your text messaging provider platform.

You need to get an account with a company that provides a '*text messaging platform*'. Ideally, this company should also provide 'voice broadcasting' services and email marketing services; allowing you to get an all-inclusive system that automates all your patient marketing using text, voice, and email in one platform. (I will be making an announcement in this chapter about a service I built that does ALL of these things and helps you market your practice to patients and prospects on their cell phones.)

Every practice should have at least three, preferably five, mobile keywords like lowback, hip, knee, etc. to appeal to different segments of patients. When you are marketing to the general population, asking prospects to text the 'mobile keyword' (like HEALTHFIT) to the short code is an instant way to get their cell phone number into your database. The interesting part is, once your 'keyword' is taken by someone else there is nothing you can do about it. Therefore, it makes sense that when you follow up with prospects using motivational quotes and inspirational messages, the likelihood of getting the prospect to convert to a patient increases significantly.

If you've been collecting the cell phone numbers of your patients as part of your patient intake (good job!), simply import it into your text messaging platform. Once the cell phone is in your system, you can send patients appointment reminders and engage them by using a combination of surveys, polls, competitions, incentives, greeting cards, etc.

Text messages are CHEAPER and get read FASTER than traditional email and snail mail, allowing you to save time and money while getting IMMEDIATE responses from patients.

Imagine the power of simple banner on your building or signs along the roadway with a way for people to simply text that they're interested in what you have to offer. Your sign or text could say something like:

- ❖ **"Text BACKPAIN to 77453 to receive a FREE low back pain evaluation"**

- ❖ **"25 Volunteers needed for a guaranteed results pain relief study. Text PAINFREE to 77453 to learn more"**

- ❖ **"Free Fall Prevention Class this Saturday. Text NOFALLS to 77453 to secure your spot!"**

- ❖ Combine <u>scarcity</u> and <u>urgency</u> in your offer and take a normal call to action like "call now to claim your 2 week pass" and make it better. For example: **"Special Bonus: Text WELLNESS to 775453 and receive an immediate coupon for 50% off your exercise program."**

- ❖ **"Special Bonus: Text HEALTHY to 77453 for unlimited 2 week passes for you and all your friends and family."**

- ❖ **"Show a staff member at our facility this text today before 9:00pm to receive 25% off on any massage package."**

- ❖ **"Hi Charles, be sure to check-in at the clinic today between 10am – 3pm and I'll give you a free T-shirt"**

- ❖ **"Special Announcement: Renew your wellness program membership by Wednesday next week and get an additional 6 weeks FREE!"**

Do you want to see this in action? Just text the word **PATIENT to 77453** to see this marketing technique in action. I'll send you a FREE book on *"The 10 Laws of Mobile Patient Marketing."*

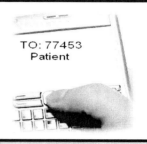

TO: 77453
Patient

BENEFITS OF MOBILE MARKETING

Get ready to revolutionize your practice with cutting edge technology for text, voice, and email marketing. With mobile marketing, anyone with an Internet connection can take advantage of the power of text messaging (SMS), picture messaging (MMS), voice broadcasting, email marketing, and social marketing including Facebook and Twitter, to reach an unlimited number of patients! All you need is an ordinary computer with access to the Internet and nothing more.

In today's fast-paced world patients are more on-the-go and yet better connected than ever before. The best way to engage these patients in real-time interaction is via their mobile phones! Expensive and increasingly inefficient direct mails, catalogs, and print ads are being replaced by mobile messaging and the mobile web. Mobile text messaging has emerged as a new way of contacting patients with unmatched speed and precision. From SMS alerts and promotional messages to mobile coupons and text-to-win campaigns; mobile marketing makes it easy to build, launch, manage, and analyze mobile campaigns in real-time. All you need is an ordinary computer with Internet to access our web-based, self-serve platform with no need to install additional software.

THE KEY BENEFITS OF MOBILE MARKETING INCLUDE:

✓ Mobile marketing enables you to send text messages to ANY cell phone in the U.S.
✓ Text message personalization – looks like it was personally sent!
✓ Over 95% of SMS messages are opened as compared to 10-20% open rate for email.
✓ Short text messages are direct, to the point, and get the consumer's full attention
✓ Mobile marketing generates significantly higher return on investment as compared to direct mail or email
✓ Mobile marketing enables creative, interactive, and engaging campaigns

MOBILE KEYWORDS

A mobile keyword is a one-word phrase that identifies your practice. The shorter it is the better.

For example, let's say the name of your practice is ADAMS PHYSICAL THERAPY and you specialize in physical therapy of the hand.

Your mobile keyword could be ADAMSPT / APT / ADAMHAND / HANDPT (upper or lower case does not matter).

Consider this example:

On American Idol, they had you text 'fantasia' to 77453.
Fantasia = 'mobile keyword'
77453 = 'short code'
This allowed viewers to vote for their favorite "Idol" whose name was Fantasia.

When patients text the mobile keyword ADAMSPT to a 5-digit short code number, they receive an automatic text message (you specify the content) AND they get added to a list that you specify. This allows you to create different offers for different lists.

For example, if a patient texts ADAMSPT to 77453, the patient will immediately receive an automated text response (that you can setup and change at anytime) with information about general physical therapy and get added to one list.

Another patient texts ADAMSHAND to 77453, the patient will immediately receive an automated text response (that you can setup and change at anytime) with information about hand physical therapy and get added to a different list. This allows you to create segmented lists and send personalized, relevant messages to your audience.

You can setup a different automated response with each mobile keyword. Users can immediately create a mobile keyword as long as it's not yet taken by another user (much like owning an internet website name). For this reason, you want to secure your mobile keywords as quickly as possible, before your competitor does.

Again, if you question how it works or how fast it works simply try it out yourself by texting **PATIENT to 77453** and get a FREE book on the "*10 Laws of Mobile Patient Marketing*". Please note that the keywords are not case-sensitive. After texting the keyword you'll receive an automated response right back!

Unlike traditional email subscriptions, mobile keyword subscriptions are controlled by the end users, your patients. People can subscribe and unsubscribe any time they want.

The new emerging mobile culture makes mobile marketing (with keywords) an exciting new frontier with possibilities that exceed regular mail, email marketing, and

Chapter 10

other traditional marketing channels resulting in an over 90% open rate (email averages are only 15-20%) and over 25% response rate.

SHORT CODES

Short codes are special telephone numbers that are typically 4 to 6 digits long. Unlike regular 10-digit phone numbers, you cannot call a short code number. They are used for texting purposes only.

Short codes act just like any other regular 10-digit phone numbers that you can send text messages to. Typically they are used by businesses and are provided to consumers who may want to request more information about a product, service, or business.

They are often used to tally votes for a contest or sweepstake (like they do on American Idol). You've seen mobile keyword and short code technology on TV shows, radio commercials, billboards, print advertising, and websites.

2-WAY SMS

Send a text message to patients. When patients reply, you can see their text message in your account or on your cell phone!

✓ This can be used for several purposes, including appointment confirmations.
✓ Never have to worry about making dreaded confirmation calls
✓ Increase productivity and save money by freeing time for more important tasks
✓ Text messaging is the least intrusive way for appointment reminders

PICTURE / VIDEO (MMS)

MMS (Multimedia Messaging Service) is an enhanced way to send text messages that include pictures and videos to the cell phones of your clients and patients. MMS takes SMS (text message) a step further by allowing exchange of text messages beyond the traditional 160 characters in length. Using MMS will allow you to send sounds, images and videos!

Picture / Video Messaging (MMS)

MMS is the new standard in mobile messaging and often gets 2 to 3 times the response rate in comparison to standard text messaging alone. With multimedia content, you can now deliver powerful messages faster to skyrocket your brand recognition, sales, promotions, and marketing.

Unlike SMS marketing, MMS mobile marketing platform delivers animated images, a sound track, as well as audio ensuring your brand identity is immediately recognized by your clients and prospects.

MMS BENEFITS:

INCREASED RESPONSE RATE

Because of its interactivity, MMS videos increase user interest and boost direct response rates from individuals that are tired of just seeing boring text. It's also the perfect way to showcase to your patients that your business is on top of the latest technologies.

MMS BROADCASTS

Keeps all your patients engaged through regular bulk MMS announcements with anything from coupons, promotions, important alerts to season's greetings!

INTERACTIVE COMMUNICATION

MMS creates a more interactive and emotional appeal on mobile devices compared to SMS through elements of sound, animation, and images giving you powerful visual branding possibilities.

TARGETED CONTACT

Send MMS messages to specific target groups based on demographics, interests, or locations. Communicate to the people you want to and get your message heard right away.

PERSONALIZED MESSAGES

Send unique, customized MMS messages to individual people one at a time so it has the most impact. Make each recipient feel special!

Chapter 10

SAVE THE PLANET!
Help save the earth as part of a Go Green initiative with MMS. Sending moving colors and messages via mobile phones eliminates the need for paper and expensive direct mailers.

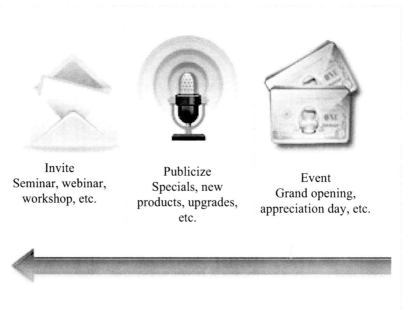

Invite
Seminar, webinar, workshop, etc.

Publicize
Specials, new products, upgrades, etc.

Event
Grand opening, appreciation day, etc.

Unlike SMS marketing, **MMS Mobile Marketing** delivers animated images, a sound track as well as audio ensuring your brand identity is immediately recognized by your clients and prospects.

MOBILE COUPONS

Mobile Coupons represent the most cutting edge method to send exclusive coupons, discounts, and special offers directly to your patients' cell phones! Your patients now need to rush to your clinic and simply show their cell phones to redeem their coupons.
With our "done-for-you" swipe and deploy Mobile Coupons, you can create a promotional campaign, broadcast it, and start seeing an immediate increase in patient visits within minutes.

1 JOIN OUR PATIENT CLUB **2** RECEIVE COUPONS VIA TEXT! **3** START SAVING MONEY!

Maximize gains from your marketing dollars with the speed and convenience of mobile coupons. You can now offer incentives like educational resources, discounts / special offers for services, and appointment reminders. You can also create unique promotion codes for each individual SMS mobile coupon and track redemption rates and revenue generated. This allows you to precisely track which coupons worked and which didn't. Now, you can constantly test, tweak, and improve the offers presented to your patients.

These are just some of the benefits offered by mobile coupon:
- ✓ Create unique promotions with personalized SMS mobile coupons
- ✓ Generate increased revenue (since you know which campaigns worked and which didn't)
- ✓ Generate more patient visits IMMEDIATELY since 95% of text messages are read within 5 minutes of receipt.
- ✓ Decrease overhead by reducing or eliminating printing and mailing costs

APPOINTMENT REMINDERS

Appointment Reminders

Text, Voice, Email

Since the health of your practice depends upon appointments and patient compliance, mobile text reminders can reduce missed appointments and increase revenue. This is the most effective way to keep your patient schedule full at all times. This feature alone will pay for the cost of your membership. Easy to use text messaging reminder feature allows you to easily queue and send automated appointment reminders via SMS. Your patients will appreciate a text message (instead of a phone call) as a non-intrusive reminder, boosting patient compliance.

It's perfect for physical therapists, chiropractors, dentists, physicians and massage therapists.

Chapter 10

Appointment Reminders

Appointment reminder service pays for itself with just a single saved appointment and is the most effective (and least expensive way) for you to maintain a full patient schedule.

The best part is that any practice or business can get setup and start sending SMS reminders in minutes. All you need is a computer with Internet access!

It's time to let your staff focus on something more important than making repetitive reminder phone calls and never bother your patients with intrusive phone calls again!

You also have options to:
- ✓ Quickly add new contacts to your database and set appointment times
- ✓ Search for an existing contact in seconds
- ✓ Create automated templates to send reminders quickly and automatically without typing each individual message
- ✓ Edit or cancel queued reminders at anytime

Physical Therapists, Chiropractors, Dentists, Physicians, and Massage Therapists
- ❖ Appointment reminders
- ❖ Prescription refill reminders
- ❖ Reminders for patients to take their medications
- ❖ Past due reminders – notice that a payment is past due
- ❖ Event and meeting reminders

3 Steps **To Setup Your Reminder:**

STEP 1 **Sign in** with your user name and password.

STEP 2 **Set** the date and time for an appointment, the send time, mobile number and message.

STEP 3 Click the "**send this reminder**" button.

It's THAT Simple!

MOBILE VOTING & SURVEYS

Mobile Voting / Polls

Mobile voting and survey capability enables you to create SMS polls and surveys to engage your patients. This feature gives you valuable, real-time insight about your practice. As people participate, every vote is categorized, tallied, and reflected in your dashboard for you to analyze in real time.

Mobile survey capability allows you to create a multiple choice questionnaire with several choices. All your patients need to do to participate in the mobile vote is to text your mobile keyword to 77453. The client will immediately receive back a text message that's customized by you with all the choices they can vote for. The client simply replies back with just the number that's tied to their choice and that's it!

Every vote / reply message and every mobile number in your account will be recorded. You know who voted, what they voted for, and this valuable insight allows you to tailor future messages to them via SMS. Keep in mind that each mobile phone can only vote once to keep the process fair and simple.

How it works:

Text the Mobile Keyword to 77453. → **Immediately receive the question and choices to vote.** → **Reply back with just the number of the choice you want to vote for.** → **Receive a thank you message that you can customize and change at anytime.**

Mobile Voting / Polls

Utilizing This Feature:

- ✓ A physical therapist who wants patients to participate in a quick survey to evaluate patient satisfaction
- ✓ A physician who wants feedback from patients about cleanliness within the clinic
- ✓ A massage therapist who wants feedback from patients about a particular staff member
- ✓ A dentist who wants to ask patients to grade their experience at the front desk and on their initial office visit
- ✓ A chiropractor who wants his patients to vote for the most important reason why they came seeking his/her services

Chapter 10 251

MOBILE CONTESTS

Mobile marketing allows you to create text contests (also known as text to win), mobile contests, and text sweepstakes. Your audience can participate in a contest and try to win a prize by sending a text message to 77453.

All participant information is automatically updated in your database for future contact.

Text contests are preferred by consumers and typically result in more entries than the web, regular mail, or phone campaigns. Mobile marketing allows you to create mobile contests to engage and entertain patients while capturing their contact information into your database.

Mobile Contests

LEAD GENERATION

Lead Generation

Getting the contact information of patients who are interested in your services should be a top priority for your practice.

Once you have your own dedicated mobile keyword, use it to attract more patients and prospects to your clinic.

Forward incoming leads to an email address or directly to a phone and have your staff follow-up with prospects quickly.

Where Do You Share Your Keyword and Shortcode:
- ✓ In your email signature
- ✓ On your car for a free trial membership
- ✓ On your business cards to get a free report
- ✓ On your direct mail postcard or magazine ad
- ✓ Promote your keyword on the radio or television
- ✓ External Signs at conventions, expos, etc.
- ✓ Internal Signs for constant reminders for referrals

TEXT TO SCREEN

Text messaging platform enables your audience to text your mobile keyword followed by a message so that it can be projected onto a large screen at your facility in real time. It's the best way to keep your audience engaged and entertained!

No more long, boring, one-way presentations. Create polls and quizzes to engage your audience, project answers onto a giant video screen, compel the crowd to participate, and then post the results on that same screen, ALL while collecting consumer data in real time!

ON-THE-GO CONTACT CONTROL

Tie your mobile phone to your account so that when you're not in front of a computer you can still send out a single text message from your phone and message all of your contacts.

SHUFFLE RESPONDER

With the SMS shuffle responder your patients can text your keyword and get a different auto responder each time.

It's great for setting up a pool of different pre-planned promotional messages to send to your patients and prospects.

You Can Send:
- ❖ Inspirational quotes
- ❖ Announcing specials, coupons, and promotions
- ❖ Health and Wellness tip of the day
- ❖ Create 10 different promotional text messages for your private practice. These will become a part of your automated shuffle responses when people text your mobile keyword to 77453.

❖ A physical therapy private practice signs up to use the automated shuffle responder to give fitness and injury prevention tips to patients.

❖ Banners and/or other signage direct patients to text "TIPS" to 77453 to receive their fitness tips.

❖ Clients/prospects can easily opt into the program by texting the keyword on banners and signs.

❖ Clients/prospects receive a special text message from the pool of different auto responders.

❖ When prospects/patients text the same keyword again ("TIPS" to 77453), they will receive a different promotional message (the shuffle responder) until the pool of auto responses has been exhausted.

❖ Opting in is easy for the customer and it's a fast way for businesses to obtain customers' contact info.

❖ Customers opting into the program WANT to receive your specials and promotions.

❖ Once the promotions are set up, the private practice owner can quickly send out mass text messages to all the prospects/patients at once – saving time and money in message delivery.

❖ Increased engagement with patients leading to higher retention and improved patient satisfaction.

❖ Automate the timing of special promotions to go out during downtime and increase patient volume in a matter of hours (not days).

RESOURCE

"Finally. A No-Nonsense, Trusted Resource To Help You Build a Zero-Stress Private Practice... With Unrestricted Access To The Most Powerful Physical Therapy Marketing and Referral Generating Systems, Strategies and Tactics Only Available To The Top 1% of Physical Therapists Worldwide..."

YOUR FREE 30 DAY TRIAL INCLUDES THE FOLLOWING RESOURCES TO HELP GROW YOUR PRACTICE ($500 VALUE):

✓ Private practice marketing checklist
✓ Audio / video training on "The FOUR pillars of referral generation"
✓ Done-for-you templates to increase referrals
  and much much more...

Attention: If you are looking for physical therapy marketing ideas guaranteed to get you more patients, stimulate referrals and increase revenue in your private practice, then read on to discover how you can get the most cutting edge "what's working" patient attraction systems delivered to you every few days as part of the exclusive 'Inner Circle'...

Dear Success Minded Private Practice Owner,

Do you want patients and new streams of revenue? The small percentage of maverick private practice owners who understand the business of private practice are 'early adopters' continue to thrive while their competitors perish, wasting time, energy and money on advertising that doesn't work.

The big difference between a struggling clinician who works 60+ hours a week and a progressive, flourishing practice owner who checks in once a while is the volume and quality of referral generation systems. The ability to consistently attract new patients with simplified, automated systems without wasting time on archaic, expensive mechanisms that no longer work.

Just imagine this for a moment...

Would you like to have insider's access to literally dozens of powerful, time tested, proven physical therapy marketing systems for getting all the patients you can handle?

You'll learn multiple ways to increase income using out-of-the-box revenue models like cash-paying boot camps, membership models and recurring revenue streams that leverage your expertise and help you spend more time with family.

Chapter 10   255

Do you think these 'push-button' strategies can skyrocket your private practice? If you answered yes to these questions, then you probably want to know how you can become a part of that 1% - the kind of private practice owner that can generate patients on autopilot, to the extent that delegating some treatments becomes inevitable. You WANT to be in that position, which is why you are reading this, isn't it?

Just one tip in the Inner Circle can change the way you manage your private practice. You can judge for yourself, especially if you have been reading my blog, bought my book and attended my live presentations. I give you the most cutting edge information as soon as it is released in any industry, since some of the sharpest private practice owners in the country are a part of my personal network.

To Sign Up, Go To: **www.nitin360.com/ptbook**

YOUR FREE 30 DAY TRIAL INCLUDES THE FOLLOWING RESOURCES TO HELP GROW YOUR PRACTICE ($500 VALUE):

- ✓ **Private practice marketing checklist**
- ✓ **Audio / video training on "The FOUR pillars of referral generation"**
- ✓ **Done-for-you templates to increase referrals and much much more...**

For example, my 'Physician Profiling' principle has helped hundreds of private practice owners establish INSTANT relationships with physicians.
or when my 'Patient Billboard' formula ignited 14 new referrals in 1 month for one of my coaching clients... or when one of my "Lead Generator" reports helped a client attract 783 emails of patients interested in low back pain within 34 days of implementation...

And the list goes on...

WHAT EXACTLY IS THE INNER CIRCLE?

Since my private coaching programs are beyond the reach for most physical therapists, I realize it locks out a lot of private practice owners who can really benefit from these maverick strategies. That's exactly why I created the Inner Circle, which is a private member portal on my blog. Each week, I craft an Inner Circle post that is hot off the press, stuffed with the latest and most cutting edge techniques for your private practice. This is content that no high priced coaching program or no amount of experience can every teach you. It's like getting spoon-fed with a high-octane dose of marketing spinach.

Here are some of the benefits associated with an Inner Circle membership!

Interviews With Successful Private Practice Owners - Monthly 'audio interrogations' packed with tons of killer information of some of the most successful private practice owners in the industry. We ask the private practice owners to break down their precise formula for excess and reveal the strategies that have made the BIGGEST impact in their business. Just imagine how many light years ahead you will be, with this kid of information!!

Increase Revenue – As the 'hidden genius' behind the success of hundreds of physical therapy private practices, I will show you how to copy my success and bring in several new patients into your practice.

Increase Referrals – You'll get all the latest strategies on how to get referrals in your practice, create multiple streams of revenue by providing patients with high value products, services and tools designed to help patients, and boost referrals.

Save Money – I'll show you where to save on everything from logo design and website building to creating your own DVDs, CDs and books you can customize and hand out to patients. You get to use all my connections and secret resources to save money as you grow your private practice and leverage your business.

Save Time – You'll get information and charts you can use in seconds, not some vague concepts you need to learn. There's no hype, just straight-to-the-point information. Why take 20 minutes to tell you about a new marketing strategy when you can learn it in 3 minutes?

Stay Current – The absolute latest, cutting-edge information that will help you put your private practice business on autopilot.

Beat Your Competition – I see the trends coming. So if I see something that is going to be a waste of time and marketing dollars, you will be the first to know it, and you will get a head start on your competition.

Exclusive discounts to all my products (plus, I have relationships with lots of vendors to get you huge discounts)

Finally All Your Questions Answered – Just ask your question and I will answer it in a new training video. It's just like having me as your personal business coach.

And too many more benefits to list here…

Even if you had to pay $197 a month to access this information, it would be the deal of the year.

However, you are not going to pay anything near that.

To Sign Up, Go To: **www.nitin360.com/ptbook**

YOUR FREE 30 DAY TRIAL INCLUDES THE FOLLOWING RESOURCES TO HELP GROW YOUR PRACTICE ($500 VALUE):

- ✓ Private practice marketing checklist
- ✓ Audio / video training on "The FOUR pillars of referral generation"
- ✓ Done-for-you templates to increase referrals and much more…

ABOUT THE AUTHOR

Nitin Chhoda PT, DPT, CSCS is a licensed physical therapist in NJ, NY and a published author **of "Total Activation: The New 5 Step Fitness Mantra" and "Marketing For Physical Therapy Clinics"** (both featured on Amazon.com). He is also a private practice marketing consultant and most importantly, a regular guy who enjoys time with his wife Ritika Gulrajani PT, DPT in their home in New Jersey. He enjoys techno music, watching DEXTER on Showtime, writing articles, consulting with clients on the phone, going into his 'batcave' (it's just an office with a bunch of computers) to find new ways to automate marketing and referral generation using technology and in general, juggles multiple roles as a writer, consultant, inventor and family guy.

Nitin has written several articles on physical therapy marketing for IMPACT, ADVANCE, and PT Magazine, in addition to his blog (the #1 ranked blog on Google for 'physical therapy marketing'). He is the founder of Referral Ignition training systems, the Private Practice Summit, the Private Practice Formula and the Private Practice Mastermind group. He has presented at the Private Practice Section Meeting of the American Physical Therapy Association, in addition to his talks at various fitness conventions in several locations across the US, Canada and Asia. He is also the creator of the Therapy Newsletter automated newsletter marketing system and Clinical Contact, a web-based mobile, email and voice broadcasting system with built-in appointment reminders to boost patients arrival rates and increase revenue.

In addition to his prolific speaking tours, he has served an adjunct faculty member on Health, Wellness and Kineseology at Millersville University, PA. Nitin has also been a guest speaker at the University of Michigan, Ann Arbor and was a keynote speaker at Shades of Brown, an international educational conference in Toronto, CA.

He has been featured on the Martha Stewart radio show, Investors Business Daily, the Bergen Record (amongst the nations 100 best newspapers) and CH 14 television, Montreal.

CPSIA information can be obtained at www.ICGtesting.com
Printed in the USA
LVOW072219080312

272300LV00005B/225/P

9 781463 751173